EVERYTHING IN MODERATION

DANIEL FINKELSTEIN

Everything in Moderation

WILLIAM
COLLINS

William Collins
An imprint of HarperCollins*Publishers*
1 London Bridge Street
London SE1 9GF

WilliamCollinsBooks.com

First published in Great Britain in 2020 by William Collins

1

A catalogue record for this book is available from the British Library

ISBN 978-0-00-835660-6

Typeset in Adobe Garamond Pro by Palimpsest Book Production Ltd,
Falkirk, Stirlingshire
Printed and bound in Great Britain by CPI Group (UK) Ltd, Croydon CR0 4YY

MIX
Paper from
responsible sources
FSC
www.fsc.org   FSC™ C007454

This book is produced from independently certified FSC™ paper
to ensure responsible forest management.

For more information visit: www.harpercollins.co.uk/green

For Nicky

Contents

Part Three: The Arrow of History

Part Four: People

Part Five: Pastimes

Part Six: Crime and the Law

Part Seven: My Times

Introduction

I suppose you could say that I really started working on this book when I was eight years old.

It was then that I began getting up early so that I could be the first one to read the newspaper. Rather to the bemusement of my parents, who had absolutely no interest in sport, I'd become a football fan, and I wanted to read the match reports and the scores before my dad came downstairs to make breakfast. After that, the paper was his.

So as soon as it arrived I would skip to the front door, lay *The Times* out on the hall rug, and, starting with the back pages, read whatever football news there was. Which wasn't much, to be honest.

After I'd been doing this each day for a couple of years, it occurred to me that the paper seemed to contain a lot of other stuff and maybe it was interesting. So when I had completed my survey of the football coverage, I turned the paper over and began again at the front.

It was at about this time that the burglars were caught in the Watergate complex. I was soon hooked on the stories of the President and his men. And on the other political battles that made the mid-1970s such a fascinating political time.

It made me rather an odd child, though. I obtained the autographs of Norman St John-Stevas and Ray Buckton (google them). I collected *Times* Guides to the House of Commons and memorised the size of majorities of MPs. When Giscard d'Estaing became President of France, my French teacher told the class about it and announced that he had until then been defence minister. I responded that in fact Giscard had been finance minister. I was, at that point, eleven.

And so I first became attached to three of the great passions of my life: football, politics and *The Times*. And much as I imagined I might grow out of one or the other of them, I never have.

My parents couldn't talk to me much about football, although they did try. My father, a bookish professor, even took me to Hendon games. Sitting in the freezing cold at half time in a recent Hendon home match I heard over the tannoy: 'Elsewhere in the league it's Billericay nil, Bognor Regis nil', and I thought, my goodness, my dad must have loved me very much.

But politics was a different matter. I wouldn't say either of them was excessively political and they were both less-than-usually argumentative people. But they did think public affairs mattered a great deal and they were thrilled that I did too.

So, over breakfast each day we would talk about what was in the news. Other things came up. Philosophy a little, mathematics a fair bit and religion too (more out of intellectual interest than devotion). But mostly it was politics.

Around the time I first became interested, 1970 or so, my parents were both Labour voters. Dad, especially, really liked Harold Wilson. As an engineer (a measurement theorist to be precise), my father felt that modern systems and planning were the way to organise a society. The talk of forging a new Britain in the white heat of technology was very attractive to him.

As I write later in this book, he was also an immigrant who had lived on welfare benefits, made his way through night school and worked in the coal mines. He found the Conservative Party of Macmillan an alien thing and suspected the feeling was mutual.

He did have one problem with Labour, however. As a child he had been deported to Siberia along with his mother, and his father had been arrested and sentenced to hard labour as a capitalist and democratic civic leader. As a result of this, my father did not trust the MPs to Wilson's left, but this rather increased his support for Wilson himself.

My mother – a maths teacher and as much a believer in scientific progress as Dad – shared this concern about extremists, but for a reason that was both different and not so different. She was a survivor of Belsen concentration camp. She was always pretty wary politically of anybody – how shall I put this – over-excitable.

By the end of the 1970s, my dad had come to the conclusion that planning the economy didn't work, and both of them became concerned about the Left. Thus began the shift that saw them vote SDP in the 1980s and Conservative after that, though very much of the Major/Cameron kind.

So this was the environment I grew up in. A generally progressive household, but a *Times*-reading one rather than a *Guardian*-reading one. Rationalist and pro-science, firmly on the American side of the Cold War, socially liberal on race and women's equality, for the welfare state and public services, for free speech and the rule of law and, above all other things, for moderation, a sense of proportion and generosity to other people.

Whether it is nature or nurture – a bit of both I think – this isn't a bad description of my own politics all these years later. My mum often used to use the phrase 'Everything in Moderation'. She mostly applied it to portion size and her willingness to try anything once, but it could pretty much be our family political slogan.

All of these hobbies and instincts I brought with me when I joined *The Times* properly in 2001. Plus one other thing: a lot of political experience.

By the age of twenty-four, I had already run for Parliament. I was the SDP's candidate against Ken Livingstone in Brent East in 1987. I was far too young. I hadn't had a proper job yet, I lived at home and I couldn't drive. I've a letter from the local Citizen's Advice Bureau somewhere that reads: 'Dear Mr Finkelstein, it was so nice to meet you, and your mother.'

But I'd become close to the party leader David Owen and he'd become a mentor. Actually he still is. I did a lot of growing up when I worked with David. During the 1987 election we had breakfast every day before his press conference. He said he found it helpful and I believe him, because he doesn't dissemble, even to your face. But I suspect it was me that found it more useful.

I learned a lot from David about national politics, fighting by his side on the party's national committee. I also learned a great deal about how to maintain your integrity and independence, how to think things through for yourself and ensure you never let being moderate make you go soft altogether.

Ultimately, of course, we were unsuccessful: the party collapsed, and I rather surprised myself by what I did next. I joined the Conservative Party.

My politics had certainly shifted a bit since my teens. I'd become quite a lot more convinced of the benefits of a capitalist market economy, quite a bit more fiscally conservative and a little more sceptical about government intervention. But what changed most was my view of political alliances.

Experience had made me appreciate that you can't build a broad enough political movement if you only worked with people who shared your views and your background completely. The world isn't full of Jewish sons of refugees or people from Hendon Central with Master's degrees in computing.

The miners' strike, the argument over CND and the obvious fact that many of Mrs Thatcher's reforms had been necessary also made me realise that I was trying to be right wing on the left. So the Tories it was.

Within about three years of joining the party I found myself round the Cabinet table briefing the Prime Minister as his head of research. It was the tail end of an eighteen-year government and politically it was very tough. But it was hard not to respect John Major or be proud of serving him. I wasn't too surprised, however, when we suffered a huge defeat.

What followed was sometimes hilariously difficult. I became a close adviser to William Hague and convinced I was supporting someone who deserved to be prime minister. He was incisive, calm, witty and kind. His qualifications seemed to me obvious. But it was difficult to get anyone to agree. These days there are lots of takers for that proposition, but at the time nothing we did made any difference. Maybe that is because some of it wasn't very good, but then again, even when it was brilliant – Prime Minister's Questions for instance – it made no difference.

It was partly as a result of this I began to grasp something very important. Something I'm embarrassed I didn't get earlier. People aren't following politics. To what is really an astonishingly great degree. What moves politics are much deeper things – demographics, how the economy is changing, instinctive and hard-to-move reactions to the party leaders. Grasping this was my first step to real understanding. I don't think there is one column in this book that isn't touched by this awakening.

It was also during this period I appreciated properly how serious the Conservative Party's problems had become. I am quite an optimistic person and sometimes I'd persuade myself that things weren't as bad as they looked. Andrew Cooper was there to put me right. I'd met him in college and he had become a hugely successful pollster as well as one of my best friends. He didn't share my Pollyannaish tendency, being instead a pitiless empiricist. And he was almost invariably correct.

I started to meet up with others over pizza to discuss how the party could become more moderate, modern and liberal. There'd be four or five of us each time. One of them was George

Osborne (also a close friend) and another was David Cameron. We shared frustration, but in David's mind the idea of what to do next began to take shape.

So anyway, all that is a long way of saying that in 2001, when I joined *The Times* after being defeated in Harrow West in the election, I brought with me years of working on the inside. But also the complication that I had publicly known political views, an agenda and friends and allies active in politics.

The stakes became higher when one of those friends became the prime minister and another the chancellor of the exchequer.

I took the view that I couldn't escape this, and I shouldn't deny it. So the best thing to do was to give readers the benefit of the understanding I gained, the insight I had, while being honest about who I was. I was an opinion writer and not a news reporter. I hope (and think) readers felt I struck the right balance.

I've read *The Times* every day since those first encounters with it on the rug, rarely missing an edition. It has always suited my temperament and mostly suited my politics too.

And that may be what accounted for the feeling I had sitting in reception at the paper, waiting for a meeting with Peter Stothard, the editor. I had a number of different job offers and they all seemed very interesting and to offer good prospects. But in the reception of *The Times* I felt a sense of excitement and also one of belonging.

I proposed to Peter a sort of online think tank: basically a blog in the days before such things existed. He was mildly interested in that, but more interested in me joining as a leader writer.

It wasn't long before I started writing columns for the paper. And three things were, I think, particularly important in the columns I ended up writing.

The first is a piece of advice I received when I first started writing a regular column for the main comment pages (or op-eds as they are known, as this sort of article initially appeared opposite the editorials).

The first columns I wrote appeared in the features pages, where I was asked to stand in for the historian and journalist Anthony Howard while he wrote a book. The appropriate style for such a column was informal, relaxed and personal. I would bring in anecdotes and talk of my own experiences.

Then Michael Gove, one of the paper's most prominent and popular writers, was selected as a parliamentary candidate and it was decided to move his column to features and that I would take over his op-ed slot.

Just before I made the move the features editor Sandra Parsons told me I should take care not to change too much. Keep it informal, keep it personal. Don't feel the op-ed pages require you to be stiff or pompous. It was wise counsel. Where stiffness and pomposity remained, it was at least my own personal stiffness and pomposity rather than being put on for the occasion.

Also important was inspiration from my brother. I have always lived surrounded by books. My grandfather (my mother's father) had been the archivist of the German anti-Nazi movement and established a library, one of the largest collections of material about fascism in the world.

Quite apart from the library, he bought so many books of his own that he was driven out of his flat above the ice-skating rink in Queensway into a house in Golders Green, in order to have enough shelf space. He devoted three entire rooms of this house to books, although he was frustrated when a structural engineer put a limit on the number of volumes he could store. Apparently the engineer was concerned that the floors would collapse under the weight.

My father then also bought many thousands of books of his own, some hundreds having been given to him by his father-in-law as an engagement present. The overwhelming majority of these were on Judaism, which was my father's intellectual hobby. And I, like Dad, started by being quite focused in my reading. Politics and history, history and politics.

My brother, by contrast, though distinguished in his field (software engineering) has always been amazingly eclectic in his reading. If you introduced someone to him and said they were an expert in the history of Chinese piracy, Anthony would invariably remark: 'How interesting, I've just been reading a book on that.'

It rubbed off on me eventually. I began to experiment more. Social science, social history, books about murders and about baseball, random books that just looked a bit interesting and might take me off on an interesting tangent. And I'd often share what I learned with readers.

Sometimes people ask me how I have managed to read so much and I've never been sure of the answer. I'm not particularly speedy. But I am pretty dedicated. Whenever I am not doing anything else, which turns out to be a lot of the time, I'm reading.

From this inspiration I had an insight. There was a huge amount of social and political science that could cast light on the news and it wasn't necessarily appearing in other people's columns. Game theory, for instance, and social psychology. And at one point in my first couple of years at *The Times* I stumbled into statistics.

During the World Cup in 2002 I began to write a column on football, using statistical analysis to illuminate the game. These columns don't appear in this book, but their influence does. I began to think about issues in a different way, understanding how concepts like reversion to the mean might aid my understanding of politics and social affairs.

Armed with all this, I settled in to write a weekly column that has appeared, and still appears, on Wednesday every week since 2005. And there hasn't been a single week in that entire period when I didn't wake up nervous on a Tuesday morning, wondering if this week's column was really going to work when you started writing it for real.

But it's got to work. It's appearing in *The Times*, after all.

Actually, Tuesday's nerves are only part of it. The most difficult part of producing a column isn't writing it. It's having the idea. From the moment a column appears, I start to worry about what on earth I am going to put in the next one. And the fear grows until an idea comes.

I might have been reading the paper and articles and books all week and be completely blank. And then, emptying the dishwasher, a column will appear to me while I'm putting away the teaspoons. Sometimes it is just the very basic argument, other times it's the whole thing.

Once it does, though, I may (in fact almost always do) need to do quite a bit of reading. I might want to use an academic study or tell a historical story or write about someone who has just died. I am fanatical about getting this stuff right and ensuring that even the most expert reader would accept that I know what I'm talking about. Because one thing I can be sure of, working on *The Times*, is that even the most obscure points will come to the attention of the expert on the subject.

Once I have the idea I have to agree it with the Comment Page Editor. Often I will give them more than one potential column and they will pick. Sometimes they – or very occasionally the editor through them – will tell me that the paper has already run too many columns on this idea and I should come back to it another time. But it's a matter of pride not to propose such ideas if I can help it.

I have often been asked whether I am told what position to take and I can honestly say that this has never happened. Well, OK, once I wanted to write a column telling Sir John Chilcot to take as long as he wanted to complete his report on the Iraq war. I unwittingly timed this for the day on which the paper was launching a series of news reports which suggested he needed to get on with it. I was politely but firmly asked if I might pick another topic and I gladly agreed. But apart from that, never.

Once I've been given the go-ahead I'll settle in and start writing. I try not to schedule any distractions for Tuesdays so that the column in my head is the one I get down on paper. How long does a column take? Well it's 1150 words and it takes usually between two and three hours to write down. But in reality it has taken me somewhere between three hours and the entirety of my life since I was eight years old.

Finally, a word about this book.

I've written something like 700 columns for *The Times* and had room in this volume for about 110 of them. The earliest column in this volume was written in 2003, the latest on the day Theresa May announced she was leaving office in March 2019 (which seemed a reasonable place to stop).

When I read them all again, obviously I was looking for the best ones, but just as important was that they should still seem relevant and interesting now. For instance, I wrote a column on gay rights which I was pleased with, but a lot of it dealt with the religious opinions of Ruth Kelly, a Blair-era cabinet minister. I thought this material would mystify readers who had forgotten the details of this political row.

Equally there were some columns which predicted exactly what was going to happen next. I am rather proud of them, but once the predicted events had happened, I concluded that the article might be more interesting to me than to readers of this book.

In some places context is necessary to enjoy the column properly, and I've added a short couple of sentences of explanation before the column begins. But in many cases they should be immediately understandable without notes.

I decided early on to group the articles together by theme

rather than chronology. Where useful – in my articles on the big political battles of my time as a columnist for instance – the sections do follow a chronological order. Elsewhere – the section on great contemporary figures – it does not.

I grouped together some political columns on the issues of the day that I think elucidate basic rules of politics. And I have also included a lecture, very much inspired by the columns in *The Times*, that has not yet been published.

There are some issues I care about that are missing and one or two columns are excluded because, while they were quite good, I've repented of the views in them (such as a horrible column suggesting that I didn't really care about Scottish independence, which I passionately do).

I haven't altered the ones that are included, even when a phrase or idea or prediction makes me wince. The only changes I have made are a few tiny excisions when I have repeated a word or when the sentence reads particularly poorly or I have made an observation more than once in the book. I have also, in one or two places, removed a reference to an event that might have meant something to the reader in the week it was written but is now just distracting. When making such a change I have been particularly careful to avoid altering the sense of anything I've said.

I've also kept the headlines from the original articles in most cases.

So here they are. My wife always observes that op-ed columns are either obvious or rubbish. I hope you will find more of the former than the latter. And perhaps one or two that aren't either.

PART ONE

The Sound of the Suburbs

When I became Comment Editor of *The Times*, I used to tell our columnists that it wasn't enough for readers to learn what the writer thought. They also had to be convinced that it mattered.

This was partly about the evidence they produced to support their argument of course. But it was also about giving readers a sense of who the writers are, where they come from, what their values are.

So I suppose I should start this collection in the same way, with columns that give you a sense of my outlook. Not everything, of course, but some important things.

The suburbs are what make Britain great

Bourgeois life is too easy a target for satire.
There's nothing better than the dual carriageway
and a job in extra-wet tissues

12 August 2015

Some years ago my father came home from an academic conference with a picture book he'd been given by his visitors, *Oulu, the Fifth Biggest Town in Finland.*

It was crammed with photographs of the highlights of this jewel of Northern Ostrobothnia. The town hall, the sawmill museum, a bicycle stand, a deserted shopping street covered in snow. There was also plenty of useful information. Since 1996 Oulu has hosted the Air Guitar World Championship. And at the end of the book was a picture of a dual carriageway accompanied by the suggestion that we might like to visit Oulu. 'Or better still, go round it.'

At first I thought this meant that the whole book had been a joke. Slowly, however, I realised that they were simply proud of the Oulu ring road and were advising us not to miss the chance of travelling on it once we'd had our fill of sawmills.

You might think of this column as: In Defence of Oulu.

It is prompted by the death of that great genius David Nobbs, the author of *The Fall and Rise of Reginald Perrin*, the man who appreciated the comedy in describing a train arriving eleven minutes late at Waterloo station owing to staff difficulties at Hampton Wick.

Nobbs chronicles the monotony of daily suburban life brilliantly. Walking down Coleridge Close and turning right into Tennyson Avenue, filling in the crossword on the journey into work at Sunshine Desserts, the three pictures on his boss's wall: 'A Francis Bacon, a John Bratby and a photograph of CJ holding the lemon mousse which had won second prize in the convenience foods category at the 1963 Paris Concours Des Desserts.'

Nobbs said that one of his inspirations was the thought that people have such strange jobs: 'You can't grow up wanting to become an executive for extra-wet strength tissues.' A life trying to think of ways to market products like Kumquat Surprise ('What about something like, off the top of my head, I like to stroke my nipple with a strawberry and lychee ripple') drives Reggie to a breakdown.

Though Nobbs was an uncommon talent, his was not an uncommon target. The futility of suburban or small-town life, the banality of commerce and management, the hypocrisy of respectable lives behind net curtains, the despair as youth trickles away into middle age.

And every time I watch Richard Briers quit for a life of self-sufficiency in Surbiton, or Kevin Spacey's character Lester Burnham melt down in *American Beauty*, or Reggie Perrin fake his suicide, I am struck by the same thought inspired by the guide to Oulu.

Sunshine Desserts is the height of civilisation. Lester Burnham was better off when he went to work in an office and looked after his family. Oulu is right to boast of its ring road, which is quite an achievement.

When we look at history we regard as heroes those who

fought and those who conquered, those who were martyrs for their point of view, those who set out on great adventures, those who built great cathedrals and pyramids.

Yet I think it is a fine ambition to have been an executive for extra-wet strength tissues. In the history of mankind how many better jobs have there been? How many have been better paid? More comfortable? Less dangerous? More inoffensively useful to their fellow man?

The HR department of a children's shoe brand has never launched a war. Nobody dies in the creation of advertisements for Kumquat Surprise. Surely the reason our ancestors struggled so hard and even fought wars is so that we, their children, could live happily on the commuter line to King's Cross, heading into work on the 8.17.

I always sigh when I hear people attack consumerism. All that hunger, and war and pestilence, all that dictatorship and torture and tragedy and they want to attack shopping?

I was brought up in Hendon Central and when I was thirteen years old they opened Brent Cross Shopping Centre. I could walk there without crossing the road. My father was a cultured man, a highly sophisticated intellectual, but he regarded the shopping centre as among the great beneficial developments of mankind.

He had almost starved as a young boy in a Soviet-imposed exile. When my father was thirteen years old he couldn't walk to the shopping centre because there wasn't one in Siberia. He couldn't drive there either, because Stalin had the car.

For him, the ability to buy a prepared sandwich in Marks & Spencer or meet my mother for a crusty roll and butter in the Tesco coffee shop represented a great advance in the condition of man. And isn't it wonderful to live in a country in which we worry seriously about becoming too fat?

People talk about the death of big ideas. The great thing about Britain is our small ideas and our pragmatism, our suburbs and our bourgeois stability. This thing – this apparent banality – that we so easily satirise is what people at the Channel Tunnel are desperate to have. They are fighting their way to be able to work in the Alpine Dry Cleaners in Hatch End. The right to purchase *Good Housekeeping* in the WHSmith on Bridge Street is as attractive a right as all those contained in the Declaration of Independence.

The Metropolitan Line from Pinner, change across the platform to the Jubilee Line at Finchley Road, is not quiet despair, it is salvation. Oh for delays caused by leaves on the line! Come bring me your apologies for inconvenience!

The heroes of history are those who do not fight wars; those who instead create a world fit for people to market non-stick frying pans and sell to each other oven-ready chips. Yvette Cooper. Jeremy Hunt. Not Julius Caesar. Or Fidel Castro.

Give me any day a politician who has been special adviser to the agriculture minister over a man on a white charger come to purify the nation and sweep away its corruption. For I well know who will be doing the sweeping and who will be the swept.

Give me special advisers and special offers. When people are trying things on in the changing rooms of Top Shop they are too busy to start transporting the Jews to the East.

We have toiled hard over centuries to create places like Oulu and Pinner, where we can live in peace and work in offices with desk chairs that swivel. Let the sun shine on Sunshine Desserts.

Not every age needs a Churchill or a de Gaulle

My mother's life taught me the value of political
moderation and to be distrustful of radical change
and big ideas

8 February 2017

A couple of weeks ago I received in the mail a copy of a book
called *Survivor*. It contained stunning portraits of Holocaust
survivors taken by the photographer Harry Borden. And one
of them was a wonderful picture of my mother, standing by
the open door of the dining room at her house in Hendon.

Accompanying each portrait were a few words from the
subject in their own handwriting. Next to hers, Mum had
written: 'I think of myself as a person, a wife and mother first
and a survivor last.'

Last week, after a long illness, she died. And I have found
myself standing by the same open dining-room door and thinking
about what she had said. Here's my attempt to make sense of it.

Whenever my mother told of her arrest and being taken to
a concentration camp by cattle truck, she would always add
that my father had spent much longer in such a truck when
exiled to the Siberian borders by Stalin.

Partly this reflected her natural modesty. She found competitive stories of suffering utterly ludicrous, and was keen to undercut her own. But partly it was to emphasise the way in which the enemies of liberty, however different they look, produce the same misery and death.

Even as a child it wasn't hard to absorb the simple political lesson. It was to be resolute in defence of democracy, free speech and the rule of law. When I was a student I was often offered dope, but refused it because Mum and Dad taught me never, ever to break the law. If you don't respect the rules laid down by a freely elected parliament, where next? My friends remind me that I refused to tape records for them because it breached copyright.

As an adult, however, I began to understand better the subtlety of my parents' politics. Actually, more than their politics, their way of looking at the world.

My mum's favourite joke was 'Apart from that, Mrs Lincoln, how did you enjoy the theatre?' Indeed, when my father died, I returned in a hurry from watching Chelsea play Norwich City and my mother looked at me and said: 'What was the score?' (It was 3-1 by the way.)

The reason she found the Lincoln joke funny was that she thought nothing so absurd as a lack of a sense of proportion. It would have been a perfectly reasonable response to Belsen and exile for my parents to have had a hair trigger, to see the next Holocaust in every event, the next Stalin in every bumptious leadership figure. Instead, they went the other way.

My mother's view was that if she lived her life as a 'survivor', she would be granting Hitler the ultimate triumph. She would live as a person, a wife and a mother. She would note not how similar events were to a fresh disaster, but how dissimilar they were.

My parents never involved themselves in a hedge (or any other) dispute with a neighbour, it was out of the question to disapprove of their children's partners, they never took sides in rows on the synagogue council. It isn't quite true that we children were never admonished, but they were remarkably tolerant. Even when I failed to realise that Copydex glue for carpets was intended for the underside.

The only time I remember being properly told off was for claiming, just before dinner, to be starving. Justly, my parents found my failure to appreciate what starving really was, offensive.

Inevitably, this all had an impact on their politics and on mine. It isn't just that we find unbelievably stupid, people who put the Nazi emblem on the European Union flag or call it the EUSSR. It's broader than that.

The great figures of history are often seen as those who are unreasonable in circumstances where reason no longer applies. Take Charles de Gaulle, for instance. He was stubbornly, almost insanely, unreasonable about small things as well as big ones. And his pettiness was his greatness. Through it he preserved the rights of France and secured its independence.

No one would argue that Winston Churchill was always reasonable or acted proportionately. Nor that, in different circumstances, Margaret Thatcher was either. There are moments in history for people willing and able to be incredibly bloody-minded and to appreciate that great acts of change or resistance are necessary.

But not every moment is like that and not every circumstance requires it. There is greatness too in the ability to compromise, to moderate, to accept with generosity the eccentricities and obsessions of others. It can be an achievement when nothing much happens.

America's first president had his wars and his monument. America's fifth president, James Monroe, cannot boast a great cathartic moment, or a spectacular military victory. Only a period in office known as 'the era of good feeling'. But I know which president I would rather have lived under. There would be no Monroe without Washington, but what would be the point of a Washington if we were never able to enjoy the era of Monroe?

And not every political event requires courage and resistance. Sometimes acceptance and understanding are the right response. I notice the imprint of my parents' politics on my view of leaving the European Union. I wanted to remain, but you know what? We'll live. Even if the worst predictions of the economic consequences are correct, which they probably aren't, we will live.

My parents thought political moderation was a virtue in itself. They regarded grand conspiracy theories as bizarre, and sweeping big ideas as unconvincing. My dad liked Harold Wilson precisely for the reason some of Wilson's colleagues despised him, because he was a pragmatist who adapted to circumstances. I think politically Mum was happiest when she supported the SDP, though she admired John Major.

My mum didn't want to live all her life as a survivor. She wanted a country that was free but also safe and stable. She didn't want a turbulent politics that sucked in every citizen. She wanted reason and moderation and a sense of proportion so that she could do more than survive.

So that she could live, and love, and nurture and prosper. And, in the end, so that she could die in peace and tranquillity in her adopted home.

Once in a while just go for it, hell for leather

Moderation is fine for every day, but for one-off moments adopt an uncompromising, Steve Jobs approach

Oscar Wilde once said: 'Everything in moderation. Including moderation.' Although probably someone else said it first. This column appeared during the London Olympics, of which I'd always been a supporter.

8 August 2012

Enthusiasm for the Olympics has its critics. Someone wrote to me last week describing the whole thing as a disappointment, while complaining that there were so many empty seats. This reminded me of Woody Allen's joke about the two Jewish women and the restaurant. 'The food here is terrible,' says one. 'Yes,' says the other, 'and such small portions.'

One argument, however, I feel I have to take seriously. It goes, roughly, like this. It's fun and all that, but we've spent billions of pounds and as many hours so that some people can run around in circles for a fortnight.

I've thought a little about how to respond to this and I feel the best way is by telling you about my one sporting triumph. I beat Sebastian Coe in an egg-and-spoon race. Not at school. As adults. He already had his gold medals. And there was none of this stuff he did against Steve Ovett, none of this coming back in his less good race later and being vindicated. He was just beaten and I won, end of.

The thing is, you see, that Seb turned out to run quite fast, faster than me (on the day). But he dropped the egg and I didn't.

The egg-and-spoon race rewards moderation. If you run too slowly you lose anyway. Run too quickly and there's a good chance that you will lose the egg. Egg-and-spoon suits both my athletic ability (although in the ten years since my famous victory, I've lost a yard or two of pace) and my attitude to life.

I am, in general, conservative with a small c. I am suspicious of big schemes, of people with a glint in their eye and a simple solution, of those with dogmatic obsessions who can't resist hammering it home. I am all for the spirit of compromise, taking one thing with another, seeing if we can't fold everyone into the solution. Naturally I suffer from the inevitable human failing of believing myself more reasonable than others think me, but you get the idea.

And the Olympics, the history of it, the conduct of the competitors and, indeed, the very fact of London 2012, is a contradiction of that idea.

At the end of last year, Walter Isaacson published his excellent biography of Steve Jobs. And it turns out that in many ways Jobs was dreadful. He was manipulative, egotistical, ready to trample over people to an extraordinary extent and his head was full of highly eccentric notions, particularly about his health and diet.

He was also simply brilliant. And there was a connection between his impossible personality and the impossible results he achieved. He insisted that his singular vision, his concept, however extreme and impractical it might seem, was delivered exactly as he had conceived it.

He was quite unwilling to compromise with anybody or even with reality. He ignored cost, or even whether the parts he wished to include in his new product existed. He thought anyone who couldn't see things as he saw them was a fool and should be treated as such. He lied and cheated to get his way. And he succeeded.

This can't be a rule for everyone's behaviour. It can't be countenanced. And even for one person, it can end in disaster, as with Jobs it often did. But the extremism, the insistence on seeing through his idea without challenge, that's what made it so good. You can't always be like that, but sometimes you have to be.

To follow the history of the Olympics is to be struck by the unbelievable dogmatism of Avery Brundage, for decades the leading light in the International Olympic Committee. He held to his ideas – that the Olympics should be for amateurs, and that politics should be kept out of it – to the point of madness. In the late 1950s he was still complaining publicly about the 'well financed' campaign in the 1930s against the Nazi Olympics of 1936.

Yet at the same time it is hard to avoid the conclusion that without this singular, blinkered, intense commitment – one that it would often have been hard for a reasonable, moderate person to justify – the Olympics would have collapsed long before London 2012.

Brundage's behaviour was hard to tolerate, but perhaps sportsmen tolerated it because, at some level, they understood his extremism. Bill Furniss, the swimming coach, describes intense sessions with the great champion Rebecca Adlington as 'sick-bucket sessions' because they push her to the absolute limit. One of Adlington's great advantages as a swimmer, her admirers explain, is her willingness to endure pain.

Who does that? And why? It is to achieve a moment, even if only a fleeting one, of uncompromised brilliance. She endures pain because she has a singular vision that brooks no opposition or interference. Not everyone can do it, and she can't go on doing it for ever, but what it produces is something worth having. And something that can't be obtained in any other way.

That's what we've done with these Olympics. We achieved something great, something wonderful, because we went all in, because we brooked no compromise, because we stopped at nothing.

We spent millions and millions of pounds on an opening ceremony and then allowed one man's vision to determine its content. It was, at points, more than slightly bonkers, but for the same reason it was worth watching. It never seemed like it was made by committee.

And then we spent billions on staging the Games themselves. We created Olympic lanes, and told office workers to stay at home, and covered Horse Guards Parade in sand so that women in bikinis could play volleyball on the parade ground. We took a ludicrous amount of trouble. We never said we couldn't. We never said we wouldn't. We just did it, whatever it took – to deliver it just right, without a corner being cut and without even common prudence calling a halt.

And what we have got has been worth it, even if it has been a bit mad. The fact that once in a lifetime we got it out of proportion has been the point. We couldn't have had it any other way.

It isn't a way to govern, of course. You'd run too fast and drop the egg, you see. I think my moderation is the right way most of the time. But I wonder if we couldn't do it just occasionally. A new airport perhaps. Some people look at the Olympics and think: 'Whatever next?' And I think that's rather a good question.

Peace and freedom: the blessings of capitalism

The great ideologies dispossessed my father. It was democracy that let him live and die in safety and contentment

7 September 2011

A little more than a week ago my father lifted his arms and did something that he had done countless times before, blessed his children as he ushered in the Sabbath. But he was doing it for the last time. When he had finished, his hands fell to his side. He died the next day, with the blessing as his final act.

He had known for several weeks that his illness was terminal, and each day he grew more tired. But through it all his mind remained as sharp as ever, which is to say very sharp. And so each night in those precious days before his death, I sat by his bedside and we talked, sometimes about his extraordinary life, sometimes about a task that still needed doing (updating, for instance, some references in the book he had been writing about Polish Jewry) and sometimes about the future of capitalism.

I didn't find these odd topics, even though he was so ill. My father cited 'conversation' as his chief hobby, along with 'not gardening', and took both seriously. Yet with him, the small talk was never small.

Throughout my life we would discuss philosophy and argue about politics over breakfast. At dinner we might talk about problems of physics and maths, with a long discussion about how many cans of drink might be fitted into a fridge of a given volume. Both my parents, I recall from one Friday night meal, felt very strongly that it is insufficiently appreciated that a centimetre is not a proper SI measurement.

The day after a debate on some ethical question I would often get a call, my father having sought clarification from a scriptural source or from one of his many reference books.

And all of this seemed so natural that it is only in writing it down now that it occurs to me it might seem a little eccentric to others. Oh, well.

Anyway, all this is to say that considering the future of capitalism counted as light chit-chat. Our latest discussions began because I had been reading some articles by journalists and commentators whom I respected, which argued that the Left had been correct about capitalism all along. Capitalism, they said, had proved to be a conspiracy of the elite against the masses. Karl Marx's prediction that it was inherently unstable had been right.

I wanted to know what my dad thought because, as far as I could see, this argument contradicted the experience of his life.

In response he began, as he often did, by telling me a story. It was one that I knew – the one about the cocoa and the bones – but one that I wanted to hear again, just one more time. In 1941, when Hitler invaded the Soviet Union, my grandfather had been released from a labour camp, where he had been serving a sentence of eight years' hard labour for having been, the communists judged, a 'socially dangerous element'.

Leaving prison, my grandfather had joined the Polish Army Corps, had traced his family to the remote Siberian outpost where they had been exiled, and had managed to send them a little money.

After almost two years of starvation, my father and his mother rejoiced that they had some cash, and, their deportation order having been lifted, the right to spend it. My grandmother decided to go to the finest restaurant in the whole of Semipalatinsk.

In they went, a waiter took my grandmother's coat and they sat down, each with a large and fancy-looking menu card. Yet as they requested items, they were told that unfortunately, today, this or that was off the menu. Eventually my grandmother was forced to ask: 'Well, what do you have?' Just bones and cocoa, came the reply.

My father never had much time for complaints that 'consumerism' was undermining the moral fabric of society. He thought it odd that people would regard it as a bad thing to produce items to buy and sell and to make a profit from them. He also thought that a gloomy view of Britain and Britons totally lacked perspective. The idea that ordinary people did not benefit from capitalism seemed to him too obviously absurd to require refutation.

However, the main benefit of capitalism was not, as far as he was concerned, money. Beyond the ability to purchase books and the occasional Indian takeaway, he was not motivated by accumulating wealth. He left an inexpensive Casio watch which, as a measurement scientist, he liked because it told the time accurately. What he really appreciated about liberal capitalist democracy is that it left him in peace. In peace and freedom.

A fellow detainee in my grandfather's prison had tried to persuade him not to leave when he was released. They could stay safely in the camp, he said, and drink the meths in the hospital. On behalf of his family, my grandfather chose freedom instead. And though it brought many trials and years without land to call home, my father never doubted its virtue.

The great sweeping ideologies had been a failure. They had driven him from his home and from his life, killed his relatives, dispossessed his family. My dad took a rather dim view of those extolling Marx's powers of analysis, which he found, to say the least, wanting. He supported capitalism for the small things that it brought – the suburbs, the rule of law, Brent Cross Shopping Centre. He was safe here. His family was safe here. The vast majority of British people are safe here.

In those last days, we discussed, too, how his life showed that it was, in any case, silly to think of Britain as some sort of free-market anarchy. My father had been on National Assistance when he first came here, had spent years in the coal mines working for a nationalised industry and had then spent the bulk of his career as a university professor.

Unlike those of us born here, my father became British on purpose, as a conscious act, one that he had thought about deeply. He never thought Britain's leaders corrupt, or that the country was going to the dogs, or that our society was collapsing, undermined by its moral decay. He lived here proud of a nation that let him live, let him learn, let him teach, and let him practise his religion. He knew what it meant to be British.

Six reasons why I'm an uber-moderniser

David Cameron must not retreat from his progressive agenda

Just before the 2003 Conservative conference George Osborne, then still shadow chancellor, gave an interview in the *Spectator* in which he said that he 'didn't take the kind of uber-modernising view that some have had, that you can't talk about crime or immigration or lower taxes. It is just that you can't do so to the exclusion of the NHS, the environment and economic stability.' I didn't really disagree with this, but it was interpreted as George (who absolutely is an uber-moderniser) distancing himself from modernisers. So I thought it an opportunity to state some of my own basic views about Conservative politics.

3 October 2007

I am about to do something dangerous, something I might regret. I am about to allow myself to be labelled. The history of this is not encouraging. A few days ago Roy Hattersley wrote about how much he wishes he had not accepted the label 'old Labour'.

And put it this way, the Tory 'wets' are no longer paying a grateful retainer to their branding consultancy.

But the boy can't help it. I am an uber-moderniser. The moment the phrase was coined by George Osborne to describe the keepers of the Tory modernising faith I realised the term fitted me perfectly.

There are plenty of people who think that what David Cameron should do now is gently retreat from all that modernising rhetoric. It is all too 'Blair', they argue, and there isn't enough in it for Middle Britain. I completely disagree. A sharp break from the strategy that lost three elections is essential. When Mr Cameron stands up later today, he needs to show that he still carries the modernising torch.

Here, then, is the uber-modernisers' manifesto.

That optimism triumphs over pessimism

Tory modernisers argue that the Conservatives must talk about more than the economy. Quite right. But we uber-modernisers worry. We think that all this talk of the quality of life can easily lead the Tories to sound gloomy, angry, at odds with today's society, banging on about anarchy on the streets.

And voters will come to associate the Tories with that pessimism, just as visitors to a car show associate the vehicle with the sexy woman sitting on the bonnet. Mr Cameron must talk of his confidence in modern Britain. A sunshine strategy, that's what uber-modernisers want to see.

When you talk about them, voters learn about you

The Tory party members would cheer a vicious attack on Gordon Brown, but it would still be a mistake. Voters will not rely on Tories to tell them what to think about the Prime Minister. Instead they listen to Tory politicians and make their mind up about Tories. Are they reasonable? Are they pleasant? Are they in touch?

Last week there was a ludicrous call for [Labour minister] James Purnell to resign because somebody, without his permission, had photoshopped his picture to suggest he had been in a group photo. In fact he had been slightly late and photographed separately. Uber-modernisers regard calling for his resignation, as some did, as an indication that Conservatives still don't get the point about being seen as reasonable and intelligent. And it's an important one, since commenting about Labour is one of the main things that TV viewers see Conservatives do.

That to win, Tories must appeal to their core vote
This may seem a bit odd. Isn't the whole point of modernising to move away from a core-vote strategy? Ah, but that depends on what you think the Tory core vote is.

Uber-modernisers argue that the real core vote for the Conservatives, the people who have elected Tory governments for a century, are the middle class, and particularly women. The experiences, views and aspirations of this core have changed massively in the past twenty years and the Tory party failed to change with it. Instead the party chased after new voters who shared traditional Tory prejudices. This group is too small, lives in the wrong places and is disinclined to vote Conservative.

A proper core-vote strategy requires a more liberal, tolerant Tory party in tune with working women and the modern middle class.

That brand decontamination comes before everything
The very start of the modernising journey was the realisation that a proposition that could win popular support became unpopular the moment it was advanced by the Conservatives.

So before you can make a successful public appeal on crime, immigration or, say, voucher schemes for schools, you first have to persuade the voters to trust the party.

You have to remove from the party's brand the idea that, for instance, it doesn't care about public services and that it dislikes foreigners. You have to show that what matters to voters matters to you and matters more than your obsessions – say on Europe – and more than Westminster gossip.

While Mr Cameron has made some progress, personally, on

this task, the party as a whole has a long way to go. Uber-modernisers are concerned that the party overestimates how far voters think it has come.

That the danger is having too much policy, not too little
When David Cameron became leader he was told by almost every commentator that he needed lots of policy. Not us Uber-modernisers.

Policies don't win elections. Victory comes from voters feeling that a party is fit for government and preferably that voting for them is something to be proud of. And policies don't tell people how you are going to govern either. The micropolicy produced in opposition by a research team too small to do it well forms only the smallest part of the real programme of a government.

So uber-modernisers were always concerned about having large numbers of policy commissions under light central control. And we were right. The confusing mess of unfiltered policy ideas has been very damaging.

In his speech Mr Cameron needs to make a proper argument, accompanied by big statements of direction on important issues, but not make lots of small, poorly thought-out policy promises.

That you must show as well as tell
It is not enough to say that you have changed. You must demonstrate it. It's what you are that matters, not just what you say.

Since party reform is one of the few things an opposition can actually do, how you handle the party is vital. That means, for instance, that the leadership simply has to succeed in getting large numbers of women candidates.

And it also means the leader has to show he is strong. Party reform is not complete and Mr Cameron must not ignore it.

There is a long way to go before there is modernisation. Too much modernisation is certainly not the Tory problem.

MPs? Well, I can't trust anyone. Not even you

The British public is feasting on hatred. One
minute it's estate agents, then bankers or
foreigners. Who will be next?

This was written at the height of the MPs' expenses scandal.

27 May 2009

I can't. Believe me I've tried. And I know it would make my
life easier. Occasionally in the last three weeks I have managed
to work myself up into a state of righteous indignation for an
entire hour at a time. I feel briefly as though I may be able to
join in. But then it goes. Nothing I can do about it, I am afraid.
The national anger, the frenzy, the fury about MPs and their
allowances just passes me by. Actually, it is worse than that. I
am afraid it makes me shudder.

When Princess Diana died I walked through St James's Park
and saw people, tears in their eyes, laying funeral wreaths for
someone they had only seen on television. I remember then
feeling outside the national mood, finding the intensity of the
mourning slightly strange.

Yet I did, at least, find something uplifting in the emotion, even if I didn't feel it myself. Sadness at the death of a young woman with two young children is, after all, compassionate, a worthy sentiment. I felt rather proud of my compatriots, if a little bewildered at their fervour.

The national mood of anger at MPs strikes me rather differently. It doesn't bewilder me as the Diana wreaths did. I can see that some MPs have behaved badly. I even think some should (and might) end up in prison. So I 'get it'. I see why people feel as they do. I understand it. I am, to use that dreadful political cliché, 'in touch' with the national mood. I just can't share it. I find it ugly, unpleasant, lacking all sense of proportion.

Robert Mugabe starves his population to death. Nothing. The Janjawid commit genocide in Darfur. Nothing. Gordon Brown bankrupts the country. Nothing. Then someone buys an unnecessary trouser press. Pandemonium.

When people are being murdered in their millions, dying in their boring, banal way, the BBC puts Question Time on at 1.30 in the morning and sticks a comedian on the panel to give proceedings a bit of a lift. Now that Cheryl Gillan has accidentally claimed for £4.47 of dog food, they move the show to prime time, bumping the Two Ronnies or whatever, so that everyone can boo Ming Campbell.

I would find it all fantastically silly if I didn't find it so worrying. It is, you see, a flashing alert signal for me when 'I was following the rules laid down by Parliament' ceases to be regarded as any sort of defence. I get worried when I see people declared guilty until proven innocent in Harriet Harman's famous 'court of public opinion' because there has been an article written about them in a newspaper. It makes me shiver when a whole category of people – politicians – are regarded as guilty, because 'they're all the same', and when it becomes routine to dehumanise them by comparing them to farm animals.

And it isn't just the MPs, you see. It would matter less if it was, I suppose. It is that all of us think everyone else is on the take, or is useless, or tasteless.

We've only just finished (for the time being) a great national furore against bankers. Bankers, they're all greedy. With their big, fat bonuses. Ripping us off, lining their pockets, making off with our savings. That Sir Fred Goodwin, he's one. Take away his pension. Strip him of his knighthood. Kick him out the golf club, him and his banker friends.

And before the bankers, there were social workers. Totally useless. They let Baby P die because they were busy ticking boxes. It's left-wing political correctness gone mad (and you don't want to go mad, or you'll have to see a psychiatrist, and there's a group of people you want to steer clear of). Sack them. Take away their pay-offs. It's time that whole profession had a clear-out.

When the opinion pollster (not that you can trust opinion pollsters) Populus asked voters their view of MPs' pay, they were virtually unanimous in wanting an independent group put in charge. 'How about a major accountancy firm?' Populus asked their focus groups. Oh, no, came the reply. We can't have accountants, they're the worst. 'Lawyers, perhaps?' Lawyers? Are you kidding? They're worse than accountants.

Although perhaps not as bad as estate agents, I suppose. Does anyone know what they do for all that money they get paid? No, neither do I. You can't trust a single one of them. Any more than you can trust a journalist. And don't get me started about journalists. Here they are, going on about MPs' expenses when they're all on the fiddle themselves. I know they are, because I read it in the newspaper.

Journalists, they're as bad as second-hand car salesmen. Or those people who sell insurance, come to think of it. Or those so-called advisers who hook you on their pensions and leave you without a penny. And there you are destitute, while Premier

League football players, who are stupid and always up until 2.30 in the morning in a nightclub with one of the millions of young women who are now out binge drinking, swan around 'earning' a million pounds a week for kicking a ball around and shouting at referees (who aren't deaf, even though they are all blind).

Mind you, at least they work for a living. Not like toffs who think they own the world (and probably do). Their sense of entitlement is dreadful, particularly the ones who went to Eton. It's a toss-up whether their arrogance is to be preferred to the smugness of middle-class people who live in dull suburbs and sound like Richard Briers and cut the grass too often.

Vicars? Wet and ineffectual. Property developers? Rapacious, reactionary. Teachers? Left-wing, long holidays. The police? Never come when you need them. Firemen? All off doing their second jobs when they should be working for us. Public-service workers? Pen-pushers in plush offices. Farmers? Always got their hand in the public purse, when they are not spreading diseases. Benefit claimants? On the fiddle, obviously. The bin man? Leaves rubbish all over your drive unless you pay him off.

The Scots, the French, TV documentary makers, hospital consultants, MEPs, traffic wardens, diplomats, council workers, people who wear sweatshirts with a hood. Let's face it, I can't trust anyone, except me and you. And I'm really not sure about you.

The other day I stumbled across an American opinion poll. It showed that a quarter of Americans, when asked, said that they blamed the Jews for the financial crisis either moderately or a great deal. Even more – nearly 40 per cent – attached some blame to us. Great.

When I witness this national mood of anger and blame, when I see people heckle politicians, and call them crooks, and lump them all together, and pass by all the good they do, I hope you will forgive me if I can't join in. I don't like it when people start mobbing up. It frightens me.

I'd never voted Tory. But changing was easy

The tribalism of British politics has always been a mystery to me. I hope it doesn't cost David Cameron his chance to govern

This article was my final column of the 2010 election campaign. The day after it appeared, voters went to the polls and the result was the beginning of Cameron's coalition government.

5 May 2010

Perhaps it's because I am Jewish. Or the son of immigrants. Or perhaps not. I don't know. But I have always found British tribal political loyalty hard to relate to.

When I was a child growing up in Hendon, there was a baker we used to use on a Friday. Good bread, biscuits not bad, but service? Hilariously, unfailingly, rude. They wouldn't just take an order, they would tell you what you should have ordered. 'Bagels? You don't want them. And anyway you had them last week. Rye bread's nicer. You're having the rye bread.' It would have been cabaret if they'd meant it to be funny.

I developed a theory. Yes, even though I was nine, I developed a theory. That's just how I am, leave me alone. My theory was that we Jews are outside the British class system. In most shops, I'd noticed, there was a little deference to the customer, a little bit of 'and what would sir like today?', even if sir was only just old enough to see over the counter. In most shops, the idea of poking the customer in the stomach and asking them if they'd put on weight wouldn't occur to the salesman. But with one Jew selling to another, a little bit of stomach poking was acceptable, is acceptable, as a matter of fact. Deference just doesn't come into it. Nor class resentment.

Now I am sure that not all Jews feel like this, but on me all that prodding left a mark. I find class hard to understand, and class tension baffling. And being a member of one tribe (British Jews), I have never felt the need to add a second.

Which creates a difficulty when it comes to analysing this election. Because I think the key to Thursday's outcome – the difference between the Tories falling short of an overall majority and winning comfortably – lies with people struggling with a deep, tribal, inherited, often class-based loyalty.

You may remember those posters: 'I've never voted Tory before, but . . .' The Conservatives put those up because they realised that, among undecided voters, an extraordinary number said that while they were thoroughly disillusioned with Labour, they had never voted Conservative before. Now, they said, they were on the brink of backing David Cameron. And then, again and again, they added this: 'My grandad would roll in his grave.'

Many pollsters assume – and adjust their polls accordingly – that a disproportionate number of these undecided voters will return to their past voting behaviour rather than following the trend. This has helped to make polls more accurate in the past. The result largely depends on whether that assumption holds good this time.

So, annoyingly, this election will be determined by people fighting a tribal urge that I've never felt and can't completely relate to. The best I can offer is this: once I considered myself on the centre left, and I don't any more. And once I, too, had 'never voted Tory', but in the end I didn't find it very difficult at all.

Being on the centre left was very comfortable. I found Margaret Thatcher's rhetoric jarring, I thought the Tory triumphalism of the 1980s distasteful (sometimes wrongly – I used to think that all those flags and 'Land of Hope and Glory' were sinister, but when I finally attended a Tory conference it was more like *Seaside Special*), it made life a great deal easier at dinner parties. The centre left, too, seemed the right place for a social liberal. Naturally on guard for the merest hint of racism, I also believed that gay rights were among the most important issues for my generation.

Beyond this, I found the certainty of the Tories off-putting. I have always recoiled from people whose eyes shine with ideological fervour. My parents' experience, imprisoned by fascists and communists, made me an instinctive moderate, suspicious of grand schemes and those who think they have found the key to the happiness of mankind. It's true that such certainty could be found on the left too, and I didn't like that either. But it seemed to suffuse the Conservative Party at that time.

But there was a problem. One I found more and more difficult to ignore. It just seemed that again and again, the Right was more, well, right. The economic policies coming out of the left ranged from the disastrous to the silly. The unions, basically a destructive force, were accorded too much respect and given too much power. The Left seemed incapable of understanding the need for a strong defence policy. So in 1992 I became a Conservative.

Some of this Tony Blair could see and put right. I liked his social liberalism, I thought him often moderate and reasonable, I shared his Atlanticism, and (I duck for cover here) I found him rather charismatic, and still do. But I am not at all surprised that his New Labour project is ending in failure. Because while he changed much about Labour, there are things he couldn't change.

Like every Labour government, this one has spent too much. On every single occasion – honestly, every time – the party has been in office for more than nine months, there has been a huge economic crisis, made worse by its public spending. Underpinning this mistake are two wrong-headed ideas that are deeply (indeed, almost unconsciously) held on the left.

The first (understandable but incorrect) is that it is cruel to say no to requests for spending and to interest groups. The second is that for every problem there must be a government response. I am a pragmatic person. I don't have some abstract, ideological aversion to ever spending taxpayers' money. But surely Labour has now tested this approach to destruction.

Yet, if we abandon this spendthrift policy, we must reform public services so that they are sustainable on budgets that grow less quickly. And Labour has failed on this too. Its coalition of old and new – a gallery to which Gordon Brown was playing for more than a decade – slowed reform until Mr Blair ran out of time and the rest of us ran out of money and patience.

When Mr Cameron called himself the 'heir to Blair', I think this is what he meant. That the Conservative Party needed to change to face the modern world, to make itself a welcoming home for social liberals and moderates, and people who felt Tory rhetoric had been too harsh. And when it did so, it would be ready to put right what Mr Blair and Mr Brown got wrong. I hope he now gets the chance to see it through.

It's human to dread change and fear loss

Good conservatives understand the value of tradition, but know when to welcome gay marriage or malls

6 February 2013

Years ago, before they knocked down the factory and built Brent Cross Shopping Centre, before the Brent Bridge Hotel came down and they put up suburban homes, before Mr and Mrs Underwood moved from next door to a block of flats at the end of the road, I bought my first record – 'C Moon' by Paul McCartney and Wings – in Hounsom's on Watford Way, just up the road from Hendon Central Station.

It was a little shop full of records, and behind the counter were two elderly (or at least to my ten-year-old self they looked elderly) ladies. In the back the brother of one of them wore a white coat and mended television sets, occasionally popping out, waving a screwdriver, to see what was going on. The ladies helped me to choose albums, adding to my collection of Beatles records, recommending Crosby, Stills, Nash and Young, selling me *Nilsson Schmilsson* by Harry Nilsson.

To get there you went past Woollon's, the pharmacist, who

also developed film and sold cameras, and then Peter's, the tobacconist, where you could buy sweets to consume at the pictures next door at cheaper prices than in the cinema kiosk.

Cross over Queen's Road and there was the Express Dairy which delivered our milk in glass bottles and sold chocolate yoghurt with a funny sort of disc-shaped hard topping. After that, Batty's, which sold stationery. I bought fountain pens there for school. (A fountain pen was compulsory, even if for me it was torture, reducing my work to incomprehensible smudges.) Then past the undertakers, with their newspaper clippings in the window from the day they buried Nelson, and you were at Hounsom's.

They've all gone now, the record shop, the sweet shop, the cinema, the lot. All except the undertakers, but I suppose we'll always need them. What sort of conservative would I be if I didn't miss them, if their disappearance didn't make me just a tiny bit melancholy? Indeed what sort of human being would I be? We all have this sadness, this dread of loss, within us. One of conservatism's greatest strengths is its appreciation of this.

The great liberal philosopher John Rawls developed his famous theory of justice by imagining the arrangements that human beings would regard as fair if we were behind a veil of ignorance. What would we agree to if we had no past and didn't know what our future held?

I am a conservative, rather than a pure liberal, partly because I don't believe you can arrive at a theory of fairness in this way. Rawls is asking what we would regard as fair as human beings if we weren't one. For what makes us human is at least partly our past, our experiences, the records we bought in Hounsom's.

And it is for this reason – even though gay rights has been one of the most important causes to me all my life – that I understand Conservative opposition to gay marriage, and can sympathise with it even while thinking it wrongheaded.

Conservatives draw strength from tradition. They do not abandon it lightly. They are right not to abandon it lightly.

It was while I was thinking about the Tory split on gay marriage that I heard *Desert Island Discs* with Tesco's former boss Sir Terry Leahy (or should that be *Dessert Island Discs*? Sorry). And Sir Terry was asked about the way his supermarket's growth had led many small shops to go out of business. Did it make him sad?

'Yes,' he replied. 'But it is part of progress. People aren't made to shop in supermarkets. They choose to shop there.' It was all there in Sir Terry's answer, the core of the modernising Conservative case.

Batty's and the Express Dairy may have been part of the fabric of my youth. But just as important to the tradition of this country is a restless entrepreneurial spirit and a belief in liberty. There is a tension between these things that cannot be eliminated. A society cannot be successful if it lightly discards tradition, but it cannot be successful either if it stifles liberty in the hope of halting progress.

The modernising case is that the latter is the greater danger. The practical political point for Conservatives is obvious. Look at the picture of the local Tory association chairmen who came to deliver the letter to David Cameron protesting against gay marriage. Consider their average age. There is, quite literally, not much political future in that.

But beyond the politics there is a social and economic argument to be made. Things do not stay the same, and it is poor history and poor conservatism to argue that they do. There wasn't a Hounsom's before the gramophone record was invented and televisions needed to be mended. And at some point before I was born, the local blacksmith must have closed down, complaining that shoppers were given parking tickets when they tethered their horse outside and that everyone was now buying saddles at Horses 'R' Us.

It would be impossible to prevent this change without extinguishing liberty. And absurd to try. You can't preserve Britain by stopping us doing what Britons do.

The job of Conservatives, and I think the most important task of modernisers, is to know when to accommodate to the modern world, when to resist and when to adapt, when something is a fundamental value and when it is just a passing here-today-and-gone-tomorrow camera shop. When people say that Tony Blair was a conservative I think he was, in the one sense that he had a superb modernising instinct. He knew when change was fundamental and permanent and needed to be absorbed.

Many of the great moments of Conservatism – introducing full votes for women, for instance, or Disraeli's expansion of the franchise or Butler's Education Act – have come when the party has completed a reform that agitators once called for and Conservatives once barely understood. It is the Conservatives' job to build the new community when the shopping moves out from the High Street, even while appreciating what has been lost.

In this tradition lies David Cameron's legislation on gay marriage. It has split the Conservative Party, as of course it would. But I cannot agree with the argument that it has done so for little reason. And this is not just because I think respect for gay people is so important. It is because the core of modernising Conservatism is to reconcile the changes brought through liberty with the traditions of the nation. This measure is not peripheral. It is the core of what David Cameron means.

Labour hasn't got a monopoly on compassion

Martin Freeman is the latest celebrity to claim
wrongly that the Left has cornered the market in
human decency

During the 2015 campaign, Ed Miliband's Labour Party
ran an election broadcast featuring an effective speech
about his values by the actor Martin Freeman. This is my
response.

8 April 2015

Dear Martin Freeman,

Do you have a moment, by any chance? I'd quite like to have
a word about the party broadcast you did for Labour last week.
I won't keep you long, I promise.

Let me start with this. It was really good. It is ironic that
everyone complains that politicians are just playing a role, but
when an actor appears in a broadcast, everyone is delighted
with its authenticity. But I think that is down to a particular
quality of yours. It's why I've always been a fan. One can imagine
knowing Tim from *The Office* and wanting him as a friend.

I also want to say thank you for doing it. I thought it was

really brave of you. You are successful and widely liked and it is impressive to be willing to put that at risk – to make yourself controversial and open to scrutiny – to advance a cause you believe in. So many people just moan about politicians. I admire you for being willing to do more than that.

It won't surprise you to know, however, that I do rather take issue with what you had to say.

I am not proposing to argue with you about voting Labour. It's not what I am intending to do myself, but there are some robust arguments for voting Labour. What I want to take issue with is something different. I'd like to persuade you to think again about the argument you made.

You begin your broadcast with the assertion that this complicated election is 'in the end simple . . . It's a choice between two completely different sets of values.' You continue with this: 'Now, I don't know about you, but my values are about community, compassion, decency. That's how I was brought up.' So you contend that, whatever the details of the argument, in the end they're only part of the story.

Instead, 'There is a choice of two paths. The bottom line is what values are we choosing . . . Labour. They start from the right place. Community. Compassion. Fairness. I think all the best things about this country.'

Now, I don't doubt that Labour does start from this right place. But the thing is – and I'm not quite sure how to put this correctly, so I'll just say it – the thing is, so do I. Community, compassion, fairness, decency, I like those things too. I try to live by them, too.

I wonder if at any point while making the broadcast it occurred to you to wonder if it could really be true that Tories sit down and think: 'Mmm, compassion, no I don't think we'll start there. Let's wait until someone comes up with something unfair and then we can get motoring!' Before letting out a sinister laugh and heading off to have tea with Voldemort.

I am pretty sure you didn't mean this – because you appear like a self-effacing, nice, considerate person – but actually what you said was both arrogant and offensive. And I suspect these are the last things you'd wish to be.

It was arrogant because it suggested that you have succeeded in living by the values you have been brought up with. That you are fundamentally a good person. I guess deep down we all think that, whatever our failings, but you actually said it out loud. On television. As a way of distinguishing yourself from me.

It was offensive because it suggests – there is really no other way of interpreting your comments – that your superior voting choice is dictated by the fact that your parents brought you up to be decent. Whereas mine?

You are either suggesting I am not a good son, or that my parents were not good parents. Either that they tried to bring me up to be kind, like you, but failed. Or that, unlike your parents, mine didn't much bother with moral instruction, sending me out into the world to laugh at disabled people and steal from orphans.

As I don't think you meant this, I think what you made was a simple intellectual error. You assumed that decency and compassion lead only to one political view and that if it isn't yours, someone reaching a different conclusion isn't compassionate or decent.

Let me give you a few examples that show that this isn't quite right. Take welfare. I want, desperately, to support poor people in their moment of need, but how much is the right amount? What are the right conditions?

Obviously compassion inclines one to generosity. Yet pay too much and it starts to make it more financially advantageous to be on benefits than to work. Some people won't exploit this but others will. And how fair – that word you use – is this to those who do work, have low earnings and have to pay for it?

I apologise if this is an obvious point, but I fear it really did seem as though, watching your broadcast, I had to make it.

What about war? We are kind, decent people the two of us, so how does that leave deciding what to do about Syria? It's not much of a guide, is it?

Or taxes? We all agree we should take money from those who can afford it, to help pay for communal services people wouldn't be able to buy on their own. Yet if we tax too much or in the wrong way, we might slow the growth of the economy, damaging the income of the least well off.

Has it been compassionate to end up spending so much that we need to borrow a fortune? Has it been fair? Or decent? You talked about young people and how important they are, but won't they have to pick up the bill for all the borrowing?

We all make different judgments about what works and what we think is sensible. I don't doubt there are coalition programmes you feel have been poorly thought through or whose impact has harmed people they shouldn't have harmed. Where the balance between keeping welfare bills low and protecting recipients has been poorly struck.

I don't object to you arguing these points with vigour. But I do object to the idea that they arise because you are a better person than me.

The idea that the Left is kind and the Right unkind is a pervasive one but one that history doesn't support. Some of the most grotesque mass murdering dictatorships in the world have come from the left. Mao, Stalin, Pol Pot. Leftism isn't a certificate of goodness.

Peace, love, looking after sick children, trees, the climate, poor people, family, hospitals, pensioners, I do like them all as much as you do, you know.

Daniel

No, I won't be asking for a foreign passport

Britons are rushing to apply for dual nationality
with EU countries but for me, citizenship has a
more profound meaning

27 November 2018

Before the mid-1960s the front page of *The Times* carried classified advertisements rather than news. So it was that on 6 May
1946 appeared notice of the funeral of Maud, Duchess of
Wellington, an appeal to find a travelling trunk that would fit
a 1939 Vauxhall saloon, an offer to purchase typewriters 'in any
quantity' and a small advertisement from a Dr Alfred Wiener.

The last read as follows: 'Notice is hereby given that DR ALFRED
WIENER of 45 Queens Court, Queens Way, London, W.2. is
APPLYING to the Home Secretary for NATURALIZATION, and that
any person who knows any reason why naturalization should not
be granted should send a written and signed statement of the
facts to the Under-Secretary of State, Home Office, S.W.1.'

I assume no one did give a reason, or that their reason wasn't
a good one, because shortly after this advertisement appeared
my grandfather became a British citizen.

That day's edition of *The Times* forms a pair with the *German*

Reich and Prussian State Gazette of August 1939 which lists my grandfather, his wife, my mother and her sisters among those who had been stripped of their citizenship for activities deemed to have harmed the Reich (my grandfather was one of the leaders of Germany's anti-Nazi movement).

Britain's decision to leave the European Union has produced a flood of applications for dual nationality from those who feel they might be eligible for a passport from a member nation. My wife, for instance, is the daughter of a German Jew and a Jewish Sudetenland Czech whose families fled the Nazis. Last week she, with the support of her father, submitted the forms necessary to become partly German.

She, like many others, doesn't feel this a particularly momentous thing to do. It is merely transactional. A matter of pragmatism. With a passport from an EU member she, and should they later wish, the children, may be able to work abroad and also move more swiftly through passport control. She is entitled to it, so why not?

For others, more complicated feelings are involved. Their application is a sort of protest against Brexit and an insurance policy in case Brexit presages a less tolerant Britain or a calamitously poor one. And there are also some Jews who worry about a Corbyn government.

I can't share these feelings. I understand and respect (and obviously, in one case, love) those who have applied for dual citizenship, but I won't be doing so myself.

As it happens, I actually probably can't become German. My wife can because it was her father who had been a citizen. In my case, it was my mother and that doesn't count. Hilariously, now that I think about it, I was very put out to discover this. The Nazis took away my family's status and now I can't get it back. Given that I don't want German citizenship, I am aware this fury is a little ridiculous.

But I think I could become a Pole. My father was born a

Polish citizen in Lwów and then exiled by the Soviets during the war. After 1945, Lwów became part of Ukraine and Dad could never go home again but he always insisted that he had not renounced his citizenship. And right at the end of his life the Polish authorities agreed.

So, although the process and the citizenship status sounds complicated, I could try becoming a Polish citizen. But I don't intend to attempt it.

This is not because of my feelings about Germany (I think modern Germany is extraordinarily admirable, and its creation a miracle of liberal democracy) or Poland (my father on his deathbed left few instructions but one was to encourage me to stand by the Polish people). It's about two things.

The minor one is that I am not a pessimist about Britain. I think things will be basically all right. I worry a little about being a Jew if Corbyn gets into power, but not enough to consider fleeing. I've got better things to do than start filling out long forms in Polish or assembling German documents. Life's busy enough. It took us a year to replace the kitchen bin when the spring lid stopped working.

But the more important reason is that I don't think obtaining citizenship is just another transaction. Acquiring a foreign passport is not like acquiring a department store credit card. I believe that being a citizen is to accept a profound bond with your fellow citizens. My grandfather felt that too, actually. Losing his German citizenship was one of the great, heartbreaking tragedies of Alfred Wiener's life because his nationality was so important to him.

In some ways I think it would be an insult to the Poles to apply to be a citizen if I didn't really mean it.

There are some who believe that patriotic attachment is dangerous because it challenges our universal rights as human beings. I disagree. I think that attaching yourself to a community with roots and practices, traditions and institutions is an essential part of defending rights. I think that it is empty to love mankind in general if you don't love anyone in particular. I feel this most strongly about Britain. When my mother arrived in Ellis Island, listed in the manifest as 'stateless', it was this country that ultimately took her in.

When my father's exile ended, it did so in a small house on the Hendon Way. Their freedom and their Britishness were not attached to each other by some intellectual argument, but by practical necessity. I have often repeated my grandmother's words – 'while the Queen is safe in Buckingham Palace, we are safe in Hendon Central' – as if they were a sort of general statement of her politics, but I think she just meant it as a statement of simple truth.

My loyalty to this country cannot be divided and it isn't for sale. It isn't in conflict with my belief in universal liberal rights, it is its guarantor.

When I was young I suffered from asthma, and an attack would often keep me awake at night. My mother would take me to her bed and read to me. Sometimes it would be Winnie-the-Pooh but more often I would choose a book of the kings and queens of England.

Only as an adult have I reflected that when the Tudor monarchs reigned, or even the Georgians, my family wasn't here. We lived under distant emperors. But then we chose these great Britons and they chose us. Their countrymen gave us a home and our liberty and peace. And I'm never going to be part of something else.

PART TWO

The Rules of Politics

Bill Clinton used to say that he'd like to find the unified field theory of politics. There isn't one of course. But I have always felt that analysis of current events can benefit from an understanding of how politics works.

In this section I have grouped together columns which dealt with an immediate issue but established a more general rule that could be more broadly applied.

Now here's a spiffing idea . . .

The Man in Westminster doesn't know best; that's why it's daft of politicians to attack focus groups

During the 2005 election for a Tory leader (which David Cameron eventually won) much of the discussion was about why the party lost in the general election that had just happened, and how to win again. As a way of emphasising their own authenticity, some candidates and commentators attacked the use of focus groups.

7 September 2005

I've come up with a really great idea, one that is bound to help revive the fortunes of the Conservative Party. Hear me out. I bet you'll think it's really spiffing.

The Tories should cancel all the professional assistance they have been receiving that helps them to discover what voters think. Instead they should simply guess.

Of course, I don't expect them to do this entirely unaided. They will be allowed to make full use of some randomly selected comments made to me on the doorstep during the 2001 election campaign, if I can remember them correctly. And I'll try and dig out some old correspondence, too, if anyone thinks it may come in handy.

Naturally, this will be a little hit and miss. Not to worry. It doesn't matter what voters think anyway. The party should just trust its instincts, rather than mess around trying to divine the views of the electorate.

What do you think? That ought to do the trick, I reckon.

My idea may strike you as, ahem, a little eccentric. Yet amazingly enough it has become a widespread view in the Tory party. So widespread, indeed, that I feel it necessary to point out that I was being satirical.

Attacking focus-group polling, the assembling of small groups of voters who are interviewed in detail about their opinions, has become a standard piece of rhetoric in the debate on the future of the Tory party. David Davis talks of 'hocus-pocus focus groups' and tried to cancel them when he was party chairman. 'I bring to politics a rejection of focus groups and opinion polls,' says Ken Clarke. Norman Lamont agrees. Lord Saatchi regrets not being firm in his opposition to focus-group polling. Simon Heffer congratulates them all. Matthew Parris thinks the critics are on the right track. The attack wins applause at constituency suppers and nods of approval at the 1922 Committee.

With so much agreement, it's a shame it's a load of nonsense, isn't it? I'm sorry to sound intemperate. Ever since I worked for some years as a Tory party official, I've sat through so many attacks on focus groups. And I've been so polite, haven't said a word, let it all wash over me. Then last week, I just snapped.

Funnily enough, the remark that did it for me didn't come from a Tory at all. It came from Jon Cruddas, who until pretty recently was a senior adviser to Tony Blair. He urged the Prime Minister to free himself from the 'dead hand of Middle England' (top piece of electoral advice, that) and blamed Mr Blair's shortcomings on his consultation of focus groups.

So here is this man Cruddas, who only enjoyed a position of power because his boss had the perspicacity to understand the need to move the Labour Party towards the centre and the intelligence to use professional polling to help to do it, and even he is attacking focus groups. Time, I decided, to stop letting it wash over me.

Now, it has to be admitted that focus groups can often be comically ill-informed. Attempts to investigate reactions to Michael Howard being Jewish ran aground when a group in Nottingham was asked to name any Jews in public life. A long silence ensued, only broken when one man offered 'Whoopi Goldberg' as an answer.

After Gordon Brown announced huge increases in spending on the NHS, I was keen to know the public reaction to the days of headlines that his new policy had attracted. Our pollsters reported back to me that not a single person in eight groups had heard of there being any announcement on anything.

Even when the groups do have views it can be dangerous to follow them. The Government's policy on soft drugs, for instance, is uncannily similar to the view that a focus group will give – the policing of soft-drug use should be relaxed so that the sale of hard drugs can be combated more successfully. The initial announcement of the new policy was therefore guaranteed a fairly good reception.

Yet there is a difficulty. What if the policy doesn't work? What if the focus groups are simply wrong, and soft-drug liberalisation leads to greater hard-drug use? The public won't put its hand up and say: 'It's a fair cop, guv. We gave you bad advice.' They will blame the politicians, and rightly so.

In fact, where focus groups that I helped to commission strayed into discussing detailed policy, the result was almost always incoherent. A polling report we were given on healthcare was headlined – THE NHS: IN A FOG.

Yet, anybody who mistakes a focus group for a meeting of

Mensa or the AGM of a think tank is obviously an idiot anyway. That is not their point. What good professional polling does is to help politicians to understand what voters think, what different language means to them, what they care about and what they do and do not understand.

The Conservative Party's problem has not been listening to too many focus groups, but not listening to them enough.

A good example is tax policy. The party has spent tens of thousands of pounds on focus groups that tell it that voters do not believe tax-cut promises. This is not an ideological point. It does not say whether voters want tax cuts, that is a different question. Nor whether tax cuts are right, that is yet another question. But it does indicate that the central message of successive Tory election campaigns has cut no ice with voters.

You'd think that one would want to know that. But apparently not. And that's why the grumbling about focus groups matters so much. It's why this is not a small argument about how to spend £100,000 of campaign funds.

The opponents of focus groups believe that they know what voters want without having to ask. They also believe that voters need to come to the Conservative Party rather than the Conservative Party moving towards the voters. They believe, they seriously believe, that the Tory party has been too responsive to the electorate.

I don't think they are quite correct about that, do you?

Why a mobile phone on a beach sends out a stark message to Gordon Brown

Brown says: let's make agricultural subsidies
history. Where can we get the wristband?

This article appeared in Labour conference week after the
speeches of Tony Blair and Gordon Brown. Mr Blair had
fought his last election as leader. There was much speculation about when the latter would replace the former,
which he did two years later.

28 September 2005

In the mid-1990s the American mobile phone business realised
that it had a problem. It could get men to buy phones, but
women just wouldn't. Women thought mobiles were just boys'
toys.

Then AT&T began screening a commercial that sent sales
through the roof. A mother gets ready to leave for work. The
house is in chaos, the babysitter has plonked the kids in front
of the television. The children start pestering their mother to
take them to the beach. 'I've got a meeting with a client,' says

the mother. Her youngest child replies with the line that made the ad famous. 'When can I be a client?'

The commercial finishes with the mother sitting on the beach, the children running around her, playing happily. She is using her mobile to talk to the client. And throughout the entire commercial, the word 'phone' is never mentioned.

Ten years ago this advert was being used to sell phones. These days it is being used to sell a message about political communications. Dave Winston, former adviser to Newt Gingrich and now pollster for the Republican House and Senate campaigns, shows it to his candidates when explaining how he wants them to talk to voters.

He explains to them that they need to touch voters and not just talk at them. They need to make them feel an emotional affinity, a real need, for what the candidate has to offer. They need to appeal as AT&T did.

The traditional method of selling a phone was to talk about battery life, access charges, the reach of the network. It was all about mechanics, never touching on reasons, never touching on people's (and particularly women's) daily lives. The traditional pitch for a mobile phone was like . . . well, it was like a Gordon Brown speech.

On Monday the Chancellor battered his audience with a long list of statistics about finance facilities and percentages of GDP. At one point he offered us the catchy slogan: 'Let us make agricultural export subsidies history.' Where do we go to get the wristband?

Mr Brown's conference address and his *Sunday Times* interview have been interpreted as closing the gap between the Chancellor and the Prime Minister. They did nothing of the kind. They simply demonstrated the size of the gulf that separates them.

This gulf is not essentially one of policy (although, of course, there are substantial differences). And it cannot be bridged by

adopting the Blairite agenda, even if that is Mr Brown's intention. However hard he looks, the Chancellor will not find the
secret of Mr Blair's appeal hidden in the conclusions of an NHS
White Paper. And he will not become a Blairite by promising
to implement a pilot scheme for an internal market in the
provision of school textbooks.

The key to the Prime Minister's success is to be found elsewhere – in his personality, in the way he mounts an argument
and in his ability to communicate with Middle England. These
the Chancellor simply cannot match.

Take Mr Brown's decision, announced at the weekend, to
commission a report on the Middle East so that he could drive
the peace process. And whom did he appoint to write the
document? That great expert on the Arab question, Ed Balls.
Isn't there anyone else he trusts other than Balls of Arabia? If
Tony Blair had done the commissioning, he would have picked
someone from far outside his personal circle – the Tory businessman Archie Norman, say. Brown lacks the trust and the
confidence.

Then there is his ability to communicate. When designing
the Republican House and Senate campaigns for particular
pieces of legislation, Dave Winston uses something called
'communications laddering'. A politician might start with the
technical attributes of a policy (say cutting tax by 5 per cent)
and then move to its technical benefits (you will have more
money in your pocket). Winston wants them to go up the
ladder identifying personal benefits that might appeal to the
emotions (so, for instance, you might be able to buy music
lessons for your children). Support the tax cut and be a better
parent.

The classic example of the successful use of communications
laddering is provided by the Republican campaign to win
support for an increase in the defence budget. Winston was
after the support of the group he termed 'security moms'.

Traditionally women have not backed higher military spending, so instead of talking about percentages of spend and the size of the armed forces, the Republicans concentrated on making families safer from attack.

Try applying Winston's model to a typical Brown speech. The Chancellor spends most of the time right at the bottom of the ladder, talking about the technical attributes of his policy ('£55 billion of debts written off for ever, the delivery of debt cancellation of 100 per cent'). Occasionally he travels up one rung and sets out a possible benefit of his programme (greater share ownership, to use an example from Monday's speech) but he very rarely moves successfully from these rational components of a political message to the emotional ones. If ever he does, it is to touch the emotions of Labour activists rather than those of Middle England.

Mr Blair, by contrast, finds ascending the communications ladder simple. He brings his arguments back time after time to real people and their concerns – to the patient anxious for the results of a diagnostic test, the young family struggling to afford their first home, the disabled person needing help to get back into the workforce.

He makes real arguments too. For all that he has a formidable intellect, Mr Brown's speech was simply relentless. That of Mr Blair was compelling.

The Brownites believe they can adopt the best bits of Mr Blair's agenda and move on smoothly. They will find it isn't as easy as that, nowhere near as easy. Mr Brown and his circle have never properly appreciated the political brilliance of Tony Blair. When he is gone they will. And they will miss it. Oh, how they will miss it.

Happy birthday!
We like you

How a car salesman and an anti-war demonstration illustrate a strategy for modernising the
Tories

At the 2005 Conservative conference David Cameron made
a highly successful pitch for the leadership on a platform
of modernisation. The favourite David Davis's speech fell
flat. This piece appeared after the conference but before
the first leadership ballot of MPs.

12 October 2005

Joe Girard sold a lot of cars. A lot. For twelve years in a row
he featured in *The Guinness Book of World Records* as the world's
greatest salesman. Let me tell you how he did it.

On birthdays and public holidays potential customers would
receive a card from Mr Girard. They might get as many as
twelve a year. 'Happy Birthday' the card would read, or 'Happy
Easter', or whatever. And then followed the words: 'I like you.
From Joe Girard, Chrysler Montana.' As Girard put it: 'There's
nothing else on the card. Nothin' but my name. I'm just telling
'em that I like 'em.' And it works. People like to be liked.

Since I was first alerted to Mr Girard's activities by the social psychologist Robert Cialdini, I have talked of them often to Conservative audiences. You see, I think the Tory party has spent a great deal of the past two decades sending out cards reading, 'Happy birthday, we don't like you.' And, naturally, it doesn't work.

I was thinking of Mr Girard again when I read the recent comments of the right-wing columnist Simon Heffer. He ridiculed the Tory modernisers for believing that the party lost elections because it was 'insufficiently nice to homosexuals'. Well, yes Simon, you gorgeous meaty boy, the Tory party has lost votes by being insufficiently nice to homosexuals. But there's worse news to come. You might be asked to be nice to some other people, too.

The reason? Because of a moderniser's strategy for reviving the Conservative Party that they are calling 'show, don't tell'.

For the last week the leadership contender David Cameron has been urged by innumerable columnists to start putting 'meat on the policy bones'. He is disinclined to oblige. He argues that the advice misses the point. And he is right.

The starting point for the alternative 'show, don't tell' strategy is the poll-finding that featured prominently in the conference speech of party chairman Francis Maude – that those who agree with a particular policy are far less likely to assent to the proposition if they know that it is a Tory policy. The Conservative Party is damaging its own cause.

This means that the central job of a new Tory leader is to put the Conservative argument in a different way; to win trust and wider support for the policies of the Centre Right, not just to outline new schemes; to embody a new attitude, talk a new language, show that he is in touch with voter concerns; to be the change, not just to talk about it.

Just as the Thatcher revolution applied some basic economics to public policy, so modernisation involves accepting some basic social psychology.

The things for which Tory modernisers are most mocked – going around without a tie, drinking cappuccinos in Notting Hill, organising focus groups, recognising how Tony Blair has changed politics and being sufficiently nice to homosexuals – are not risible at all. Dressing like the rest of Britain, sounding like the rest of Britain, setting as policy priorities the things that voters care about most and relating better to upper-middle-class people in metropolitan areas are important.

Take dress. Few things have brought more ridicule down upon Tory modernisers than dressing differently. What a trivial thing to worry about. Yes? No. Dress matters.

As Cialdini states in his book *Influence: The Psychology of Persuasion*: 'We are more likely to help those who dress like us.' He cites, for instance, an experiment conducted in the early 1970s when experimenters, dressed either as 'straights' or as 'hippies', approached students and asked them for some change for the telephone. The students were far more likely to help if the experimenter was dressed as they were. Similarly marchers in an anti-war demonstration were much more likely to sign a petition proffered by a person dressed like them. Indeed many of them signed without bothering to read it first.

Most of this isn't rocket science. And I think that this is what bothers the critics. Sounding moderate, shaping your political programme around the priorities of the electorate, avoiding pointless attacks on harmless groups (why, for instance, do Tories go on about people studying golf-course management? What did greenkeepers do wrong?), eschewing silly partisan name-calling. It all seems too simple. The critics yearn for some huge ideological betrayal that they can then denounce. They are almost begging Mr Cameron to disappoint them with some policy sell-out that they can disagree with.

Yet a policy sell-out wouldn't help. Of course it will be necessary to change Tory policy priorities and, in time, there will certainly need to be policy development in new areas. This is a critical part of demonstrating that the Conservative Party's culture has changed. But the central insight of 'show, don't tell' is that until the Conservative Party is once again listened to, liked and trusted, its policies, changed or not, will make no impact at all.

The Tory peer Lord Ashcroft had the pollster Populus track public recognition of Tory policies during the last campaign. Recognition that the Tories had been campaigning for a tax cut reached a peak of 3 per cent. Fewer still believed that they meant it.

This is the reason that David Davis's conference failure was so devastating. He didn't trip over the platform and bang his head on the lectern. He didn't talk gibberish: he's an intelligent man. It's just that suddenly everyone could see that he can tell but he can't show, that he can talk of change but he can never be the change.

There has been so much new policy during this leadership campaign. This candidate wants to restore advanced dividend tax credits, that candidate wants to lengthen the contract period for charitable provision of public services, a third candidate wants a new charities tax regime. But can you recall which candidate wanted which policy?

Exactly. Putting policy meat on the bones just isn't the point. David Cameron should go on ignoring those who tell him that it is.

Top Tory tips: climb the ladder, check out the ceiling and see the cheese

How optimism trumps over pessimism in life and in politics

30 November 2005

This is what happened when John Lennon first met Yoko Ono. It was at an avant-garde art exhibition at the fashionable Indica Gallery in London. In the middle of the room, Yoko had placed a ladder, on the top of which lay a magnifying glass. This could be used to read some tiny letters written on the ceiling. So the Beatle duly ascended, picked up the magnifying glass and read the scribbled word. And all it said was this – 'yes'.

It was that word that made Lennon stay. As he told countless interviewers in the coming years, if the scribbled word had said 'no', he wouldn't have hung around.

Now, as a Beatles devotee, I'm perfectly well aware that in addition to being a genius, John Lennon was an idiot. And anything to do with the absurd Yoko Ono has me on my guard. Yet I watched a TV programme last week that made me wonder if Lennon wasn't onto something after all.

David Davis and David Cameron were on *Sky News*, taking part in another debate (surely it must be over soon, somebody, please, please, do something) when an argument began over the new licensing legislation. This does not sound very promising, I agree, but, as it happens, the exchange turned out to be one of the most significant of the entire leadership election.

'We have a situation where the centre of many cities and towns in this country are no-go areas for decent people,' said Mr Davis, giving 8 o'clock as the curfew for decent people and arguing that the Government was making things worse. I have listened to Conservatives making Mr Davis's point in roughly similar language countless times and thought nothing of it, so David Cameron's reply took me by surprise. 'We must not make everyone who wants to go out and have a drink on a Friday and Saturday night sound like a criminal,' he said.

The moment I heard this I recognised the debate the two were having. An unresolved, half-buried Tory argument was rising to the surface. Should the Conservative Party paint the skies blue or should they paint them black?

Ponder for a moment which of the contenders was correct and it is obvious that they both are. Eight o'clock may be on the early side, but Mr Davis is right that many people avoid town centres at night because of the drunken, rowdy behaviour of others. And Mr Cameron is right that it is madness for the Conservative Party to regard every young person in town in the evening as indecent. Lots of people are just out to have a good time, and there's nothing wrong with that.

It is precisely because both men are right that the strategic choice they each made is so fascinating. The same set of political facts can be expressed in two entirely different ways with a completely different emphasis.

In the very early days of opposition, after the devastating result of 1997, the Conservatives debated these alternatives openly, even giving the different options labels as a shorthand.

The party could be pessimistic about all the great threats over-head (painting the sky black) or it could be optimistic about the possibilities for Britain (painting the sky blue).

But the debate never came to a conclusion. The 'realities' of opposition kicked in, taking over from the academic discussions. Without fully realising the choice it was making, the Tory party began to paint the skies black, became the pessimistic party.

This country is being strangled by regulation and taxation, criminals are taking over our streets, family life is collapsing, immigration control is a joke, alcoholism and drug abuse are rife, the constitution is crumbling and we are being subsumed in a European super-state. Oh yes, and no one decent can go out after 8 o'clock.

Eight years later it seems clear that this choice was the wrong one. And Mr Cameron's intervention in the Sky debate suggests that he realises it too.

A Blue Skies party might say this – that this country is already prosperous but untold opportunities lie ahead for all if we build a flexible low-tax economy; that one of the greatest advances in social policy of the last thirty years is that we now know that crime can be beaten with the right policies and that in other countries this is happening; that immigration can be an immensely positive thing and that assimilated communities have been enormously successful and will continue to be so provided we get the system under control; that many cities outside London are booming and that there is now so much to do after 8 o'clock. I could go on, but you get the idea.

In the mid-1990s President Clinton's chief strategist Dick Morris came to a similar conclusion. The Democrats, he said, reminded him of a group of tenants who would greet the collapse of their roof with chuckles because it meant trouble for the landlord. Changing that attitude, which he found very difficult, was one of the keys to Bill Clinton's extraordinary political recovery from a landslide mid-term defeat in 1994 to re-election in 1996.

The reason that optimism is a superior political position to pessimism is really quite simple – association. Why do you think car companies advertise their products with attractive women? It makes their cars seem sexy. Why do fundraisers serve you a meal before they pitch to you? It makes them seem warm and generous. Why did the Persians slay the messenger who brought news of defeat? It's all because of association, the linking of message, messenger and environment. John Lennon is not alone in wanting to see the word 'yes' at the top of the ladder.

A Black Skies party is itself viewed as dark, threatening, likely to bring about precisely the problems it warns against. The public slays the messenger that brings it bad tidings.

It doesn't have to be like this. My mother likes to describe pessimists as those who can only see the holes in the Emmenthal. It's time for the Tory party to wake up and see the cheese.

Let me flog you a used car

Combine a subtle sales technique with some tests
on mouthwash and you get an election strategy

Mr Cameron became Conservative leader in early December
2005. This appeared after he faced his first Budget as opposition leader.

29 March 2006

It is one of the most famous campaign posters ever produced
– a scowling caricature of Richard Nixon, accompanied by the
slogan: 'Would you buy a used car from this man?' And the
reason why this political attack, of all the many thousands, has
resounded over the decades is simple – the ability to sell a used
car is a pretty good test of both a candidate and his political
strategy.

I'll tell you what set me thinking about flogging second-hand
automobiles – last week's Budget.

Gordon Brown is a great believer in dividing lines. He wants
the voters to be able to see clearly the choice in front of them,
with Labour, naturally, on the popular side of the divide. So
his speech aimed to frame the debate over the rest of this
Parliament.

Whatever else David Cameron may do, Mr Brown hopes

that the choice at the next election will still boil down to this – the party that invests in public spending versus the party that cuts it.

On the face of it, this would seem to present the Conservatives with a nasty dilemma. Do they go for a tax-cutting agenda, hoping to overcome the scepticism of voters over such promises and their fears about the impact on services? Or do they abandon lower taxes, and with it a crucial part of what might make a Conservative economic and social policy work if the Tories were to win?

And here is where the used cars come in. The Tories should skip around Mr Brown's trap. They don't have to choose between remaining a low-tax party and abandoning tax cuts (no choice at all for a Tory). Instead they have to choose between these two strategies – lowball and highball.

As part of his lifelong work charting the way in which human beings are influenced, the social psychologist Robert Cialdini spent time undercover as a second-hand car salesman. It was during this period that he was introduced to one of the most successful selling techniques – lowball.

The customer is offered a car at a low, low price. Enthusiastically, he agrees. Then, deftly, the cost advantage is withdrawn. A calculation error is claimed, or the salesman's offer is 'overruled' by the showroom manager. A particularly popular version is to offer the buyer an inflated trade-in price for his old car. Then when the deal has been agreed in principle, an 'independent' valuer arrives and reduces the offer. Knowing how much his old car was really worth, the customer accepts the new valuation as fair. The sale goes ahead.

Lowball is a very effective and common method of persuasion. It takes advantage of our great desire to remain consistent once committed. In yesterday's papers the al-Qaeda supergrass trial provided a frightening example of lowball's potential power. It was alleged that the defendants were aiming to recruit young people to fight in Afghanistan, and then later tell them that this had become logistically impossible and they would need to target Britons.

What has this got to do with politics? Lowball is frequently on display in elections. The Blair-Brown strategy before the 1997 general election was a classic lowball strategy. Voters were told that income tax rates would not be increased, yet, once Labour was elected, tax began steadily to rise.

Now take a look at their methods. At first the tax increases were stealthy, almost hidden (changes to advanced dividend corporation tax for instance), later the rises were more blatant (national insurance) and justified more openly. This is instructive. You see, lowball need not be dishonest (the direction of travel can be made clear even if the distance of travel isn't), but if it is dishonest, voters will not complain. That is lowball's power.

By the time Labour got round to raising taxes openly, voters were convinced that this was what they voted for. Just like the customer with the undervalued trade-in motor, when Mr Brown told taxpayers they would need to pay more, after all, to fund the NHS, voters reacted by shrugging. Hadn't they always known, deep down, that the initial valuation was unfair? That they would have to stump up more? A Tory lowball strategy, an honest one, would involve being clear about wanting lower taxes and public service reform but it would be gentle and cautious about the speed and extent. In power, slowly, it would be able to go farther and with public consent.

There is an alternative, of course, and some people urge it on the Tories. Highball. The party distinguishes itself from Labour with a radical, exciting, enticing programme. It tackles public prejudices by making the big arguments right now, upfront.

There's just one problem with highball. No party has ever gone from opposition to power on a highball strategy. Margaret

Thatcher in 1979? Definitely lowball. Tax was mentioned but no big promises, and reassurance was provided at all stages. Radical Thatcherism came later, when it could take the committed voters with it.

Of course, it could be objected that the analogy breaks down because a tax-cutting Tory party wouldn't be threatening costs, it would be tempting people with a benefit. This is a misunderstanding. A radical manifesto involves this cost – risk. And social psychology, something called prospect theory, tells how voters will react to this, too.

If you offer someone a choice between receiving £15,000 and a gamble in which they could be given £10,000 or £20,000, then mathematically the two alternatives are the same. Psychologically they are not. A complicated experiment involving testing people's reaction to adverts for antibacterial mouthwash (don't ask) proved that we would prefer the £15,000 gain to the gamble. But fascinatingly, if we were told that we would certainly lose £15,000 or we could gamble and might lose either only £10,000 or as much as £20,000, we prefer to gamble. We are more cautious about expected benefits and are prepared to take more risks when a possible loss looms.

Our caution, our commitment, our consistency – lowball is the only possible choice for the Tories. Anything else, and the voters will say: we're not going to buy a used car from those people.

Guess the weight of the ox: then you will see what's wrong with our politics

Social science suggests we need to change the way
we reach political conclusions

5 April 2006

This weekend I had my handwriting analysed at a birthday party. I basically regard graphology as nonsense, but my friends had taken infinite trouble with the rest of the proceedings. Cliff Richard, for instance, sang 'Congratulations' as Denise Van Outen jumped out of the cake, neither of which happened at my last birthday to the best of my recollection. Having my handwriting analysed seemed the least I could do.

Anyway, the lady looked at the way I signed my name and said that I liked to connect up ideas from apparently unrelated areas. Fiendishly clever insight, that.

And so this column will set out to prove her right. In just under 1,000 words I intend to link the suspension of an academic at the University of Leeds, the weight of an ox, the outcome of the 2002 football World Cup, the recent dissenting speeches of Stephen Byers and Alan Milburn and the state funding of political parties. And, of course, cakes, graphology and Denise Van Outen.

Let's get going. On Sunday, a group of academics wrote to a newspaper complaining about the disciplinary proceedings instituted by the university against one of its lecturers, Frank Ellis. Dr Ellis has been suspended for arguing that racial groups have different average IQ levels, and that those of blacks are inferior to whites. His defenders protested that some evidence suggested he was correct.

Yet the academics who suspended Dr Ellis and those who defended him are making an error. In fact, the identical error. They are confusing the correctness of Dr Ellis's views with whether he should be allowed to continue his academic career. These are not the same thing at all.

In the autumn of 1906, as recorded by James Surowiecki in his excellent book *The Wisdom of Crowds*, the scientist Francis Galton visited the West of England Fat Stock and Poultry Exhibition. While there he found his eyes drawn to a guess-the-weight-of-an-ox competition. Butchers and farmers were taking part, but so were ordinary visitors without any expert knowledge. Galton was interested in how bad their guesses would prove to be.

Galton was to be surprised. The average of the 800 guesses during the day was almost exactly right and, crucially, much more accurate than any individual expert assessment. What he had discovered was something counter-intuitive – that even the wildest incorrect guess plays its role in helping to produce an accurate average guess.

Dr Ellis is a lecturer in Russian and Slavic Studies. He probably has as firm a grip on the study of IQ and ethnicity as he does on the study of ox-weighing. But his view is useful in both, regardless of its correctness. Allowing mistaken views to have a voice in the academy is a vital part of determining the truth.

Galton's observation suggests something else that is important too – independence. Let me use an example from an area about which I know a good deal more than I do about fat stock – football predictions. A Swedish study conducted during the last World Cup showed that groups of experts were far worse at predicting match outcomes than complete amateurs (in this case, US students with almost no football knowledge).

There were a number of reasons for this – experts try to be clever-clever, for instance, and factor in things that do not affect the outcome – but one of the most important was the experts' lack of independence.

When experts make judgments, they do not make them alone. Their forecasts are based on the collective wisdom, wrong or right, of other experts. They reinforce each other's errors. This makes their collective guess, the average of their guesses, far less accurate than if they had each guessed independently.

All of which brings me, as surely you knew that it would, to the state funding of political parties.

Divining the truth requires the greatest breadth of opinion to be taken into account, not excluding even the wildest and silliest ideas. And it requires the greatest achievable independence of opinions, so that all are adding in their own view rather than recycling someone else's mistake.

Now consider modern British politics. Here all the prizes go to uniformity, the acceptance of collective responsibility, the exclusion of fringe opinions and the squashing of dissent. The ability to read and remember the 'line to take' from party headquarters is valued far more highly than creative contributions to the public debate. Recent speeches by Labour's Mr Byers and Mr Milburn urging their party to develop a fresh agenda were remarked upon only because they departed from 'party discipline'. Their content, such as it was, was ignored.

The whole of British politics is, in other words, a giant conspiracy to reinforce error. The exercise of independent judgment is rare, the tendency to recycle the conventional wisdom of experts is great. And once an error is made, the unspoken rules say that it must be persisted with, and everyone is required daily to offer their fresh support for yesterday's mistake.

It is this, and not the massively overstated problem of sleaze, that is really corroding British political life.

And the state funding of political parties will make it still worse, certainly in the form that is being considered. The State will bestow its financial favours on central party organisations. Private fundraising will be severely restricted. Discipline will be rewarded, the maverick punished and independence of view militated against.

If there has to be state funding, if it cannot any longer be resisted, then surely it should be to the individual Member of Parliament rather than to the party. If MPs want to contribute to the centre then they can. And yes, I know, there are some pretty eccentric MPs out there. But that, you see, is the whole point.

Enough substance, Mr Cameron. Stick to style . . . because you're worth it

Politics is more like Budweiser than like Crest toothpaste

In the year after his election as leader, there was constant criticism that David Cameron wasn't moving quickly enough to elaborate on his agenda. An important theme of my columns was to argue against this. What follows appeared on the morning that Mr Cameron was due to give his first speech to party conference as leader.

4 October 2006

I am worried about David Cameron. I fear he will have too much policy. I am concerned that there will be too much substance and not enough style.

In 1975 Volkswagen introduced the Rabbit on the American market. And it was good. It was economical, it didn't break down and its hatchback design was an improvement on its rivals. 'The best car in the world for under $3,500,' bragged the company in full-page advertisements. It probably was. But sales were disappointing.

In his book *How Brands Become Icons*, Douglas Holt explains why. The traditional view of branding was that it was necessary to identify a unique selling proposition – Crest toothpaste has distinctive cavity-fighting ingredients, Dove soap is gentle on the skin because it contains one quarter cleansing cream – and then tirelessly communicate this benefit to consumers. Holt calls this 'mind-share branding', trying to imprint a view of the brand's unique benefits on the minds of consumers. Yet, Holt says, for many brands this approach is not enough. He dubs these 'identity brands'.

An identity brand – Nike, Budweiser, Jack Daniel's – is valued not so much for what it does as for how it makes consumers feel about themselves. One of the earliest identity brand adverts was L'Oréal's slogan, 'Because I'm worth it.' The brand is bought largely to help the purchaser to define their identity. Volkswagen recovered when it stopped selling itself on its maintenance record and started selling itself as the provider of the sort of car that a creative individual would drive.

To promote an identity brand you tell a story, one that resonates with people, one that they want to be part of. Corona turned itself into the party beer with adverts that told stories of people drinking it on the beach at spring break. Mind-share branding works differently: it works by pounding on about the benefits of the product. But Holt believes that this is suitable only for 'low-involvement' goods or business-to-business services.

Political parties, in fact political causes, are classic identity brands. Voters make choices in order to make statements about themselves, to establish their own identity, as much as they do because of anything the parties offer them. When people announce their voting behaviour, they often say 'I'm a Tory' or 'I'm Labour, me'. What was the slogan of the anti-war movement a couple of years back? Not 'this war is wrong', or 'this war is expensive', or 'there are no weapons of mass destruction'. It was this: 'Not in my name.' The ultimate identity slogan.

Most pundits, however, think of parties as mind-share brands. So here we all are in Bournemouth asking the Tories where the USP is, where the policies are, as if it were policies, benefits, the technical qualities of the brand and its products that determine elections. They don't.

Naturally (this is the media we are talking about, after all, and high mindedness is our USP), there is a more high-minded case for policymaking. To start off with, policymaking tells us what parties are going to do in government, doesn't it? It informs voters what to expect, doesn't it? Well, actually, no, not really.

Let's take the most often-cited case – tax cuts. If a party that might govern for a decade or more lets you know what is going to be in its first budget, how well informed are you? If they set some targets for the NHS and a planned reorganisation of regional health authorities, how much do you really know about the way they will run the health service?

Between 2001 and 2005 Tony Blair committed this country to two major wars. Were they in his manifesto? Of course not: how could they have been?

Policymaking, then, is a bit of a con. Manifestos pretend to be an entire programme for government when in reality even the most detailed of them only cover a few items. Voters don't make judgments based on these programmes and they shouldn't either.

What matters is not such bogus 'substance', it is the governing style of the prospective rulers. Are they strong or weak? Interferers or liberals? Atlanticists or Europhiles? Moderates or extremists? Localisers or centralisers? Tax cutters or big spenders? Tied to vested interests or independent of them? Free traders or protectionists? In touch or out of touch? These are the sort of questions voters should ask.

Big emblematic policies – favouring the continuation of the NHS, supporting school vouchers, opposing the Euro and so on – can help, to a certain extent, to provide answers to such questions. Much more than that they can't do.

But even if a manifesto doesn't tell you what sort of government you are going to get, at least it is useful for the party taking office. Erm, no again.

I used to be director of the Conservative Party policy unit. There were four of us. The Government probably has as many people assigned to the development of policy on the export of carpets. We did not remotely have the ability to determine sensible policy on the myriad of detailed issues we would be facing in government. We couldn't costs things properly or make the right trade-offs. But that didn't stop us trying.

Labour has spent much of the past five years undoing stupid things it committed itself to in opposition and then did in its first five years. The problem with politicians, you see, is not that they don't do what they say they will, but the opposite – they try to do what they said they would do, even after realising it wasn't a good plan.

So if policies don't win elections, inform voters or help with governing, why do the media keep asking for them, and why do politicians keep offering them? Simple. To keep us all entertained.

Let's review yesterday's papers, shall we? Full pages on a stray remark about autism at a fringe meeting, reports of a tax revolt that wasn't happening, a Tory donor questioned by police and a huge story in the *Daily Mail* informing us that a new family tax policy was about to be announced. The *Mail* provided us with costings and everything, which was clever of them considering that the policy doesn't, as far as I can discover, exist.

Why did these stories appear? Partly to fill the space normally occupied by policy announcements – crackdowns on internet porn, a five-point plan on dental hygiene, you know the sort of stuff – that are carefully handed out to newspapers to make sure everybody is usefully occupied. Without it the space gets filled one way or another. And some media outlets decide that they will make up their own policies if none are given to them.

The Conservative Party conference has been rich in useful information about the sort of prime minister Mr Cameron will be. He declared from the platform, for instance, that he belongs to the centre, an extraordinary, unprecedented remark for a modern Conservative leader to make.

But soon all those policy groups will report and we'll be done for. We'll stop learning all this useful style stuff and 'substance' will rule the day. Let's hope David Cameron puts it off as long as possible.

Ooh matron! I'm sick of fizzy populism

Labour could regret having a snap election

When Labour gathered for Gordon Brown's first conference speech as Prime Minister in 2007, it was at the end of a summer in which he could do no wrong politically. Everyone seemed to be talking about him as a political genius and saying he would call an election and sweep back to power. I listened to his address and then, at the height of this fever and before it broke, I sat down to write this column questioning the whole thing.

26 September 2007

So rubbish is the new brilliant, is it? Here's the theory. Yes, Gordon Brown was really boring on Monday. Yes, he had nothing to say, but took sixty-five minutes to say it. Yes, his statements of belief were astonishingly incoherent. Yes, his stunning strategic move was to pinch the clothes of the Tory party, failing to recall that they were the garments the Tories wore when they lost three elections.

There was remarkable agreement in Bournemouth that the Prime Minister's speech was poor. Even his most enthusiastic supporters weren't claiming it was Demosthenes.

But what you have got to understand is that it was all done on purpose. He meant to be dull, you see. The cheesy rhetoric showed that he was too busy running the country to be bothered with crafting good phrases. His shopping list of cheap populist promises was not a worrying revelation that there is nothing there, it was a clever move to dish David Cameron. His lack of a single funny joke was designed to emphasise his seriousness. It was rubbish, but, hey, wasn't it fantastic?

It's remarkable how such an eccentric theory has taken hold in the media, but it has. I just keep reminding myself that moods pass. Noel Gallagher's visit to Downing Street was hailed as a masterstroke, Cool Britannia was regarded as a vote winner and it was believed to be miraculous that Mr Cameron could ride a bicycle.

So I dedicate this column to two assertions. That rubbish is rubbish is rubbish. And that Gordon Brown can call a snap election if he likes, but he might not win it.

As Mr Brown spoke, I realised I was listening to something vaguely familiar. And then suddenly it came to me. He was repeating the standard Tory platform speech from the 2005 election, right down to the pledge to clean hospital wards.

The pitch was exactly the same. In place of the tricksy Tony Blair, let's put in a hard man who can get the job done, someone who acts rather than emotes. And with the hard man comes a series of hard pledges all about foreigners and guns and drugs and things. These promises come straight out of focus groups. You make liberal use of the two phrases that get applauded at both party conferences – 'matron' and 'cancelling contracts'. The very words of Middle Britain. How can you lose?

Here's how.

Once upon a time Coca-Cola believed it was onto a winner. In focus-group tests, consumers said they preferred Pepsi. So you make Coke taste more like Pepsi. New Coke was born. And it was a fiasco. In his book *Blink*, Malcolm Gladwell explains why – consumers preferred Pepsi when they were asked to compare a sip of that drink with a sip of Coke. But when they drank a whole glass? Coke came out on top. Individual policies on immigration and hospital wards pass the sip test, but voters may not want a whole glass of fizzy populism.

Look at it another way. Politicians often wonder why people don't vote. This is the wrong question. The real puzzler is why on earth anybody bothers voting at all. If you multiply the chance of influencing the outcome by the difference that a change of government might make to your life, you might calculate that the benefit to you is so small that it is not enough to risk, say, the probability that on the way to vote a caravan full of violins falls on your head, having been pushed off a third-floor council house balcony by a drunk dentist.

If a rational view of personal interest cannot explain people's voting behaviour, what can? That they vote to make a statement about themselves. As the identification of party with class has declined, for instance, so has voting. By supporting a party, voters are declaring what sort of person they are. They want to be able to say that this is something they did for the country and they want their party label to declare that they are a good person, who does the right thing for the country.

A string of policy pronouncements may chime with individual preoccupations without satisfying even those who agree with them. Mr Brown could easily find in an election campaign that his message doesn't work as well as the focus groups seemed to promise.

It might reasonably be objected that Mr Brown may not have crafted the perfect message but that doesn't matter because he's fighting the Tories and they are in a mess. Quite right. Except that it is not only the Tories he is fighting – it's also the Government's record.

The public have not made up their mind about Mr Brown. They are reasonably impressed with his handling of the various problems in the summer and reassured that he appears to be moderate and a human being. But they are very sceptical of New Labour politicians bearing gifts.

He says he is going to jail for five years those who illegally carry a gun. Where? He says contract cleaners will be sacked if they don't meet cleanliness standards. Aren't they now? He says he's going to toughen up border controls. Yeah, right.

Mr Brown has excited expectations of change, but he cannot meet them merely by talking. He has to demonstrate change. And if he goes to the country now, he won't have done. That's why his poll lead is not stable. How long since he was last on even terms with the Tories? Er, a couple of weeks back, wasn't it?

Of course, the Tories present a tempting target. It's very hard to see them winning a majority in the autumn. But is it so hard to see them depriving Labour of its majority? There are serious contradictions in the Tory strategy. Perhaps even insoluble ones. A quick dash to the polls might allow Mr Cameron to go to the country without even trying to resolve them. Anyone who can't conceive of Mr Cameron appealing to undecided voters in a burst of television exposure is demonstrating a failure of imagination.

An autumn election? It is not hard to see Gordon Brown calling it in haste and repenting at leisure.

Curse of the Premier
of the Month

After Gordon Brown's supposedly glorious
summer the reality dawns that he was never
much good even then

19 December 2007

Congratulations, James Gordon Brown. For you were the Barclays Manager of the Month for September. I'm just sorry, as you opened the champagne, that no one reminded you of something every football fan knows. The Barclays Manager of the Month trophy comes with a curse.

I want to introduce you to some statistical work on the fortunes of Premier League gaffers. You see, I think it can help us answer a puzzling political question.

Back in the summer the media portrayed Mr Brown as a political demigod. Now he is written about as someone who would be lucky to win third prize in the East of England tiddlywinks competition. The standard narrative is that he changed. He started brilliantly, but when he called off the election, he lost his way. But is that really right? Perhaps the standard narrative is just a way for the media to get itself off the hook. Perhaps the truth is simply that the summer's reporting was hyperbolic nonsense.

And this matters. It matters because of the light it sheds on the coverage of politics and the light it sheds on what is really going wrong for Gordon Brown.

But first – the football. Every month, one Premier League manager is honoured for his team's performance. And most fans do not regard this as a blessing. They note that no sooner has the boss of their team been photographed with the trophy and a sheepish grin, than their side begins to lose. The curse of Barclays Manager of the Month strikes.

Now I am not a big one for curses normally, but this one? There's something in it. Here's how it works. The boss who wins the award does so because his team did better than anyone expected that month. This might indeed have been because his team had genuinely improved. However, that's not usually the reason for the run of good results. The reason is that victories and defeats come in clusters.

A team that have the ability to win 50 per cent of their games will not ordinarily do so by winning and losing alternate fixtures. They will win a few, lose a few, perhaps have a draw in the middle somewhere. And guess what happens to you if a cluster of victories happens to coincide with a calendar month? Come on down, manager of the month. The problem is that a cluster of defeats is quite likely to be on the way to even things out.

The whole idea of a manager of the month, in other words, is ridiculous. A few weeks is far too short a time to judge whether real improvement has taken place. And handing out a trophy for a cluster of victories shows a touching faith in the ability of people to change.

Forgive me switching sports for a moment. Over in America the baseball manager Billy Beane has built a successful team upon a recognition that players don't change. In *Moneyball*, his bestselling book on Beane, the journalist Michael Lewis records how most baseball managers ignore the flaws of promising youths because they think these flaws can be eliminated. Beane picks them knowing that he will have to live with their flaws. Players don't change.

The coverage of Mr Brown this summer made both these errors. It assumed, as the Barclays Manager of the Month does, that a cluster of victories is the same as a real improvement. And it demonstrated a touching, but misplaced, faith that politicians can simply change who they are and eliminate their flaws.

The result was a ridiculous overestimate of some fairly prosaic acts by the incoming Prime Minister. Did he deal with the terrorist attacks brilliantly? Not really. He didn't have all that much to do. Was his handling of the floods a triumph? Hardly. The Audit Commission has been damning about the inconsistent, badly targeted government assistance. Foot-and-mouth? I think it has to be a 'no' on that one too. And coming back from holiday early was a good stunt but maybe even that wasn't smart. The man has looked exhausted ever since.

And now, in an attempt to make the narrative work, the summer's political genius has become winter's dunce. Nothing can go right for this comic character. Vince Cable captured this point and made people laugh when he said that the Prime Minister had within a few weeks turned from Stalin into Mr Bean. Witty. But honestly, how likely is it?

Gordon Brown has been a consistent character – his virtues and his defects. His brooding intelligence, his inability to make a decision, his relentless drive, his attachment to a closed clique. These things weren't going to change. He wasn't a new man in the summer and he isn't a dolt now.

Isn't this all just history? Not quite. The standard narrative rather underestimates the troubles facing Mr Brown. It describes his difficulties as a few extraordinary incidents hitting him in quick succession. That's something he can turn round once he catches his breath. But understand his difficulty as an underlying problem that existed in the summer and you see the hole that he is in.

People have turned against the Government not because of a few bad media stories, but because people wanted change, felt Mr Brown might bring change and now feel that he won't. It is the long-standing disaffection with New Labour he is really suffering from.

What does this analysis tell us about the coverage of politics? That we are too inclined to ignore long-term trends because we are busy covering immediate incidents. That we are carried away with the idea that people change, merely because change makes a good story. That we often record the noise rather than the signal.

We are too inclined to believe that a week is a long time in politics. It isn't – any more than a month is a long time in football management.

Some sage advice: ignore the results

It's opinion polls, not local elections, that count.
And where's the fun in knowing that?

30 April 2008

Forty per cent of British women who go on a holiday to Spain have sex with a stranger within the first five hours of their arrival. Believe this? Then you are ready to follow this week's local election results.

Nearly one quarter of young drug users have smoked cannabis together with their parents. Convinced? Then you are missing your vocation. A job awaits you as a political reporter.

The cod survey is ubiquitous. Britain's favourite flavour of yoghurt as determined by 132 respondents on the Yoghurt Council website; the ten top musical acts of the last millennium (winner Robbie Williams, runner-up Mozart) as nominated by listeners to LBC; the news that 38 per cent of people prefer their vacuum cleaner to their spouse (according to a survey of vacuum cleaner retailers).

Most of these start their life on the PC of a hopeful PR executive and end it in the news-in-brief column of a free-circulation newspaper. But imagine if a cod survey were to dominate political debate for a week, become the lead item on the news, create a massive storm that swirls around the feet of the Prime Minister. Well, imagine no longer because that is precisely what is about to happen.

At the end of this week, millions of voters will go to the polls and elect thousands of local government representatives. And the results will matter to those who live in the areas involved. But they will also be reported as providing a useful guide to the state of national opinion, a verdict on the Prime Minister and a glimpse of the result of the next general election. Such reporting is a preposterous error.

Ask a politician to respond to an opinion poll finding and chances are you will get back this cliché: 'I don't believe in polls, I believe in real votes in real ballot boxes.' Michael Heseltine even gave this answer once when he was asked about the views of Polish people. Journalists pretend to be cynical when they hear this cliché. But really it represents our view too. Surely real voters going out to cast their ballot in proper elections are giving us a clearer view of the political picture than opinion polls?

No, they aren't.

Let me start with the question. Any pollster will tell you that tiny changes in wording can make a big difference to the outcome of a survey. If, for instance, you remind people that the Liberal Democrats exist before asking about voting intention, the number who say they are Liberal Democrats increases.

But here we are not talking about tiny differences. We're talking about trying to find out who you want to be prime minister by asking who you want, say, to be mayor of london. It is hardly surprising if this does not prove very enlightening.

Next, there is the nature of the sample. This week's local elections do not take place in every part of the country, so one can only guess at what might have happened in the places that are not going to the polls. But there is an even more serious problem with the sample – it is a self-selecting group of enthusiasts.

The surveys that I mentioned at the beginning of this article – the holiday sex poll and the cannabis poll – were real examples. They came from magazines that asked their readers to write in with their drug and holiday experiences. Naturally, respondents were people happy to share details of their love life and drug use and sufficiently motivated to put pen to paper. Not exactly representative.

Those who vote in local elections are a similar bunch. Not sex addicts and drug users, but unusually enthusiastic about their own peculiar vice – picking their local councillor. Angry protesters and political junkies form a much bigger proportion of the local vote than they do in a general election. The sample in local elections seems so much better than that provided by pollsters, because it is so much larger. But unfortunately it isn't properly balanced.

And finally – a minor point this, but worth noting – there is the fact that not every seat is contested by every party. Quite often voters will go to the polls to find that there is no Labour candidate, say.

None of these is merely a theoretical point. The proportions of votes cast in local elections and those cast in general elections are wildly different. But there are analysts who will play with the figures and claim they can tell you what it all means. They will dominate the coverage next weekend and the Prime Minister's future may depend on what they had to say.

For them I have two questions. The first is – how? How can you really adjust properly for the different questions voters were asked and for the unrepresentative enthusiasm of the sample?

The other question is – why? Why would you bother? Who would construct a poll by, to start with, asking millions of people in only some parts of the country to go down to their local school if they want to and opine on an entirely different matter; and then, reverse-engineer the results?

Surely you would just ask 1,000 or so voters in a representative sample what their general election voting intention is? You would use a poll, with all its imperfections.

But that would mean admitting that anything we will find out on Thursday, we already know more accurately now. And where's the fun in that?

Everyone agrees he's got to go. So why hasn't he?

Bobby Kennedy and the Brazilian football team explain why toppling Gordon Brown is only a possibility, not a certainty

By 2009 the frenzy over Gordon Brown fighting an election as a genius had turned into a frenzy about him being deposed. A challenger was expected at any moment, but I was dubious. This article appeared the day before Labour did disastrously in the European elections, a fiasco that was widely anticipated.

3 June 2009

John F. Kennedy, always the cooler, more considered of the Kennedys, watched his brother Robert dive off a sailboat into frigid waters off the coast of Maine, laughed and shook his head. He remarked to his close aide Ted Sorensen: 'Well, that either showed a lot of guts or no sense at all, depending how you look at it.'

Sorensen recalled these words when he found himself riding in Robert Kennedy's campaign plane, supporting a presidential bid that most of the old JFK team, including him, believed was doomed. Bobby Kennedy's 1968 campaign, taking on a sitting president in his own party, either showed guts or no sense at all. It depended how you looked at it.

Robert Kennedy hated President Johnson. 'He's mean, bitter, a vicious animal in many ways,' Kennedy complained. His young advisers thought LBJ was sure to lose in the end in 1968 whatever Bobby did. And if LBJ lost, and Kennedy stayed out of the race, then Kennedy would go down with him. It would be 'eclipse – irretrievable', his trusted aide Adam Walinsky warned him. Yet still, Kennedy had hesitated before running.

There were good political reasons for this hesitation. In his compelling book on Kennedy's 1968 effort, *The Last Campaign*, Thurston Clarke explains how the more seasoned 'honorary Kennedys', JFK's extended family of advisers, joined forces with the Democratic establishment to urge RFK to stay out. He couldn't win the nomination, they said. He'd just spoil it for Johnson. And in the background there was always the possibility, the nagging thought, that it could all end in tragedy. As it did. Friday marks the doleful anniversary of Bobby's assassination.

So why did Kennedy do it? Why did he take the plunge? What turned his confident public statements that he would not run into a decision to go for it? In one word – Vietnam.

Kennedy could not support Johnson through the campaign as a war that he hated continued to escalate. Political considerations could be balanced. This couldn't. He could not stay silent; he had to make the case. And when he had finally decided to take the plunge he told friends: 'I don't know what is going to happen, but at least I'm at peace with myself.' Clarke believes that, in the end, Kennedy felt morally compelled to stand.

The decision Kennedy agonised over – to challenge for the crown, or not to – must surely be in the minds of some of Gordon Brown's Cabinet today. Those that are left, that is.

Surely they can see what the rest of us can see. That Labour led by Mr Brown is doomed to terrible, catastrophic defeat.

That no one, no one, could lead Labour to a worse defeat than he. That waiting it out for another year does not bring dignified defeat for a united government.

What could possibly be stopping them, then? Why is the departure of Gordon Brown as Labour leader still only a possibility and not a certainty?

The first reason is what one might call the Bobby Kennedy reason. Mr Brown's critics do not have a Vietnam War to compel them to act. They only have the hedged-about political considerations that led RFK to hesitate. If cabinet ministers were to call for Mr Brown to go, what would they cite as the reason? Merely that Mr Brown would lead Labour to defeat? That may be of interest to the Labour Party, but hardly to the rest of us. It certainly doesn't constitute a moral case for action.

When Michael Heseltine stood against Margaret Thatcher, he offered a clear change of direction. So did John Redwood when he challenged John Major. Both felt that they could no longer stand aside, that they needed to make their case. They believed that their moment had come. Is there anyone in the Cabinet of whom that is true now? Upon what grounds?

If Mr Brown survives, there is something else he can thank – the fact that there is a market failure in the market for political coups.

It is tempting to use social psychology to analyse the behaviour of the Labour Cabinet. One could suggest that they are adhering to a social norm, going along with the group. Just as hundreds of followers of the Reverend Jim Jones drank poison just to fit in, so cabinet ministers are keeping quiet as they all commit suicide together.

But this description doesn't quite fit. Because, unlike Jones's followers, most individual cabinet ministers are only too aware of what is going on. And they don't want to die.

So economics provides a better way of understanding why they still might not act. A market failure can exist where it is impossible for people to gain the full benefit of the costs that they incur by acting. And this may yet save Mr Brown.

The benefit of Brown's demise – increased support for Labour – is shared among most members of the Labour Party. The cost – the risk of sticking your head above the parapet and then finding no one else has joined you – is concentrated on the person doing the head-sticking. It could be in everyone's interest for Mr Brown to go, but still in no one person's interest to start the movement against him. Naturally someone could decide to move, heedless of this calculation. But market failure explains why such an obviously sensible thing for Labour to do might yet remain undone.

There is a final reason. Let's call it the World Cup reason. Brazil were the best team in the last football World Cup. In any game they played, they were favourites. Yet it still remained unlikely they would win the whole tournament. And they didn't. The reason is simple statistics. A string of things, each of which are probable, taken together become improbable. It was very likely that Brazil would win any one individual match, but unlikely they would win them all.

It is very probable that Labour will achieve such a bad result tomorrow that the party will be jolted. It is very probable that in the next week one or more Labour MPs may announce that it is time for Mr Brown to go. It is very probable that Mr Brown could be forced out if there were a revolt. But for all three things to happen? That's a great deal less probable.

It is hard to believe, isn't it, that Gordon Brown can carry on like this. It's extraordinary to think he might. But, really, he can. He shouldn't do, he might not, but he can.

Keep plugging away. The brand is a winner

Tories think that the job of changing their party's image is complete. It isn't – and complacency could be fatal

This appeared as the 2010 election campaign was under way and responded to a feeling that the Tory campaign was underpowered and inconsistent. It picks up again on the issue of brand and deepens my analysis.

10 March 2010

In 1915 the Coca-Cola company decided that it needed to do something about its bottles. The firm's bottlers were complaining. They felt that the straight-sided containers they were using weren't distinctive enough. So Coca-Cola set a challenge to glass manufacturers. Could someone out there come up with a better bottle?

Yes, was the answer. The Root Glass Company of Terre Haute, Indiana, proposed the swirling, curved 'contour' bottle. It became, and remains, one of the most recognisable and best-loved brand icons. And Martin Lindstrom, the brand guru and author of the book *Buyology*, thinks he knows why. The Coca-Cola bottle is, he says, 'smashable'.

If you drop the famous Coke bottle on the ground, and it smashes into a hundred pieces, you would be able to pick up just one of them and still recognise what it is. Lindstrom lists some other brands of which the same is true. A bit of a Harley-Davidson, a scrap of an iPod, a drop of Guinness, Lego. These brands are all smashable.

But the Conservatives? I suspect there's only one sense in which anyone thinks they are smashable, and it's not Lindstrom's.

A smashable brand is consistent, the same through and through. Its values guide every part of the design, its identifying features suffuse everything, there isn't a detail that is left out, that isn't true to the whole. And all appeal to the emotions. One study, using brain scans, shows that smashable brands light up the same part of the brain as religious imagery.

These brands share something else. Their owners understand that there is much more to their appeal than one simple function, however good that function might be. In fact consumers purchase the product as much for what it says about them, and how it makes them feel, as for what it does. The product is much more than functional, it is part of their identity.

You can divide the last five years, or even fifteen years, in politics into two sorts of period. You can divide it into the periods when the Conservatives have remembered and cared about their brand and the periods when they haven't. Periods when they have understood the need to build a consistent and coherent picture in voters' minds of who they are, and periods when they have doubted the necessity, or have believed the job done, or have chased other goals.

And I believe that you can divide the periods in one other way. The periods when they have cared about their brand and been successful, and periods when they haven't cared and have not been successful.

Now the election campaign is upon David Cameron's Conservatives, and the polls are closing, and the leadership team has a choice. What sort of period are the next two months going to be?

To anyone who doubts this account, I recommend a superb new history of the last decade in Tory politics, published this week. Peter Snowdon's meticulous narrative, *Back from the Brink*, records the highs and lows of the party both before and after David Cameron captured the leadership.

As Snowdon records, one of the events that propelled Mr Cameron into the leader's chair was the presentation to the 2005 Tory conference of opinion research on the Conservative brand. Tory immigration policy garnered significantly less support the moment voters were informed which party supported it. Informing voters that the immigration policy they had just been asked about belonged to Labour made no difference to their support. The brand problem was confined to the Conservatives.

The party faithful realised what this meant and chose a leader who might alter perceptions. And in a hectic, but hugely successful, period after David Cameron became leader, his team concentrated on just that task. Everything – policy initiatives with Bob Geldof, photocalls with huskies, being seen out biking, dropping health policies that seemed to favour opting out of the system, shifting Tory attitudes on issues like gay rights – was geared to make the party, and particularly its leader, seem different.

These Tories, the message was intended to say, are modern, energetic, determined, tolerant, they listen, they are at ease with today's Britain. They understand that people are fed up with knockabout politics as usual. They support public services, particularly the NHS, they will protect the low-paid and they understand that, as Mr Cameron put it early on, 'we're all in this together'.

The Tories are still living on the capital from this spell. But every so often, they forget. They start thinking they have changed the brand already, that the work has been done. They have self-indulgent little rows, as they did over grammar schools. They coast. They start wondering if they need a retail offer to the public, some big (probably expensive and therefore impossible) initiative. They lose sight of the fact that their best moments (Mr Cameron's speech without notes and his response on expenses, George Osborne's big calls on taxes and debt and spending) have been when they have been reinforcing their new brand.

Politicians and pundits alike overestimate the impact that individual policy initiatives have on voters. Focus-group research suggests that most voters don't know what 'Whitehall' is or what 'hung Parliament' means. The BBC has done research which shows that the term backbencher is lost on those watching its news bulletins. All that get through are very broad messages about the character of a party, about who it is, about its brand. And this is transmitted in many ways big and small, but particularly through pictures and spontaneous public appearances.

The old negatives that dogged the Tories – that they will cut the NHS, get rid of tax credits, favour the rich over the poor, the South over the North – dog them still. They, and particularly David Cameron, have made some progress in persuading people that the party has changed. But not enough. And certainly not enough to stop plugging away at the message. Every day. All the time.

Eighty two per cent of people think it is time for a change. Less than half say they will vote Conservative. The voters are out there to give the Tories a landslide, but the party needs to help them over the finish line. They just need to show a bit of (Coca-Cola) bottle.

This isn't Fox: The Movie. It's messy, real life

Why doesn't the PM simply fire his defence secretary? It's about being human and about being in control

The details of Liam Fox's resignation as defence secretary in 2011 are too arcane to reprise. But the incident was classic as an example of a prime minister hovering over whether to sack someone involved in a messy controversy in which the facts were disputed. In the end a degree of clarity was achieved sufficient that Mr Fox had to be replaced. But this article was written before that, at the stage of contested allegations and calls for him to go. It looks at the unwritten rules that apply in these situations, situations that PMs encounter repeatedly.

12 October 2011

So what were we supposed to do? The 1997 election campaign had begun when *The Sun* let us know it had a sensational story for the next day's paper. A married Conservative MP and ministerial aide, Piers Merchant, had been photographed in a park, apparently kissing a 17-year-old hostess who worked in the Casa Rosa nightclub in Soho.

We were manning the press office at Conservative Central Office and naturally our first step was to phone Mr Merchant, who I'd always rather liked, and ask him about it. He denied it. Totally. He wasn't having an affair. She had suggested a walk in the park and then she had kissed him, unexpectedly and without invitation. He alleged a tabloid sting. Trust me, he said.

We phoned back the journalists. Come off it, they said. Listen, we followed him. We know. Trust us. It was an affair. He's lying.

So what were we supposed to do? In the end, what we actually did was, well, nothing. And all these years later, I still don't know the truth about that kiss. It all still seems a bit murky. Although it does have to be acknowledged that a few months later the MP was embroiled in a second story involving the same woman and had to resign his seat.

The lesson of this story is that in these scandals you are expected to move decisively, taking a clear position. Anything else is weakness, dithering, tolerating sleaze. But often you can't honourably do so. You don't know the whole truth. You may never know it. And you can't really act without knowing it, because that's not fair on the accused.

The result? You end up breaking what is possibly the most important rule of politics. The rule that says that you must always seem to be in control of circumstances.

The Liam Fox story provides a perfect example. That Dr Fox has shown poor judgment is not in any doubt. But the fact that he is still in office and that the Prime Minister has not turned against him is not as complicated as it seems. It's less about calculations and party balance, and more about something very human.

David Cameron doesn't know any better than anyone else the nature and consequences of the Defence Secretary's relationship with Adam Werritty. But he does have a different responsibility. If he sacked Dr Fox based on concern about where the stories might go in future, he would be ending a man's career. And all to make it easier for him, David Cameron, to get through the next 48 hours.

The Prime Minister would be inflicting a terrible blow on someone he has worked with closely (Dr Fox is rather liked by the Downing Street team, even though they think he is, ahem, 'a card'). He is reluctant to do this just to make the story go away.

This stance, however, is risky. If, as is obviously possible, more emerges that makes it impossible for Dr Fox to continue, Mr Cameron might look as though he wasn't firm, strong, on top of things. And once you've lost a reputation for being in control of the situation, it is very hard to win it back.

It's very odd, this political imperative that you must look in control. In dealing with a strike, for instance – or, as Presidents Obama and Clinton discovered in different ways, a budget fight or a party split – being seen to be in control usually ends up being of greater importance than the innate popularity of the stance that you took.

The Government is discovering this with its deficit position. Even though people are wary of its policy, they like that the Government is clear, has a direction, seems to be in control of what it is doing. Politically speaking, if inflation runs out of control or the deficit target is not being met, that may prove a much bigger threat to the Government's position than the grinding hardship of the austerity programme. So there's no doubting the power of this feeling that control is so important.

But I have often wondered: where does it come from? Why do people feel like that? After all, with a little thought, we accept that in reality a prime minister can't be in control of circumstances, because circumstances are circumstantial.

I think the cultural critic Neal Gabler provides an insight in his dazzling book *Life: the Movie*. The book argues that in the last century entertainment has driven all before it. The demand to be entertained has been by far the most important political and cultural force, supported by the development of entertainment technology.

There is no field, in Gabler's view, that has escaped the impact of entertainment; everything has succumbed to its overwhelming power. Reality has simply given in. The media, shopping, crime, even our personal identities, all have become branches of the entertainment industry. We all see ourselves as leading actors in a movie named after us, and work at our image and relationships to fit with the plots and characterisation that we have in mind for ourselves.

Some take this idea a very long way. Walt Disney spent his life trying (and succeeding) to create an entertainment empire that was a world of his own, one that he could control. I think Steve Jobs was rather the same, an entertainment entrepreneur, trying to control his own life and ours. But most of us don't go that far. Beyond the fairly limited sphere of our own immediate existence we are content to be spectators, watching the show.

And our attitude to politics reflects this. We see political narratives rather like films: we expect them to proceed at pace, to go somewhere, to have a conclusion. That's what we've become used to – life as entertainment. And we expect, however unrealistically, that the protagonist should drive the narrative on, staying on top of it, remaining ultimately in control and triumphing over adversity.

The fact that real life cannot provide us with this neatness, with the clear resolution of a movie, leads to disillusion, to confusion and disdain. And, knowing this, politicians will do a great deal to keep up the illusion, making small bets about what will happen next so that they can anticipate it and seem in control.

While David Cameron is grappling with the truth about Liam Fox's actual life, voters are watching him in *Fox: the Movie*.

This politico has a lesson for 'the real world'

Let me offer the banking industry a little advice:
this disaster won't go away until you face some
hard truths

Revelations about the manipulation of interest rates brought
more bad publicity for bankers. I gave them some advice.

4 July 2012

Being the generous, warm-hearted person that I am, I'd like to
return a favour.

You see, if you have worked in politics, as I did for a while,
you will forever have been in receipt of advice from business
people.

You get advice from all sorts, of course. Ken Dodd once
kindly sent through a sheet of jokes, for instance. But there is
a special quality to business advice. It was usually offered only
when the business person had fought, and lost, the battle to
conceal that they thought you were a fool, a battle some fought
less assiduously than others.

A common theme is that the person proffering their insights
lives in the 'real world'. This, apparently, is a place somewhere other

than Pinner. And it is the home of wisdom on how to run things. Given how much succour I have been given by citizens of the real world it would be churlish now, at their time of need, not to reciprocate. I feel that the banking industry is in want of my advice.

You bankers may think, in common with others in business, that you know how to organise things and make things happen. But dealing with a mammoth, self-created public fiasco involving resignations and front-page humiliation in the newspapers? Perhaps you will allow me.

The banking industry is in the middle of a political crisis. And before it can emerge from it, there are a few political points it must understand:

This is not a PR disaster. It's a disaster

In politics it is common to blame trouble on bad communications or bad communicators. Almost always, this is blaming the wrong thing. Motions to Conservative Party conference used to bemoan the failure to present the Community Charge in its best light. Presentation was not the problem with the poll tax.

Political difficulty cannot be overcome until its source is understood and removed. People can tell, and do very quickly, the difference between changing the way something is presented and changing the reality.

Bankers may be thinking how best now to present themselves. Instead they should be thinking how to change the industry to regain public trust.

The change required is bigger than you think

A common feature of attempts to change perceptions of a political party is that, when they begin, the scale of the operation required is underestimated. Both Neil Kinnock and William Hague perceived that their parties needed to change, but neither engaged in a programme radical enough to succeed. Nor were their parties willing to let them.

It will be very hard for the banks to regain public confidence. It will require imaginative demonstrations of a change in behaviour that, at the moment, seem hard even to identify, let alone enact.

You will think that the whole thing is a bit unfair. You must accept that it is not unfair
Faced with a public outcry, politicians often believe that they have been misrepresented – that the whole thing is down to the press mischief-making. And this gets them precisely nowhere.

During the expenses scandal many MPs thought that they had been unreasonably traduced. And some of them were right. But making this protest misunderstood the public mood. Voters wanted to feel that the entire political class understood that practices that seemed all right to politicians were, in fact, not all right.

What is happening in banking now is analogous. Many bankers will feel that it was not they who made the bad loans, or who needed a bailout, or who manipulated Libor. But even if they are right, this misses the point.

The entire industry either engaged in practices directly, or chose to ignore practices that, now they have been exposed, they cannot defend. This encompasses both the recent shocking disclosures about Libor and the risks taken before the financial crash. The response now needs to come from the entire industry. A slightly sulky feeling that bankers are being picked upon by a population that doesn't properly appreciate them is simultaneously understandable, inappropriate and totally counterproductive.

You need to understand what the public cares about and how they think
Politicians vastly overestimate the amount of attention that the public is paying to what they do. This leads them to believe,

for instance, that a performance at Prime Minister's Questions might change public opinion. The truth was that everyone was busy at work. They didn't notice it.

People's political opinion is shaped by their direct personal experience of public policy and by a few very big colourful issues that might come to their attention.

They also believe very strongly that what people get out of a deal should be linked to what they put in. And they are constantly on guard against those people who try to withdraw from the favour bank without depositing. This is why welfare fraud is such a huge political issue.

A recent poll featured in *The Times* suggested that more than 30 per cent of 16- to 23-year-olds did not realise that bacon came from pigs. While this may be a little bit of an exaggeration, it at least hints that if you were to ask the same sample whether the Vickers report is right to ring-fence retail banking you might not get back a very illuminating answer.

The banking industry's response to the crisis now upon it must be bold – lurid even – and it must make a direct personal impact. Otherwise people won't notice. Regulatory change will not be enough.

The big issue is remuneration. The banks will get nowhere until they address the bonus issue properly. The response must also involve the deal that customers get from banks and how they behave towards those to whom they lend money. They will also need to cooperate properly with criminal investigations.

You think it will blow over. It won't
In politics most things pass over people's heads. The things that don't, though, stick around. You live with them for years. This is one of those things.

Glad to be of service.

There's only one solution to the PM's dilemma

How do you appease rebels and yet pursue policies they oppose? Appeal to swing voters – and show you are a winner

In early 2013 the Conservative leadership was in quite a lot of trouble. With poll ratings low, it faced a lot of internal dissent from people who wanted to change the leadership and move to the right. Game theory seemed to me to provide an explanation.

13 March 2013

You know when you are a child and you do something stupid and everybody laughs? Yes? And your mum tells you not to be upset because 'we are laughing with you, not at you'? Well, if the Conservative Party's mum tells it that, she's lying. People aren't laughing with it, they are laughing at it.

I hope the laughers among you will excuse me a minute if I explain to those being laughed at what is going on.

The Conservative Party is in a difficult political spot and has, essentially, only three assets. The first is David Cameron. Of course there are lots of people who don't much like or admire him but he has always been more popular than the party with swing voters.

The second is the large constituency of voters who accept that Britain is in an economic hole and want to stop digging. They don't want to borrow more, and realise the need to take difficult decisions to deal with the deficit. And the third is that the Opposition has pitched itself too far to the left, under a leader who has yet to convince.

It is quite possible that none of this will produce a Tory victory, but equally obvious that if it doesn't, nothing will. Even if the party's leader and its central economic policy were agreed to be wrong, changing them at this stage can't possibly bring victory.

So the laughers are laughing at the laughed at (who include me) because they've spotted that Tory dissent is targeted at the only things that just might provide salvation. And they are hugely amused that the dissidents can't seem to see it and that the leadership can't do anything about it. Are these people mad?

Let me try an answer.

There's a bit near the end of Joseph Heller's *Catch-22* when Yossarian explains that he is no longer interested in the war effort and is not willing to die. It won't change anything, he reasons, because the war is essentially over. 'From now on,' he tells Major Danby, 'I am thinking only of me.'

Danby gives him a superior smile: 'But, Yossarian, suppose everyone felt that way.' To which Yossarian replies: 'Then I'd certainly be a damned fool to feel any other way, wouldn't I?'

Yossarian's reply is the perfect example of a common co-ordination problem that game theorists call the prisoner's dilemma.

Two prisoners are being interviewed separately. If both stay silent, both get a light sentence. But if one confesses, that prisoner goes free and the other gets a heavy sentence. The best solution for the pair is for neither to confess, but for each individual the right strategy is to confess. As a result, both confess. By doing so they incriminate each other and both get a heavy sentence.

The Tory party has not gone mad. It is just suffering from a prisoner's dilemma. Each person is behaving rationally in their own interest, but the outcome is bad for the group.

Supporting a government that is in political difficulties imposes a cost on an MP. You find yourself defending it wherever you go. It is difficult to know quite what to say when growth doesn't go up. You feel a bit silly and stuck for an answer when a journalist asks you why your party is 10 per cent behind in the polls. You find yourself under pressure at a party meeting for a policy you were never all that sure about in the first place.

So the natural thing to do is to join in with the critics, or develop your own special critique. Then perhaps do it publicly to show you really mean it. It is a relief to be able to speak your mind and not to have to say nice things about colleagues that you might not really think. Suppose everyone did that, Yossarian? Well, you'd be a damned fool to do anything else, wouldn't you?

In *The Art of Strategy*, their superb book on game theory, Avinash Dixit and Barry Nalebuff explain the sort of politics that results. In order to make an impact you exaggerate the intensity of your position, but not so much that 'you are thought of as a crackpot . . . The trick is to take the most extreme stand consistent with appearing rational.' Quite a good description of the politics of Nigel Farage.

Understanding that Tory dissenters are perfectly rational, even if the result of their behaviour is not, is the key to responding. First, it is not possible to solve the prisoner's dilemma by appeasing the dissidents. Doing so misunderstands their motivation. The more the leadership moves towards them, the further away the dissidents will move to keep the original distance.

It was, for instance, entirely predictable that announcing a referendum on Europe would be followed by more intense opposition to Mr Cameron. Those wishing to enjoy the fruits of dissent simply moved their opposition from Europe to something else – the leadership, the economy.

Second, it is not possible to produce unity by calling for it and even less possible to do so by insulting the rebels. Again, this fails to understand the rational basis of dissent. It treats people as mad who are not mad.

It is true that one solution to a prisoner's dilemma is for the game to be repeated in the context of a long-standing relationship of trust between the prisoners. This sort of trust and loyalty used to exist in the Tory party and was one of its great strengths. But it isn't any more. It hasn't existed for more than a quarter of a century.

Which leaves really only one answer. The leadership needs to change the payoffs in the game. A prisoner's dilemma is created by the particular structure of incentives and punishments, and the best way out is to change this structure.

The dissidents calculate that the Conservative Party is likely to lose the election and that even if it won, they wouldn't really share in the victory. They anticipate receiving what game theorists call the sucker's pay-off. They pay all the costs of party unity but get no benefit. For each individual, this makes rebellion a better personal strategy than cooperation.

To get the dissidents on side Mr Cameron therefore needs to maximise the chances of victory. If he is winning, the dissenters' incentive to rebel is vastly reduced. This produces the apparent paradox that he can increase the unity of the Right only by capturing the centre. He has to appeal to swing voters and not to the core vote. His best shot at unity is to follow his instincts about how to win over voters toying with Labour.

But he also needs to reassure dissidents, through better party management, particularly in the Commons, that everyone will share in victory, not just existing loyalists.

In other words the right strategy for David Cameron for dealing with plotters and rebels is to ignore their advice, while not ignoring them.

What happens in Syria will not stay in Syria

If Assad is allowed to cross Obama's red line without consequence, America is giving a green light to other evils

This article appeared as MPs were being recalled to Parliament following the Syrian government's chemical weapons attack on its own citizens. Two days after it was published, MPs rejected the Government's plan for a military response.

28 August 2013

Let's say that there is an epidemic of a disease that kills about ten of every 10,000 children. A vaccine is developed that eliminates the chance of getting the disease, but there is a problem. The vaccine kills. And five out of every 10,000 vaccinated children die as a result of receiving it. Would you vaccinate your child?

If your answer is that you would – after all, the vaccination halves the chance of death – you are relatively unusual. Most parents in a survey said they would not vaccinate. Because the vaccine kills.

This example is provided by Tobias Moskowitz and Jon

Wertheim in their excellent sports book *Scorecasting*. The authors are investigating what psychologists call 'omission bias' – our tendency to judge harmful actions more harshly than equally, or even more, damaging inaction.

Basketball referees are taught that there are four types of calls – correct calls, incorrect calls, correct non-calls and incorrect non-calls. It is better to make a correct call than an incorrect one, obviously. And if you fail to call an infringement when you should, you will be criticised.

But every referee knows that it is far better to make such an omission than to make a call in the dying moments of a game and be wrong. So what happens? In sport after sport, the referees blow their whistles far more in the earlier parts of the game than in the closing stages, thus penalising those infringed against. Omission bias.

Yesterday morning the Conservative MP Adam Holloway, opposed to taking action in Syria, provided as his chief argument that the outcome of intervention was impossible to predict. And he is quite right. In fact, he pierced to the heart of almost every foreign policy dilemma. The outcome of action is always hard to predict.

When Winston Churchill prevailed in his War Cabinet and decided to press on with war against Germany, it was impossible to know what the result would be. Victory seemed quite unlikely. When John Kennedy exposed the Soviet missiles in Cuba, it might have ended in disaster. When Tony Blair put pressure on Bill Clinton to threaten escalation against the Serbs, he couldn't be confident the Serbs would capitulate.

In each of these cases the decision to act could only be made if omission bias was overcome, if the consequences of action were compared with the consequences of inaction. And if the leaders were prepared to take risks that might turn out badly. As indeed later happened, in many critical respects, to Tony Blair in Iraq.

So the mistake the otherwise acute Mr Holloway was making was to fail to observe that while the outcome of intervention in Syria is impossible to predict, so is the outcome of not acting.

Syria is the Iraq of the non-interventionists. We did nothing and the situation got worse. And the worse the situation got, the more we used it as an excuse to do nothing.

Thus we are told that the opposition is now controlled by Islamic fundamentalists, while the liberal dissidents are nowhere. But this is hardly surprising when every force in Syria is being provided with support and weapons – except for the liberal dissidents. In Iraq we invaded to find no stockpiles of weapons of mass destruction; in Syria we did nothing and it turns out they did have stockpiles of chemical weapons and they used them.

Non-intervention has been a disaster. An interesting illustration of omission bias is that no one will launch a public inquiry into it. Non-intervention was an incorrect non-call. And who cares about those, right?

It is true that to change this policy now, to do something rather than sit there, is risky. And we have let the situation deteriorate so badly that the risk is greater than it was at the beginning. But the risk of not doing something is great too.

The Syria that will emerge if Bashar Assad wins will be a profoundly dangerous place. The choice is not between secular, but comparatively safe, repression under his Baathists and the triumph of the friends of al-Qaeda. As the leading Syrian expert Andrew Tabler has explained in both his recent book and a series of papers, victory will cede Assad a rump country in Western Syria ruled by repression, with parts of the state run by other terrorist groups.

Assad will hold power only with the support of Hezbollah and the Iranian Revolutionary Guards. They will be engaged in a running battle with Sunni insurgents who will turn to foreign allies to assist a jihadist struggle.

In addition to the hundreds of thousands who will die in Syria, the establishment of both an Iranian hold on Syria and a jihadist insurgency supported from Kuwait, Qatar and Saudi Arabia, will spread through the region and fuel international terror.

As Tabler puts it: 'Las Vegas rules do not apply to Syria: what happens there will not stay there.'

All this if we do nothing. But what reason is there to believe that acting might be any better? Is there anything we can do that has any point to it at all? Or are we being urged to act just for show?

The right place to start is with the Cold War. Much of what we did in the Cold War, and particularly much that America did, was just for show. It may not have achieved an immediate improvement in conditions on the ground, but it demonstrated that the Western allies were united and committed to resisting tyranny.

America took a decision it did not have to take – that it would engage with the world, spill blood and dollars to defend liberty against tyranny – and the results were hugely to the benefit of mankind. It got itself involved in an apparently irrelevant war in Korea, a place most Americans couldn't care less about, that ended in stalemate and a country divided between two dictatorships. And the war was hugely unpopular at home, and nearly resulted in disastrous military defeat.

Yet the Korean War signalled to the Soviet Union that the United States would act if it pushed things too far. Something happening in Korea, miles and miles away, was a vital moment in the postwar history of Europe.

So if all we in the West now do is act for show it will still be worthwhile. If, having described the use of chemical weapons as a red line, we do nothing, what lesson will Iran learn, as it develops its nuclear programme? We could be paying the price of an incorrect non-call for years.

But this is to take the most pessimistic view and to advance the minimum case for action. Creating a safe zone, protected from the regime; meeting the secular and moderate opposition there and helping them with arms, advice and technology so that they have a stronger voice; forcing Assad to the negotiating table; all these are possible.

No one can be certain that acting will produce this outcome, or that the outcome will be desirable. No one can say for sure what the 'end game' is. Once we start, the whole thing is open-ended. But the point is that if we don't start it is open-ended too and no one knows what the end game of inaction is either.

One of my favourite cartoons pictured a couple walking briskly down a street, with a cruise missile about to fall on the street next door. The caption read: 'Come along, dear, don't let's get involved.'

Syria won't go away just if we close our eyes.

71 days to go and Ed has no campaign in sight

If you're up against an opponent with a strong economic record, you need a strong alternative theme. Labour is still looking

In the run up to the 2015 election I was pretty sure what the Conservative Party should do. On 21 May 2014 I wrote: 'After the European election, the Conservatives' big task will not be to beat UKIP, or to do a deal with it, or to make Nigel Farage look foolish. It will be to shut up, shut up, shut up about UKIP and talk about the economy. They must be a clarifying economic party running a clarifying economic campaign. Nothing else will work.'

Meanwhile Ed Miliband was gaining plaudits for the way he was leaping on issues, jumping from topic to topic. He'd just had a good political week attacking a Tory donor over his tax affairs. I realised that despite the good press he was getting, he was on the wrong track.

25 February 2015

When I was doing my A levels, Dayvilles opened an ice cream parlour that I passed every day on my way to school. It offered thirty-two varieties of ice cream, something I'd never seen before. And one day I went in and just stared at the products.

I intended to buy something, but I couldn't decide what. The sheer choice was mesmerising. I pointed at a tub, then changed my mind and pointed at another. I stopped altogether in order to ponder further. At which point the man behind the counter burst out: 'Oh for Christ's sake, it's only a bloody ice cream.'

While I acknowledge that this makes me sound like Forrest Gump, my mama always says that politics is a little like an ice cream. The available range of issues on which to campaign is dazzling. But in the end, you have to pick. It's only a bloody ice cream.

When is Ed Miliband going to decide what his election campaign is about? He may not have noticed, but it's nearly March.

Let me take you through the political science. In her compelling book *The Message Matters*, the American academic Lynn Vavreck reviews the effectiveness of American presidential campaigns since the Second World War. The data strongly suggests that economic prosperity, or lack of it, decides the outcome. But not all on its own. The campaign messages matter too.

If the economy is in your favour – things are going well and you are in power or things are going badly and you are in opposition – the decision about what sort of campaign you should run is almost made for you.

You must be the 'clarifying' candidate, as Eisenhower was in 1956, Lyndon Johnson was in 1964 and Bill Clinton was in 1996, talking about the economy because the fundamentals favour you. All were successful, as was Barack Obama in 2008, running against the incumbent party as a clarifying candidate in a weak economy.

If the economy favours your opponent, you, as the 'insurgent' candidate, are at a significant disadvantage. But there is something you can do. You can find an alternative issue, something else to campaign on. It is possible to win.

Richard Nixon in 1968 won while talking about crime and disorder and the values of the silent majority. In 1976, Jimmy Carter won by campaigning on Watergate and the need for a cleaner politics. In 2000 George W. Bush ran as a compassionate conservative against a broken society.

These are all Vavreck's examples, but it is easy to provide British ones. In 1997, for instance, the economy was strong. Tony Blair ran as the insurgent as a fresh face who would end sleaze, bring change and stop Britain's public services running down. He left John Major's economic clarifying campaign (on which I worked) nowhere.

The rules for selecting an issue aren't difficult and the data is clear here, as well. Don't try to run as a clarifying candidate, talking about the economy, if the fundamentals favour your opponent. This will never work. Find an alternative issue, or preferably a bundle of issues tied together, on which you enjoy a clear advantage over your opponent and which your opponent cannot neutralise.

Once you have found this issue or theme, stick to it. It is difficult enough to make non-economic issues central, and you certainly won't succeed if you are not absolutely relentless. And find imaginative ways to dramatise the issue that you have chosen.

Ed Miliband has, so far, managed to break every one of these rules.

It was, I suppose, a reasonable punt earlier in the parliament that Labour would be able to run on the economy, that they and not the Tories would be the clarifying candidates. It has been quite a while since that was the case.

For months, even years, now, the party has been hopping around, trying to find an alternative. Three weeks ago it seemed they had selected the NHS. But like the squeezed middle and the cost of living and the British promise and one-nation Labour, no sooner had they identified an issue than they moved on from it.

For the past two weeks they have jumped on bankers avoiding tax and MPs having second jobs. The Labour leader has actually done quite – even very – well. But this won't succeed as a campaign.

Tax avoidance and MPs' behaviour are potentially powerful as vote movers, because many people have a strong feeling that others are taking out of the economy while they, the hardworking people, are putting in. They are being cheated in the deal.

As long ago as his 2011 conference speech, Ed Miliband seemed to understand this feeling. He hit on the idea of making the end of the 'something for nothing' society his promise. The notion required some development. It needed strong counter-intuitive Labour policies on crime, benefits and immigration to broaden the attack beyond rich people and politicians. It needed constant repetition.

Yet after leaving the stage in Liverpool, the Labour leader hardly ever talked about the 'something for nothing' society again.

At this late stage it will be very hard indeed to return to it properly. All by themselves, without development, bankers' tax avoidance and MPs' behaviour are not issues where Labour enjoys an advantage. Certainly not the sort of advantage that Vavreck regards as essential for an insurgent campaign to work.

Ed Miliband may believe that voters see him as an outsider, naturally able to stand apart from tax avoidance and the pay of MPs. They do not. Lord Ashcroft's focus-group work shows that the details of the issue disappear, as people dismiss Labour in the same way as they dismiss the Tories. As part of the existing system.

As a result, the issues that Ed Miliband is promoting, tempting though they are, will help outsiders such as UKIP and the Greens. If they help anybody at all.

The strange thing is that with the NHS, Labour has a ready-made issue that can work. They haven't turned their position into a compelling theme or laid the groundwork and this makes it much harder. But nonetheless they enjoy a strong lead on the NHS, people care about it and the Tories can't neutralise it.

Yet to be successful, they have to be relentless. Particularly having started so late. And they just aren't. Their current behaviour, frankly, is baffling.

Picking up a newspaper, alighting on a story and shouting out 'Oy, Stewart, have you seen this? Let's put out a press release' is not a campaign. It's a double scoop of Tutti Frutti.

Bad news for Labour: you're stuck with him

Those who imagine they can replace Corbyn don't understand the party and don't know the lessons of history

This was written at Labour conference in Brighton in the week of Jeremy Corbyn's election as leader. The consensus then was that he wouldn't make it as leader to the next election, whenever that was. I did not agree.

30 September 2015

Will Jeremy Corbyn be Labour's leader at the next general election? I want to start my answer in exactly the wrong place.

In Brighton. On the day the Labour leader addressed the party conference. A rebel unexpectedly propelled to the leadership late in life after years as a London MP. And while enjoying the backing of many activists, unable to get the party's grandees to support his policy of unilateral disarmament.

It is 1935, and George Lansbury – who became leader in 1932 at the age of 72, essentially because no one else was available – is trying to persuade the union bosses who dominate the conference to support his pacifism. Instead he attracts a stinging attack from Ernest Bevin, the transport union leader.

A week later, ill and fed up and unable to square his conscience with party policy, Lansbury resigns. His fellow MPs ask him to continue, but he turns them down.

The reason this is the wrong place to start a consideration of Mr Corbyn's prospects is not because it's the tale of a leader from eighty years ago. It's because I am beginning my analysis with an anecdote rather than statistics.

In his important new book *Superforecasting*, the scholar of the science of prediction, Philip Tetlock, warns that compelling narratives about how something might happen or has happened in the past are often misleading. The right place to begin a forecast is with a cool statistical view.

So when considering how likely someone is to buy a cat, it's a mistake to try to imagine what that person might do. Instead, you should use an objective calculation – what proportion of people have cats?

The correct way to predict whether Jeremy Corbyn will still be Labour leader in 2020 is not by dreaming of all the ways he might lose his job. Nor is it by identifying an instance of something similar having happened in the past. It is by asking this: what proportion of Labour leaders have been deposed in the middle of a parliament or without fighting a general election?

This provides what one might call the base rate of Labour coups. We can then vary it to take account of the particular circumstances of Jeremy Corbyn.

And here is the answer. The base rate is 0 per cent.

The party has had seventeen leaders and it has not pushed out a single one between elections. Labour has only deposed a leader once in any circumstances. This came immediately after the 1922 election, when John Clynes was superseded by Ramsay MacDonald, who was returning to the leadership upon re-election to Parliament.

On Monday, here in Brighton, I asked a former Labour minister and shadow minister for whom I have a great deal of respect how he could possibly recommend to the British people that they make Jeremy Corbyn prime minister and John McDonnell chancellor. Given everything I know about his politics, this would be totally irresponsible, I said.

He calmly replied: 'This will not be a problem. Jeremy Corbyn will not be the candidate.' Yes, I said, but what if he is? 'He won't be. I guarantee it.'

I do not believe he is in any position to give such a guarantee. I understand why moderates are desperate that the leader does not last. If Mr Corbyn is the candidate for prime minister it will make their position at the next election impossible – squashed between their careers, their party loyalty and what they know to be right for the country. Yet such desperation does not make for good predictions.

I think that, looked at as objectively as possible, Jeremy Corbyn is far more likely than not to be Labour's leader at the next election. I believe the chance of him still being there is 80 per cent. Perhaps even a tiny bit more.

The reason why the base rate in ejecting Labour leaders is so small is simple. There is a market failure in the provision of political coups.

A market failure exists when something that is clearly in the interests of a large group is not provided because no individual thinks it is worth the burdens, costs and risks of providing it. And such is the case with the Labour leadership.

The rules for replacing the leader set out in Labour's constitution are opaque and contradictory, as if these were mechanisms they don't imagine using. However, it seems to be the case that an election can be called if 20 per cent of MPs nominate someone else in the run-up to a party conference. That person would then have to defeat the existing leader in an election by members, affiliated members and registered supporters. The same electorate that gave Mr Corbyn 60 per cent in the recent contest.

A challenger who can't win is possible, I suppose. But otherwise an individual has to come forward capable of actually being leader. Someone outside the current left–right divide (so that they can actually win broad support) and with good future prospects. Dan Jarvis, say. Or Keir Starmer.

Why on earth would it be in their interests to take such a vast personal risk? The risk of losing and being seen as the Right's pawn? All in the cause of maybe (but probably not) winning a leadership that they could get much more easily a year or two later in more propitious electoral circumstances for Labour. The good sense to avoid that would seem to be a qualification for leadership all by itself.

The Conservatives did, it is true, depose Iain Duncan Smith. But this is because party rules did not require an alternative candidate. Mr Duncan Smith faced a vote of confidence resulting, as the rules stipulate, from anonymous letter writing. So the market failure did not exist.

There is, of course, the alternative thesis that Mr Corbyn gives up. He realises he can't hack it. Or he resigns on principle when losing a policy battle. Yet how often does this happen? What sort of politician really does that? Let's include Lansbury and the base rate is 6 per cent.

Five years is a long time. Mr Corbyn is already 66. His MPs don't want him and policymaking is chaotic. John McDonnell and Len McCluskey could fall out and the People's Front of Judea would split with the Judean People's Front. Mr Corbyn could become so unpopular that the risk of running for the leadership is reduced. I guess.

It's possible to tell a story of how Mr Corbyn might fall. But the chances of him going are dwarfed by the chances he will stay. The moderates have to face the fact that it is overwhelmingly likely that in 2020 if they recommend voting Labour they will be recommending putting Jeremy Corbyn in No. 10.

PART THREE

The Arrow of History

In 2016 I was invited to give the Sir Isaiah Berlin lecture in Hampstead Synagogue, to which Berlin had belonged. I chose to ask whether history had a direction, a logic.

This lecture forms the central part of a section which also includes my articles on how we understand the past and how it helps us understand the future.

The 2016 Isaiah Berlin Lecture

Is there an arrow to history – and if so, which
way is it pointing?

By looking backwards can we determine any sort of pattern
in human affairs which lights the way to the future?

24 November 2016, Hampstead Synagogue

It is my privilege, my rather daunting privilege, to be asked to
give the fourteenth Sir Isaiah Berlin lecture.

I encountered him only once. I shook his hand when introduced to him by Professor John Gray in the entrance hall of
the Athenaeum.

But intellectually I encounter him all the time. Not just because
he is a champion of liberty, and liberty is so precious, but because
I am a political practitioner and I believe that no one has come
closer than him to understanding what politics is there to do.

He understood that the things we value – liberty, justice,
fairness, and many others – cannot all be realised at the same
time and made compatible with each other.

He returned to this point in his last essay 'My Intellectual
Path' in which he wrote the following:

Liberty and equality, spontaneity and security, happiness and knowledge, mercy and justice – all these are ultimate human values, sought for themselves alone; yet when they are incompatible, they cannot all be attained, choices must be made, sometimes tragic losses accepted in the pursuit of some preferred ultimate end.

But if, as I believe, this is not merely empirically but conceptually true – that is, derives from the very conception of these values – then the very idea of the perfect world in which all good things are realised is incomprehensible, is in fact conceptually incoherent. And if this is so, and I cannot see how it could be otherwise, then the very notion of the ideal world, for which no sacrifice can be too great, vanishes from view.

We have to choose. When we choose more of one desirable thing we may suffer loss in another.

This lecture is about the choices we face now.

I have only lied to a journalist once. I felt I had to.

It was 1997 and I was working for John Major. One of my jobs was to come to the front after his election press conferences and field any extra questions the reporters might have.

The day before the general election I was standing at the centre of a ring of journalists when James Blitz of the *Financial Times* asked me this: 'Danny, are you going to win?'

Now, bear in mind that we were about to suffer the worst election defeat for the Conservative Party since 1832. I knew that we were not going to win, and he knew we were not going to win. He knew that I knew, and I knew that he knew I knew.

But instead of saying, 'No, of course not James,' I instead said this: 'We are cautiously optimistic.'

Hidden deep in this lie is an answer to the question I want

to examine today. Does history have an arrow? Does it point the way forward?

I am not a determinist. I do not believe anything in human affairs is inevitable. I even think that view is quite dangerous.

I do not believe, either, that because something has happened in the past it will therefore happen again. But I do write a football column that, with some success, uses past behaviour to indicate what is likely or unlikely to happen next. And it would be rather odd if it did not.

So what I want to do today is to see whether we can discern patterns in history that help us understand what might come next. I want to use them to help us explain the political battles of the moment even if they cannot tell us with any confidence who or what is going to win those battles.

I am going to argue that there has been an arrow to history and look at the direction it has been pointing.

And my starting point is with the lie I told to James Blitz.

Why was I so keen to avoid telling the truth about our political position that I told James something we both knew wasn't true?

It is because I appreciated that for John Major's adviser to admit that we were going to lose was powerful information, information that would make our pretty shaky position even worse.

The reason the information is powerful is that people follow each other, they copy each other, they are anxious to know what others are doing so that they can do it too.

The social psychologist Robert Cialdini has conducted a number of experiments that demonstrate the impact of what he calls social proof.

One was a test of how best to persuade people to save electricity. Cialdini first asked respondents what information they would find persuasive. Information about the cost? About the environment? About social responsibility? When respondents ranked them, one piece of information came bottom with almost everyone.

Almost everyone seemed certain that being told how much electricity their neighbours used would not influence them at all.

But when Cialdini then experimented with using various kinds of information it turned out that only one thing changed behaviour at all. People saved electricity if they were told that their neighbours were using less than them.

Another experiment was with hotel towels. In many rooms there is a card that tells you that you can help the environment if you hang your towel back on the rack rather than allowing it to be washed. But most of us ignore it, thinking this is just about the hotel's laundry bill.

What words can they put on the little card in your bathroom that will encourage you to hang your towel back on the rack during your stay?

It turns out that if you tell guests that 75 per cent of people hang their hotel towel back up, it increases the proportion who do it on any given night from 38 per cent to 48 per cent.

And if you tell them that 75 per cent of people staying *in their room* hang their towel back on the rack it increases the proportion who hang from 38 per cent to 58 per cent.

We are sensitive not just to what others do, but most particularly to what others *like us* do.

By the way, this means that when we say that there is an obesity epidemic we may think we are striking a blow against fatness. In fact people just think: 'Oh, I didn't realise that *everyone* was fat. I'll have another canapé.'

Let's now try and unpick the reason for this human foible.

Ask yourself this. Why do we cooperate with people who do not share our genes?

We all know why we cooperate with people who share our genes. It is to help perpetuate our genes. But why otherwise cooperate?

The answer is that we have found it an effective strategy for survival. Reciprocity is a good evolutionary strategy. A vampire bat will regurgitate blood into the mouth of another unrelated vampire bat if it believes that bat is on the point of death. The first bat expects that this favour would be returned if it found itself in a similar position.

And this works. It is very powerful.

The only problem is if you do a favour for someone and they do not do it back. We are always on our guard to ensure that this does not happen.

Together this explains quite a lot of our political behaviour.

First, our fairness norm is not, as many think, that we should all be equal, but that we should get out in proportion to what we put in. People think markets and profits and trade are fair, for instance, as long as it's a fair exchange. Because a fair exchange is no robbery.

You remember the hotel towels example? Cialdini tried another experiment. He promised people the hotel would donate a little bit of money to an environmental charity if they put their towels back. It didn't really work. The improvement was not statistically significant.

But then he tried this: The hotel has already donated money to an environmental charity and would be very grateful if, in return, you were to hang your towel back on the rack.

Fascinatingly this worked. People are programmed to reciprocate favours. It triggers our fairness norm. If I pay you a compliment you say thank you. If I ask you how you are, you say fine and how are you.

Second, the political issues that produce the biggest reaction are those that appear to offend against the fairness norm. Welfare is a good example. As strong as people's view is that we should ensure that no one is without any welfare provision, we all also bang on constantly about welfare fraud, about people taking out when they aren't putting in.

Bankers' bonuses were not a very big political issue when they were merely very large compared to everyone else's salary. They became hugely sensitive after the crash when people felt bankers were taking out what they were not putting in.

Thirdly, we find ways to ensure that we are trusted by others and know which others to trust. One of the quickest is to see if others behave like us and, conversely, to demonstrate that we are trustworthy because we behave like them.

We copy each other's cheating behaviour and back the winner in elections in order to fit in, to try to demonstrate that we are trustworthy.

I must emphasise that I am not recommending this behaviour, I am simply noting it.

An example of where it can lead us astray is in our attitude to immigration. Consider our reaction to migrants in the light of what I have just told you.

Immigrants are thought to offend against the fairness norm because they have access to social services like the NHS that people think they haven't paid for. And they don't look like us so we don't trust them.

This is sadly quite a powerful effect. Although both television and open markets are increasing the sense we have that people of different backgrounds are indeed very much like us, we still have a very long way to go.

But important though this is, let's not get diverted. I want to explain the role that reciprocity plays in directing the arrow of history.

In two brilliant books on evolution, *The Moral Animal* and *Non-Zero*, Robert Wright looks at the way that reciprocity drives technological development.

In order to make ourselves richer we are always looking for more people with whom to trade. But we have to be able to trust those people and to ensure that when we do something for them, they return the favour.

This has led us, Wright says, to develop generation after generation of information technologies. Counting, to keep score of favours; writing, to record transactions and exchange information; printing, to disseminate the rule of law and so on.

And with each we can see the process.

Step one. We seek to get richer. We are materialistic, we seek to make our life more comfortable.

Step two. We do this by trying to expand the number of people with whom we can trade.

Step three. As we succeed, material goods keep more people alive. So population grows. There are more and more people with whom we can trade, providing us with more and more opportunities to get richer still.

Step four. We develop technologies that allow us to do this trade and to keep a record of it. Crucially this allows us to trade with and to trust people we cannot meet with directly. The rules and the recording ensure that we can deal with an invisible and unknown individual with some confidence that we will have a fair exchange rather than a robbery.

Step five. At the same time the technology shakes up the existing structure of power and wealth. As a result it is often resisted by those who feel threatened by it. Scribes and kings, for instance, resisted allowing the spread of writing. Dictators resist the rule of law and the use of the internet.

Step six. As we seek to expand the number and geographical range of people with whom we trade, we slowly develop broader governing and social structures.

We therefore move from families to hunter groups, from groups to villages, from villages to groups of villages, from groups of villages to cities and regions, from cities to states and so on.

And this too alters the existing structure of power and wealth and is resisted.

So I believe that history has an arrow. And we can work out which way it is pointing.

To seek to get richer and to succeed; to do it by finding new technologies; to use those new technologies to expand the zone of trust; to develop new governing structures to cope with this expanded area; and at each stage to see the change resisted by those who feel that there might be an adverse impact on their wealth or power or merely feel that the change is unwelcome because it disturbs settled arrangements.

So what does this now mean for modern politics and political debate?

First it means that we are going to have a political battle over globalisation.

Donald Trump's new chief strategist, Steve Bannon, has responded robustly to suggestions that he is a white supremacist and an anti-Semite. He is, he says, merely an economic nationalist.

His argument is that international trade is exporting what he thinks of as American jobs to Asia. This, he claims, only advantages globalists who get rich at the expense of everyone else.

This argument is, I think, economically illiterate but politically shrewd. It is economically illiterate because it ignores the extent to which people are consumers as well as producers and the extent to which the production of goods and services often mixes components from different countries.

There is no question but that the broad mass of mankind and even those within a single country are the beneficiaries of international trade.

But it is politically shrewd because the costs of international trade can be concentrated on particular groups. They are at best unsettled and at worst impoverished by trade. Their discomfort is available for those who wish to exploit it.

Who might those groups be?

Those who feel particularly settled and feel change to be a threat, those who have relatively low skills and education, those who feel the current social structure advantages them. The biggest swing to Mr Trump and the politics of Steve Bannon came from older white males. These also provided support for Brexit.

It is interesting to look at some of the ways that the battle over globalisation has manifested itself.

There has been, for instance, the battle over political correctness, which looks on its surface to be entirely unrelated to economic concerns or to new technology and globalisation. Go beneath the surface and I think the link is clear.

In their book *The Hidden Agenda of the Political Mind*, Jason Weeden and Robert Kurzban make the following argument:

New information technology helps those who are educated to make their way in the world, to trade, to advance. If you have high human capital – you are well educated, intelligent and well connected – there are few things in the age of the educated that can stop you from exploiting your talent. Save for this – barriers to civic equality.

Prejudice and barriers against traditionally subordinate social groups – women, Jews, gays, and so on – are two of the few things that can stand in your way.

So the strongest supporters of political correctness are highly educated people belonging to subordinate social groups. As a Jew with a master's degree who is both economically and socially liberal I am the biggest possible cliché.

Now consider who might be least supportive of political correctness. People with less human capital, worried about change, who belong to dominant social groups. Elderly white males.

The argument over political correctness is at root economic.

The other way the row over globalisation has manifested itself is, as you might more readily accept, in a debate about governing structures.

The drive to create international structures is, as I have already discussed, the natural result of the slowly expanding zone of trading and trust. It is simply the latest iteration of something that has happened throughout history.

You would expect the attempt to create law that governs international dealings, as we have more and more of those dealings. And you would expect that attempt to be resisted by those who feel themselves less able to control the new political structures.

In the recent Brexit referendum Britain divided into two countries, Remainia and Leavia.

Remainia were the classes who saw new opportunities abroad as a promise, Leavia were those who saw them as a threat. Remainia, broadly, were people with more human capital and younger. Leavia those who were less educated or older.

I am not arguing that absolutely everyone could be neatly identified in this way. Some highly educated people supported leaving the EU because they think it an obstacle to globalisation.

But age and social background were pretty good ways of establishing how someone was likely to vote.

This too is at root economic.

It isn't entirely surprising that the inhabitants of Leavia are worried about the direction that history's arrow is pointing.

Trade is successful because it allows countries to specialise in providing goods and services where they enjoy a comparative advantage.

Yet this means that high-wage countries will specialise in providing high-end goods and services. Those who are unable to join in, who lack the skills to join in, may feel, may even be, left behind.

Even though closing a country to international trade would simply make everyone poorer the political impetus behind economic nationalism is obvious.

It's not hard to see the fights ahead.

Almost all international trade treaties involve some of the same problems as the EU. The World Trade Organisation and the proposed transatlantic deal (the TTIP) both require international decisions to be made about rules by bodies that inevitably challenge the sovereignty of the parties to the treaty.

Thus any replacement for the EU in the form of bilateral trade deals will raise questions that Brexit was supposed to answer. We haven't had, in the UK, the political rows over trade deals they have had in the United States. This is partly because we haven't had the power to make our own trade deals. Complaints about the EU have taken the place that in America is filled by complaints about NAFTA.

The era in which trade becomes hotly controversial in Britain may have, with Brexit, only just started.

The Left has correctly anticipated that we would have an argument about equality as new technology and specialisation makes some people richer while replacing the jobs of people with fewer skills.

What they failed to anticipate is that this battle over equality would turn into a row about immigration, about internationalism and about economic nationalism. They have been left, so far, completely perplexed by this development.

As they have been by religious fundamentalism. Because fundamentalists often belong to minority groups and see themselves as victims of prejudice, part of the Left sees them as allies in the campaign for equality. Yet another part recognises that they are, in many cases, enemies of liberty.

The rise of fundamentalism is another way on which the political battle has not developed in the traditional left–right mould.

The arrow of history suggests why. And it suggests that we are going to have a battle over globalisation. That battle has now begun, has become, in fact, a central feature of world politics and is visiting itself on Britain.

It is worth noting that on past form, globalisation would win. But that does not, of course, mean that it inevitably will. Past form, as they say, may not be a guide to future performance.

The arrow of history also points the way to changes in political power.

The development of new information technology always proves challenging and unsettling. Throughout history, it wrests powers from elites and hands them to new, emerging, broader groups.

And this is plainly happening now.

Consider, just as an example, the MPs' expenses scandal.

This would not have happened were it not possible to steal the whole of the archive of expense claims, with all the associated correspondence, and put it on a memory stick the size of my thumb. It could then be analysed on someone's desktop computer.

There are any number of other examples. The rise of Wikileaks for instance. Or the Sony pictures hack.

The microprocessor has put processing power on everyone's desktop, inevitably spreading power from those who hold it to those who seek it.

What is happening is much bigger than the vulnerability of organisations to leaks. Bigger even than the pressure it puts on organisations to be transparent or have transparency thrust upon them.

New technology allows, indeed insists upon, an entirely new relationship between those who govern and those who are governed.

Consider the experience of shoppers. Twenty, even ten, years

The Arrow of History

ago, when buying goods – videos for hire, books, records, whatever – we would go to shops and choose from among a few items. There could only be a few items because each took up physical space on the shelf. So we had to choose from the big, blockbuster items. The shop wouldn't stock niche items because it took up too much space for too few sales.

Now consider purchasing these goods. Where are Blockbusters? HMV? Tower Records? Borders? Gone, the lot of them, and replaced by online vendors like Netflix, Apple Music and Amazon. And these vendors have unlimited shelf space. They don't need to sell just the blockbuster items. They can sell, and you can buy, some pretty niche items.

Now think about political parties.

Mass-organised political parties didn't really exist before the second half of the nineteenth century. As politicians began to need support outside Parliament, they had to organise themselves to reach a mass audience through a few blockbuster channels – newspapers, and later television and radio. The limited shelf space that these mass channels had, meant there wasn't much room for anything but a very few of the big messages.

So there was a premium on discipline and uniformity. And only the leadership really had access to the mass party audience.

The mass media and the modern political party therefore grew up together. And now they may die together.

The era in which everyone uses just a very few media channels, with very limited shelf space, to reach a mass audience, that era is over. Now everyone can, potentially, reach a mass audience. The political party is not a necessary intermediary. The discipline it seeks is no longer one it can enforce.

I recall a few years ago a video made by the MP Sion Simon with the assistance of Tom Watson. Mr Watson held the camera while Mr Simon satirised David Cameron. With a few remarks about Mr Cameron's family that were judged in poor taste he

147

landed himself in a great deal of hot water. He made, not to put too fine a point on it, a national fool of himself.

But this is not what struck me. What struck me was that while I had on occasion managed to make a national fool of myself and my allies it had cost me millions of pounds and the weight of party headquarters in order to do so. Mr Simon now only required a video camera and Tom Watson.

Just about anyone has the ability to reach a mass audience with very little cost or equipment.

The election of Donald Trump illustrates how important this now is.

Mr Trump was elected from entirely outside the political party system, with a tiny staff and a tiny network of donors. Opposed by much of the media, he was able to reach his audience directly.

Why, people asked, don't they get the guy off Twitter? The answer was because it was helping him win. Franklin Roosevelt was the first radio president, using his fireside chats. Kennedy was the first television president. Obama, the first internet president, brilliantly using late-night comedy skits and entertainment.

Donald Trump may be the first social-media president, using Twitter with a brilliantly literate understanding of how it works, of its language and its impact.

It is common to observe that there is a decline in respect for traditional institutions – banks, the police, the courts. Much less commonly observed is that this decline is really just a function of a change in the power relationship. The centre has lost control to the edges, because the edges have the technological equipment to subject the centre to scrutiny.

So the arrow of history is pointing us to a new more fractured politics, much less deference, much more pressure for accountability and transparency. We will have many more sources of power and a much flatter politics.

*

Third, the arrow of history strongly suggests that the search for and development of new technologies will carry on.

The search for new technological ideas and developments has been a historical constant. Yet at each stage we are inclined to marvel at the changes that have arrived while entirely underestimating those that are just around the corner.

In 1995 one of my great modern heroes, Bill Gates, wrote a book called *The Road Ahead* about the future of information technology. In many ways the book was far sighted. But it missed one thing. He didn't regard the internet as of central importance.

After the hardback came out, he realised his error and rewrote the book for the paperback edition.

Since then we have seen not just the rise of the internet but also of the tablet computer and the convergence between television and computing.

Soon the satnav may make way for entirely driverless cars.

Yet believing these are significant may simply reflect a failure to appreciate what significant means.

By the very nature of things it is impossible to know what the next great wave of technological change is. But it is hard to believe that what we have now learned about genetics and neuroscience will not be at the heart of it, bringing with it huge opportunities and huge moral challenges.

The arrow of history suggests that we will use this knowledge to help us determine who we can trust and trade with. And this will pose big questions.

Just to give one tiny example: the more we know about genetics the more difficult it will be to insure people as the risks faced by one individual become easier to measure and therefore harder to persuade other people to share.

As we learn more about people's capacities we will also face a clearer choice, and a bigger dilemma, about how much we judge that individuals are to blame for their actions.

I provide these only as illustrations of the very profound

changes we can expect, and expect quite soon. Quite apart from the direction in which the arrow points, we must anticipate more, and more unsettling, change.

I want to add one final way in which the arrow of history suggests that the world will change, although doubtless there are many other ways which I will not mention.

As we trade with and trust more people and as the technology to do it reaches new places, we will see the rise of new powers, countries that are enriched by more-open trading and therefore emboldened diplomatically.

In many places in the world where there has been no middle class, a middle class will grow, and in places where the struggle to survive has been all that matters the politics of relative prosperity will take its place.

Western powers will develop new relations with countries that are now sources of imports, exports and investments.

We will also see a political battle take place over the nature of these rising powers. Will they tend towards commercial nationalism or Western-style liberalism?

I tend towards optimism over the medium term. It is hard to see how trading and a middle class and information technology will not together produce an insistence, as they have elsewhere, on democracy and the rule of law. But as with all such struggles it is impossible to be certain of the outcome.

Taken together, the arrow of history is pointing to a political battle over globalisation, democracy and liberty, all at a time in which politics is becoming more volatile and unpredictable and in which technology will pose moral and economic challenges that will be hard to answer.

We have entered a period of great change and political uncertainty in which the political and social arrangements that people have become used to are being overturned as people alternately embrace and resist change.

I don't think it is entirely wrong to feel some apprehension about this turbulence. My father was a survivor of exile in Siberia, my mother of Belsen. I always tell my children how lucky I feel that in my life I have experienced none of this. I have lived in peace and never too far from Brent Cross Shopping Centre.

When people start using 'metropolitan' as a term of abuse rather than a description of the train line to Pinner I think it's reasonable to be nervous. When the elite are held up for abuse, it is people who read books who are being attacked rather than people who live behind golden doors in great towers.

But along with a degree of nervousness there has to be determination to rise to the challenge.

Tony Blair argues that we are moving from the left–right divide to a new political divide. The divide between open and closed, between, one could say, the open society and its enemies.

I think this analysis is characteristically acute.

And open societies are more prosperous, freer, more stable, and more cohesive. They are better able to allow the talented to rise and protect the vulnerable.

The biggest questions now are how we ensure that the battle is won by those who believe in open societies.

There is no point in pitching into a political battle that is then lost, emotionally satisfying though the fight be. And there is no point thinking that because the arrow of history points in a certain direction, the battle cannot be lost.

It can be lost. And even if it is won in the end, it may be won only after I'm dead. Timing that I regard as sub-optimal.

So we have to consider how best to ensure that those who resist change because they find it threatening, or not in their interest, can be helped to feel differently.

We have to consider how much this has to be done by compromise, even though this risks conceding territory and accepting arguments on issues like immigration and trade that aren't quite right.

How much can be done by economic incentive, though this risks creating economies where very large numbers of people are dependent on state payments?

And how much can be done by being bolder and braver in debate, advancing the case for openness, free trade, migration, although this may be politically naive?

Sir Isaiah would certainly appreciate all these dilemmas but he would also insist that we have to make choices. And so we will.

1968 violence:
blame the bulge

Sorry, Tariq, it wasn't ideology that caused the
unrest (and other conflicts) but demographics

26 March 2008

When I was a small child I thought that the Vietnam War was
taking place in a car park.

Every time I watched the news, I heard reporters talking
sombrely of that conflict, accompanied by pictures of violent
encounters. Some of the soldiers wore uniforms and charged on
horses, others were clothed in denim. It wasn't clear who was
winning, but I remember the smoke and the chaos, and a young
man lying across a car bonnet being hit with a club. The young
man was carrying a poster on a stick, which even to my infant
mind seemed an odd thing to carry into a war zone.

Ever since I grew up enough to understand this error, I have
been amused by my childish naivety – confusing the Vietnam
War with the protests, indeed! But at the weekend, reading
Tariq Ali's account of the events of 1968 ('It turned violent.
Like the Vietnamese, we wanted to occupy the embassy'), I
realised that what I had displayed all those years ago was not
naivety at all. It was a precocious talent for political analysis.

The 1968 protests are not best understood as their instigators would have them understood – as the antithesis of war, as the street carnivals of the peace movement. The protesters should instead be seen as having some similarities with the warriors they were opposing. Both were trying to solve a problem with violence. The protesters sought to resolve political conflict in the street and through confrontation. Many of the leaders were not wishing for an end to war, but for victory by the North Vietnamese. In my confusion between the protests and the war I had accidentally seen things clearly.

Now I am not trying to make a point about who was right and who was wrong, who had the bigger weapons and who did the killing. Instead, I am trying to rescue the protests of 1968 from the romantic memories of the participants. I hope in this way to try to show why they are still relevant.

Every attempt to revisit 1968 majors in ideology. Tariq Ali talks of sexual revolution, the liberal author Paul Berman writes of the democratic ideal and the struggle against fascism, the French intellectual Bernard-Henri Lévy sees the common thread between the fight for liberation against Western oppression and the Prague Spring. Meanwhile, the playwright Tom Stoppard found little of any value. He thought the whole thing was merely embarrassing.

I am with Stoppard. This is not, however, just because I think the slogans of the *soixante-huitards* silly and their flirtation with communism disgusting. It is because I believe all attempts to explain 1968 in terms of ideas are doomed to failure. The events of 1968 were not about ideology, but demographics.

Consider this. Young Americans were the group most in favour of the Vietnam War, according to contemporary opinion polls. This remained the case even when the war became unpopular. Here's another fact – young people in this country are the group most in favour of the Iraq war. If you see the events of 1968 as ideological, this opinion-poll data is hard to understand.

Why aren't young people more idealistic and pacifistic than others? And if they aren't, why wasn't Grosvenor Square packed with rioting old-age pensioners?

However, if you see the *événements* as the product of demographics, the data is easy to comprehend. Young people, particularly young men, tend to see violent solutions to problems as more acceptable than do other groups in society. In 1968 there was a bulge in the number of hot-headed young males.

Some of them chose protest violence on the streets of Europe, others riots in America's ghettos or dissent in Eastern Europe, while still others supported foreign wars. They were united not by ideas but simply by youth. Tariq Ali appears bewildered that the anti-Iraq war movement hasn't evolved into something similar to the *soixante-huitards*. This isn't because idealism has died. It is because there is no youth bulge. And it is the youth bulge, not anything they said or did, that gives a reason for the 1968 riots to be remembered.

Violent conflict in seventeenth-century England, the French Revolution, German nationalism in the First World War, the 1979 Iranian revolution, the Cultural Revolution in China and most twentieth-century revolutions in developing countries took place where large youth bulges were present. And academic studies suggest that the number of deaths in armed conflict is much higher in countries with a large youth bulge, even when controlling for income and inequality. Between 1989 and 1993, violence in the former Soviet republics varied with the size of their young male population, even where the initial political conditions were similar.

The social scientist Gunnar Heinsohn in his book *Sons and World Power* argues that when 15- to 29-year-olds make up more than 30 per cent of the population, there is a good chance that violence will follow. There are 67 countries in the world where there is such a bulge and there is violence in 60 of them. He cites the Palestinian territories and Afghanistan as examples and contrasts them with, say, Tunisia or even the passing of the youth peak in Lebanon.

With our blithe conviction that we can always make things better, we are convinced that political education and economic amelioration will work to bring peace where there is conflict. Heinsohn suggests that it might make things worse. Educated and well-fed young males tend to greater violent unrest.

The only hope? That young men eventually grow up. In Northern Ireland, the vast majority of victims and perpetrators were young men. But one day Gerry Adams decided he was getting too old to strap on a gun. And the rest is history. Our only alternative in, say, fighting al-Qaeda may be to hold firm and wait it out.

The real lesson of the 1960s isn't Turn On, Tune In, Drop Out. It is Press On, Calm Down, Grow Up.

Understand Chelsea versus Sheffield, and you will see the Iraq game plan

A statistical view of history helps understanding

1 November 2006

Clear the area, then stand well back. I am about to deal with a very serious subject in a manner that will seem frivolous, self-serving and in defiance of common sense. My job will be to persuade you that I have been none of those things. Wish me luck.

I intend to explain my view of the Iraq war by drawing an analogy with Premiership football. Told you.

I strongly supported taking action in Iraq. I believed that the containment regime established after the Gulf War was breaking down. Experience suggested that every time Saddam began to think that international pressure on him was lessening, he would respond by becoming more aggressive. I feared that this aggression might at some point involve him using weapons of mass destruction again.

So, after 9/11, I concluded that leaving him in power was too great a risk and that, for various practical reasons, now was the best time to act. Others, of course, reached a different view about the balance of risk.

Many of these were to be found among the MPs calling for an inquiry into 'the way in which the responsibilities of government were discharged in relation to Iraq'.

Another of the critics was my colleague Matthew Parris. In these pages a few days ago he made a robust attack on those who supported the war. He declared that he did not believe that current difficulties had been caused by failures of military conduct or planning. 'The strategy failed', he said, 'because of one big, bad idea at its very root. Your [the neocons'] idea that we kick the door in. Everything has flowed from that.'

There are a number of ways of replying to such critics and you'll be familiar with most of them – the war isn't over, so we can't judge its full impact; there have been many good results of removing Saddam as well as bad ones; almost everyone believed there were weapons of mass destruction; the military planning was lamentable and Matthew's assertion that this is irrelevant is merely that – an assertion. And so on. But I am not going to use these arguments here.

Instead, I intend to make a much harder argument. I intend to make the case that you cannot judge the quality of a political decision by its outcome.

And this is where football comes into it. Last weekend Chelsea (Premier League champions) played Sheffield United (down at the bottom of the table). If I had offered you £5 if you could pick the winner, which side would you have chosen? Chelsea, right?

Now, seven out of ten times this would have been correct and you would have won the fiver. A couple of games might have ended in a draw. But once every so often, Sheffield United will pull off a victory. The pundits will pore over the game trying to work out how it happened, but no one will be completely certain. And you? You might feel mildly foolish.

Yet did Sheffield United's victory mean that your bet was the wrong one? Of course not. To have predicted a Sheffield victory would have been silly, since most of the time it would have been wrong.

Naturally, the critics will have suggested that you were too quick to assume Chelsea's superiority in this particular game. You should have been more careful, looking at Chelsea's injury list or Sheffield's morale this month, or whatever. But this would have risked allowing your choice to be influenced by things that are entirely irrelevant. Experience strongly suggests that a cooler, more consistent view is better in the long run. That's how professional gamblers can win over time. You were right to back Chelsea even though they lost.

You cannot, in other words, judge the quality of a decision by its outcome.

This football stuff, of course, is only an analogy. Questions of war and peace are deadly serious and there is more at stake than a fiver and mild foolishness. The principle, however, holds.

The outcome of any political decision is uncertain. You use your best estimate of the probabilities of different results and make a choice. Even if you have calculated the probabilities correctly and made a sensible choice, the outcome might still be a poor one. Only an analysis of the results of repeated decisions can provide a proper insight into whether your choice was a good one.

This may seem obvious but, in fact, we rarely look at decisions in this way. Let me use Vietnam as an example. Forests have been cut down printing books about why the decision to prosecute the Vietnam War was wrong. But what if it wasn't? No one can doubt that the war was a disastrous episode, that it ended badly. But you can't judge the decision by this one outcome alone.

What if, instead of viewing the Vietnam War as a single episode, you view the decision as one of a long series? America decided to confront Soviet influence aggressively wherever it reared its head. Mostly this strategy was successful but, naturally, sometimes individual decisions produced a calamitous outcome. Luck plays a role as well as error. The Cuban missile crisis is viewed as a great triumph. It is separated by the thinnest margin from being the worst event in the history of mankind.

Apply this to the Iraq war. The critics believe that Mr Blair should have defied the request from our closest ally and chosen to stand aside and do nothing about Saddam.

They reach this point with two sleights of hand that make the decision to go to war seem impossibly stupid. The first is to criticise the known outcome of the course taken without reference to the unknown outcome of the course not taken. Not prosecuting the war would have meant leaving Saddam in power, followed in due course by his mad, murderous sons. If you ignore the possible result of allowing this, then, of course, the war becomes difficult to explain.

The second thing the critics do is to consider the Iraq war as an isolated decision, rather than one in a long series. It can't be looked at like that.

Even if you consider the history of policy towards Saddam alone, the decision to remove him is simply one among many. But the Iraq invasion also has to be seen as one decision among many in the War on Terror, in the recent history of liberal interventionism and in the long course of the special relationship.

On the whole, I believe that robust partnership with the United States, and a strong military approach to dangerous, aggressive dictators with nuclear ambitions, is a better foreign policy than the alternatives. And on the whole, I think that believing intelligence reports about weapons of mass destruction is a more sensible thing to do than ignoring them.

That's why I supported the war in Iraq. And why I still believe that decision was the right one.

Mr Blair's final magic trick will begin shortly

How politicians are remembered by history

There were many reports in the press of Tony Blair, in his final months in office, working on his legacy. The theory I advanced here has, I think, been borne out by events.

7 February 2007

The next five years will be the most important of Tony Blair's premiership. I wish I could tell you that this insight came to me while watching *Newsnight*, or reading the *Economist* or something. But I am afraid it occurred to me while watching the magician Derren Brown perform a trick with a briefcase.

For some time now I've found it useful to think of successful politicians as people who tell tales. Yes, yes, I know you do too, but I don't mean it in that way. I mean that the best way for a politician to describe what they stand for is for them to relate their ideas in the form of a story.

Bill Clinton and his advisers, for instance, brilliantly wove together his return from political defeat and recovery from scandals into a story in which he was the repentant but triumphant hero, the Comeback Kid. Margaret Thatcher is thought of as an ideologue, but was really a narrative genius. Hers was the tale of a doughty underdog who rises from suburbia to smite the pessimistic establishment and save a once great but now declining nation.

One of my criticisms of Gordon Brown is that he lacks a real story, that his speeches are full of statistics and abstract ideas rather than narrative accounts of his own task and the nation's future. He genuinely believes, bless him, that he can draw a picture of what he stands for and win over voters by revealing a surprise plan for a written constitution or whatever.

There is, however, a problem with seeing politicians as people who tell stories. A narrative has a beginning, a middle and an end. A political life just keeps going. Take Disraeli, for instance. The commonly accepted idea that Disraeli was the ultimate one-nation Conservative, a Tory populist, is at odds with much of the story of his career. It is a myth that grew up after his death and proved incredibly powerful. Whatever Disraeli did, whatever he was, it is as a one-nation Tory that he is remembered. And the Disraeli myth remains an important part of Tory debate.

Which is where Derren Brown comes in. Have you ever watched him? I hope you have. He is simply fabulous. And he's produced a book, *Tricks of the Mind*, which is as good as he is. This book explains how magic tricks work. Not how each one is done, you understand, he couldn't do that or he'd be crossed off Ali Bongo's Christmas card list. No, what he does is to set out the way tricks achieve their effect, the way they leave you feeling a sense of awe and bewilderment.

And the parallels with politics struck me immediately. Brown's central point is that 'magic isn't about fakes and switches and dropping coins in your lap. It's about entering into a relationship with a person whereby you can lead him, economically and deftly, to experience an event as magical.'

Magic, he says, 'exists only in the head of the spectator; and though your skills may have led him there, it is not the same as those skills'. He also provides an interesting account of what goes on in the head of the spectator. The more obvious it is to them that they must have been fooled, the more inclined they are to emphasise the wizardry of the magician. As they tell tales to their friends they exaggerate what they have seen, overrule any objections, try their hardest to infect others with their enthusiasm. It's a process you can see in politics any day of the week.

Now, the difference between magic tricks and stories is that stories end, but magic tricks don't. As Brown puts it: 'It is an interesting maxim in conjuring that much of the magic happens after the trick is over.' Brown builds up the tension as his trick reaches a climax, and then, as the audience is relaxing and its concentration wanes, he carries out the final part of his trick and works hard on how the audience will remember the experience.

Seen as a story, the Blair years are over. Seen as a magic trick, the most important moment for the Prime Minister is at hand. It is now, as the tension goes, as our concentration wanes, that he can begin to shape how we remember the whole experience.

This may not be welcome news for Mr Blair or his wife. They probably think it is time to relax, go and make some money and pay off all those mortgages. But his premiership isn't finished. It'll never be finished. What he does now, what he says now, will be critical. If he chooses to quit public life altogether, and allows himself to be seen as simply a moneymaking, holiday-taking machine, it'll not just be the retired Blair that will be damaged, it'll be the reputation of his entire period in government.

Yet even if he is inclined to take this advice, and keep trying to shape our view of the sort of prime minister he has been, one problem still stands in his way. I'm not sure that, even now, Tony Blair has worked out for himself what sort of prime minister he has been.

Three quite different, incompatible accounts pop up in his speeches and interviews. There is Blair the Labour leader, the loyal servant of his party, the man who finished his conference speech with the extraordinary promise to his party that 'whatever you do, I'm always with you. Head and heart.'

Then there is Blair the creator of New Labour and the third way, the man who believes in big-tent politics, who thinks that with goodwill everyone can agree, who believes that the contradictions between, say, equality and efficiency can be swept aside.

And finally there is the battle-hardened Blair, tempered by Iraq and disappointment. This Blair told the *Today* programme that he thought he had been too eager to please in his early days and that sometimes it seemed as if you can't please any of the people any of the time. This Blair seeks something bolder than New Labour and stands apart from the party he's led. It's hard to see this Blair being with Labour 'whatever you do'.

Tony Blair is not the only one who will shape our memory of his period in office, of course. He'll be called a fraud and a war criminal and all sorts. He'll have a tough fight arguing that it wasn't all just a colossal waste of promise.

But if he doesn't know who he is, what are the rest of us supposed to make of him?

There have been times in his political life when it seemed as if no one could pull off a magic trick like Tony Blair. The question of whether he is a true political wizard or just a kid with a conjuring set is about to be answered.

Would you pass or fail the Kinnock Test?

The British voter never gets it wrong. At every election in the past 80 years the right party has won. Discuss

14 August 2008

I can't remember if I've told you about the Kinnock Test. I don't think I have. But it's my party piece. Perhaps that's why I don't get invited to very many parties.

The Kinnock Test is this – do you, on reflection, think it would have been a good idea for the country if Neil Kinnock had been elected prime minister in 1992? Naturally I don't bother asking Tories this question, since, on the whole, their answers wouldn't be interesting. But I find the responses I get from Labour people endlessly fascinating. Particularly the replies I get from Blairites.

You see, for all that the Conservatives fell apart in the 1992 Parliament, I still think it was clear that a Kinnock government would have been worse. No one needs to tell me how bad things got by 1997, because I was there (I always insist on the retention of that comma). But still I assert with confidence that the voters did the right thing putting the Conservatives back in power.

Neil Kinnock was entirely unsuited to being prime minister. His endless whirling speeches showed that. As John Major pricelessly commented, as Kinnock didn't know what he was saying, he never knew when he had finished saying it. And alongside this unsuitability was Labour's programme, still only partly modernised and containing a ragtag of unfunded spending promises and threats of greater regulation.

Some Blairites understand this. They would, as I would cheekily put it, pass the Kinnock Test. Party unity might make public confession difficult but I reckon Alan Milburn and Stephen Byers would both pass the Kinnock Test. I would think Blair's old pollster Philip Gould would pass it too, for all that he worked incredibly hard to get Kinnock elected. And Blair himself? That's a no-brainer.

On the other hand I am sure that Charles Clarke thinks Kinnock as premier would have been a capital idea. And Blair advisers Alastair Campbell and Peter Hyman would fail the test too. James Purnell? Pass. David Miliband? Fail.

The Kinnock Test is thus an important way of classifying Blairites. A Blairite who thinks Kinnock would have been a good prime minister must believe that Blair's changes were mainly necessary in order to get elected. A Blairite who passes the Kinnock Test accepts that Blair's changes were required in order for Labour to be fit to govern. There is quite a big difference between those two positions.

As I pestered my centre-left friends, one of them provided a striking response. Not only, he said, did the electorate get it right in 1992, he couldn't think of a single election since universal suffrage in 1928 where the voters had got the election wrong. And you know what? I think my friend has got a point.

The proposition is that in every contest in these last eighty years the party that was more fit to govern has been victorious. Sometimes both of the main offerings were weak and unappealing, often the winner wasn't much good, but always the winner was better able to conduct the business of government than was the loser.

There are a number of elections for which this proposition is, if hardly uncontroversial, still clearly correct. I thinks this holds for 1931 (where the National Government swept home, Labour having collapsed in disarray), 1935 (another National victory); 1945 (Labour's landslide); 1955 and 1959 (Tories defeating a divided and incoherent Labour opposition); 1964 and 1966 (Wilson's triumphs over the tired and outdated Tories); and for 1979, 1983, 1987 and 1992 (the market revolution having to be drummed into Labour's head until they at least partly got the point).

My contribution is to admit that even though I voted Conservative in 1997, 2001 and 2005 and wanted to see the party advance, it wasn't ready to govern.

This leaves a few contests to argue over. In 1929 Stanley Baldwin probably deserved to lose, having run on the slogan 'Safety First' – an unbelievably complacent thing to do with unemployment running at 10 per cent. And Labour probably deserved its first proper chance to govern, even though it made a mess of it fairly rapidly. But the question of who was the better isn't clear cut. Then again, neither was the election result – the Tories had more votes, Labour more seats and no one had a majority. Right, in the circumstances.

Some might wonder about Labour being overhauled by the Conservatives over the two elections of 1950 and 1951. Yet this is because, since its passing, the Attlee Government has been canonised. At the time it was exhausted (in some cases literally dying), weak, out of ideas and incapable of responding to the aspirations of consumers. It needed to be replaced – right again.

When I have tried this out with colleagues, it is the elections of 1970 and 1974 that lead to the most debate. Those on the left give 1970 as the big error by voters, while those on the right think that in 1974 voters gave the wrong answer to Heath's question: 'Who governs Britain?' In effect, the electorate answered: 'The unions.'

What made it hard for voters to get it right in those elections, of course, was that no right answer was available (and don't say the Liberals, who were led by a man about to be charged with conspiracy to murder). Both Heath and Wilson were on the wrong track entirely. But I think it was, on balance, the best of a bad job to put Heath in and then to boot him out. In 1974 Wilson's crew weren't fit to govern but Heath's management of the economy had been so spectacularly, bewilderingly bad that turning to almost any alternative might be excused.

Do the victors just feel like the right answer because they won? Probably, a little bit. But I think that there is more to it than that. I think the history of the past eighty years shows that for all its terrible flaws, there is still something rather wondrous about British democracy.

Berlusconi's antics are everybody's business

The private lives of leaders reveal their character.
And character may be the most essential element
of leadership

22 July 2009

I am going to write about Silvio Berlusconi and his so-called private life. But before I do, I want to ask you a question. Could you write a serious biography of Mao Zedong and miss out the girls and the drugs? If you did, it would be a little-read book.

Mao liked the girls. Even in his mid-seventies, this four-times-married man regularly invited three, four or even five women at a time into his oversized bed. The word 'invited' overstates the extent of the willing cooperation of the other participants.

Actually, Mao liked the boys, too, requiring that handsome young male attendants came to his chamber to give him nightly groin massages. He was pretty keen on the drugs too. He suffered from sleeplessness and, while trying to resolve it, became addicted to sleeping pills. In the 1930s there was Veronal, then sodium amytal and, finally, chloral hydrate, which induced euphoria in him.

There was something else he was pretty keen on. Brutal, sadistic murder. He liked to participate if he could, particularly enjoying slow public executions. The use of *siu-biao*, a twin-edged knife with a long handle, was a particular favourite. If he couldn't take part, he would enjoy hearing accounts of torture. Seventy million people died unnecessarily as a result of Mao's policies.

In her book *Evil Genes*, a tremendous volume on the psychology of dictators and other manipulative individuals, Barbara Oakley draws on accounts of Mao's vices to pen a sharp portrait of him. She concludes that he was 'a perfect borderpath'. In other words, his symptoms – his addictions, his selfishness, his dysfunctional personal relationships, his sadism – suggest that he suffered from a recognisable condition, borderline personality disorder.

Tony Benn (who, by the way, described Mao in his diary as the greatest man of the twentieth century) used to have a phrase that he repeated in almost every interview in the early 1980s. Do you remember it? 'What matters is not the personalities, it is the issues.' And it is certainly possible to attempt to explain Mao and his terrible crimes entirely with reference to ideology and the failings of communism.

But Oakley's account, which emphasises Mao's personal failings, is far more convincing, isn't it? Especially when one reads in most of his biographies that he didn't much believe in communism at all. It merely helped him on his way.

Mao's is an extreme case, but it is an instructive one. It is impossible to describe the actions of political leaders merely by looking at their public life and professed ideas. It is necessary to understand their private lives and character. Every historian realises this, which is why all serious biographers do their best to get under the skin of their subjects and to tell the story of their life off-stage.

All of which is my way of answering Italy's big political

question of the moment – does Silvio Berlusconi's relationship with escort girls and younger women behind his wife's back really matter? – with the resounding response: 'Yes, of course it matters.'

It is not necessary to resolve every disputed Italian allegation to conclude that Mr Berlusconi has not been behaving with great propriety. Nor can one view the promotion to senior positions by his party of attractive women with little political experience with anything other than a raised eyebrow – or even two raised eyebrows. But worse than all of this is Mr Berlusconi's assertion that none of this is anybody's business besides his, and his consequent refusal to answer any questions about it.

The private life of a statesman is not, and cannot be, entirely private. It provides an insight into his character. And character is an essential part of leadership. Indeed it is probably the most important part of it.

Take Bill Clinton. His numerous extramarital affairs might be considered nobody's business but his and Hillary's. Indeed, the couple made that explicit argument during the New Hampshire primaries while denying that Bill had had a relationship with Gennifer Flowers.

Except that we now know two things. First, that the denial was a lie and that he did have a relationship with her. So the future president was a fluent liar. And, second, that his sexual relationships were the mark of a man who, whatever his other great qualities, was neither trustworthy nor self-disciplined.

Every voter can make his or her own mind up about whether these characteristics disqualified him from the presidency. All I am saying is that it would have been nice to know about them.

Now, anyone advancing the idea that people's private lives and what they reveal about their character should remain private, always receives in response three initials: JFK. We now know – journalists knew at the time but didn't report it – that John F. Kennedy was an inveterate womaniser. And yet his reputation is as a great president. His womanising and party lifestyle? Irrelevant tittle-tattle.

Except that it wasn't. One biography after another has revealed how Kennedy's inappropriate behaviour was a security risk. His relationship with a gangster's moll corrupted his election effort. And David Owen makes a compelling case, in his book *In Sickness and in Power*, that JFK's out-of-control drug use influenced his conduct in arms negotiations.

Silvio Berlusconi is an ally in receipt of state secrets. He is the dominant Italian politician of the era. So of course his character matters. And of course the answers to persistent questions about his conduct can help us to understand his character.

You cannot behave as Mr Berlusconi has behaved and argue that it is a private matter. The parties, the girls, the gifts – they are issues of state.

The political class is losing, not gaining, power

The idea that politicians were once pure, and
lived in the real world, but are now cut off from
it is a poor account of history

9 April 2014

Roy Jenkins only slept one night in 10 Downing Street in his life. It was on the evening in 1946 that his father died, in St Thomas' Hospital, just across the river from the House of Commons. Arthur Jenkins, the MP for Pontypool, had been Attlee's close aide. On the night of Arthur's passing, Attlee's wife, Violet, came down to the hospital and took Roy home with her.

It was while I was reading this story, in the new biography of Jenkins by John Campbell, that I caught Nigel Farage on the television, during his debate with Nick Clegg, talking about the 'political class'. Which he is not very fond of. And the conjunction of television and book set me to wondering. Is this theory about the rise of the political class, which we hear so much about, any good either as history or as political analysis?

Perhaps I had better summarise the theory before I go on. The idea is that at the beginning of parliamentary democracy, in the Georgian era, politics was deeply corrupt and incestuous. Then came the Victorians.

During the long reign of the Queen, a higher moral tone was achieved as well as a clean politics that lasted long after her death and into the modern era. Then, in the middle of the 1980s, things began to go wrong. Politics became incestuous again. A class has been rising that ignores the political and moral proprieties of its predecessors.

The rising political class is driving out from public life those with experience of anything other than politics. It is, unlike in times past, deeply entangled with the media. It is personally and financially corrupt in a way that would not have been tolerated in the past. And it is a tight social grouping rather than being drawn from all backgrounds.

Well, the problem is this. The more one considers this notion, the worse an account of history it appears. And as a result it is in danger of advancing an idea about modern politics that is precisely wrong. For what we are seeing is not the rise of a political class that has not existed until recently but the fall of a political class that has always existed.

Let us, only as an example, start with Roy Jenkins, whose entire career (by the way a very great, and in many important ways admirable, one) was lived before the so-called rise of today's political class.

Almost everything that we are invited to regard as a special feature of our current politics can be found in the life of Jenkins.

He was born into politics and from a very young age was determined to pursue a political career. He entered Parliament in his twenties (he was 25 when he first ran) as the protégé of the party leader, a status he gained through family connection. Attlee was the principal speaker at Roy's wedding, commissioned the young man to edit a volume of his speeches and acted as his sponsor when he entered the Commons.

He became a Labour MP without experience of business life

and having had a short period in the Army from which, by his account, he learnt little of life. He wasn't a political adviser but that's because few such jobs existed then. He did apply to be international director of the Labour Party, but the job went to the young Denis Healey.

I know that Roy did not regard experience of life as necessary to being an MP, not just from the account in his biography, but from my own conversations with him. When I was 23 and regarded myself as too young to be a parliamentary candidate, he set about persuading me that I was wrong.

Has politics become, in the past two decades, a class in which personal connections have taken the place of ideological differences which dominated in former times?

Among the very best friends of Roy and Jennifer Jenkins were the Conservative MP Sir Ian Gilmour and the Liberal MP Mark Bonham Carter. Roy was sleeping, at the same time, with the wives of both of these friends, and all six of them, the Jenkinses, the Gilmours and the Bonham Carters, knew about it.

Striking though this may be, none of this cross-party behaviour was that unusual. Roy's close ally, the Labour leader Hugh Gaitskell, was having an affair at the same time with the right-wing socialite wife of Ian Fleming.

This is just the life of one man. There are any number of stories that join it in contradicting the idea that the political class has risen in the past two decades.

MPs now join the House without experience, unlike in the old days? Gladstone was 22 when he became an MP, so was Palmerston. Russell was 21 and so was Peel. William Pitt famously became prime minister at the age of 24.

Media proprietors nowadays entangled with political life? In the events that resulted in David Lloyd George becoming prime minister, Max Aitken, the owner of the *Daily Express*, was so entangled that the memorandums from one member of the Cabinet to another are in his handwriting.

Lord Northcliffe, the owner of *The Times*, was offered a seat in the Cabinet by Lloyd George. Northcliffe's brother, Lord Rothermere, the owner of the *Daily Mail*, became a viscount as part of a deal struck by Andrew Bonar Law to remove Rothermere from office when he courted controversy as president of the Air Council.

Corruption a modern invention? Has anyone tried reading the biography of Reggie Maudling, with its eyebrow-raising tales of the former Chancellor's business dealings?

These politicians all lived their lives before the social revolution that led people to be more questioning of authority and before the technological revolution that has spread power and influence to every owner of a smartphone. They were protected by a degree of deference that has now gone.

A proper reading of history increases rather than reduces concern about a political class, yet it refutes entirely the idea that such a class is rising. Instead it is falling. The life of Roy Jenkins, with all its glory and all its secrets, couldn't be lived now. There has never been a time when the behaviour of politicians is exposed in the way it is now, is questioned in the way it is now, is challenged in the way it is now. We live in a more open and more democratic age where privilege is still possible, but privilege without question is not.

Labour leadership hopefuls stuck in the past

Andy Burnham and Yvette Cooper want an
inquiry into the miners' strike, which shows that
the Left has still some learning to do

17 June 2015

On 30 November 1984 David Wilkie was driving his taxi cab
to Merthyr Vale on his normal route. He was 35 years old and
had three young children, two of them under the age of six.
His fiancée was pregnant with a baby that was due within a
few weeks.

As he turned on to the A465 at the Rhymney Bridge round-
about, two men dropped a 46lb concrete block on to his cab
from the bridge 27ft above. Wilkie was killed instantly.

The assailants were striking miners aiming to prevent the
driver from taking his passenger, a pit man who was working
during the dispute, to his colliery. And when the National
Union of Mineworkers' official for South Wales heard what had
happened, here's what he did.

He made his way quickly to the union office and began to
shred documents. When he was told that his fellow union
members had killed the young father, he said: 'My knees began

to shake. Because I thought, hang on, we've got all these records we've kept at the NUM offices, there's all those maps on the wall. We are going to get implicated in this. I remember thinking I've to get to that office. I've got to destroy everything. And I did.'

Five years later Kim Howells entered Parliament as a Labour MP. He served as a government minister for more than a decade.

Last week the Independent Police Complaints Commission announced that it would not investigate alleged misconduct by police thirty years ago during the so-called Battle of Orgreave. Officers had clashed with striking miners who were trying to prevent lorries leaving the Orgreave coking plant.

Its decision did not end the matter. Of course it didn't. There were immediate calls for a 'Hillsborough-style' inquiry to find out what happened. Yvette Cooper, the shadow home secretary and a Labour leadership candidate, called for one. And her leadership rival Andy Burnham has written to the Prime Minister telling him that there is no time limit on justice.

Well all right, let's investigate Orgreave. Let's have an inquiry. But not just into Orgreave and certainly not just into the police.

There is no question that there were many things badly wrong about the policing at Orgreave that day and in the days leading up to it. There was excessive violence, breaches of rules and perhaps, later, perjury too. So let's inquire into that if people feel it would serve a purpose.

Yet while we're at it, let's have an inquiry into the way thousands of people were trying to stop lorry drivers going about their business in a free country. And about the barrage of bottles, stones and broken fencing thrown at the drivers.

Let's inquire into the intimidation of working miners in their homes and as they made their way to their jobs, choosing to work rather than obey a strike called without a ballot.

Let's inquire into the death of David Wilkie and try to find out what was in all those maps and papers Kim Howells felt he urgently needed to dispose of. Let's find out what the hundreds of miners in Merthyr Vale were thinking when they decided that the appropriate reaction to the guilty verdict on the men who orphaned Wilkie's young children was to walk out in support of the killers rather than the dead man.

Let's have an inquiry into the way that Arthur Scargill brought the dispute about and the role of his union and its supporters in the encouragement of what became major incidents of public disorder. Let's look at the role of left-wing fringe organisations and outsiders in mobilising menacing groups designed to frighten others into complying with their political demands.

And maybe we could call someone from the KGB and the former Soviet government before the inquiry. We could try to find out more about how they funnelled money to the NUM.

We could call Colonel Gaddafi too if he wasn't dead. It would certainly be illuminating to learn more about the visit to Tripoli made by the NUM chief executive. Roger Windsor went to visit the dictator in his tent within a few months of the Libyan murder of WPC Yvonne Fletcher to arrange the receipt of £1 million for the strike fund.

Let's delve into the reasons for the strike and inquire into whether it was really possible to accede to a demand with menaces. We can investigate whether it ever made sense to argue, as the strikers did, that you should mine coal whatever the economics. We can discuss whether it could possibly have been sustainable to try to maintain pit jobs indefinitely.

Let's have an inquiry into the sort of jobs they were fighting to retain – horrible, dangerous work. And we can ask the *Guardian* about its campaign to stop investment in fossil fuels for environmental reasons. Maybe they now think Mrs Thatcher was right.

And let's have an inquiry into the power of the miners' union. Let's look at the way it brought governments down and stopped the country working. And let's ask what might have happened to the Labour Party and to the country if Arthur Scargill had won the war he waged.

The inquiry being demanded into Orgreave isn't a real one. It isn't an attempt to establish the truth, the whole truth and nothing but the truth. It's a partial one, a one-sided propaganda inquiry, attempting to win a political battle that was lost thirty years ago and deserved to be lost.

It joins the many other attempts to insist that the strike was just Billy Elliot with the singing miners and their hearts of gold. The rewriting of the history of the strike through art has been extraordinary.

Yes, the miners were brave but they were also foolish. Yes, their cause had dignity but it was also often thuggish. Yes, anyone deserves sympathy when their way of life is threatened but no, nobody has the right to insist on their way of life regardless of the costs or the consequences.

Nobody has the right to mass in their thousands throwing bricks and trying to bring down a freely elected government. And we are lucky that it was stopped.

In calling for their Orgreave inquiry Yvette Cooper and Andy Burnham demonstrate that while saying they have learnt the lessons of 2015, they are still struggling with ones from 1984.

Rees-Mogg's Brexit history lesson is bunkum

Far from making the same mistake as Sir Robert
Peel in the nineteenth century, Theresa May
should follow his example

This article appeared as the battle lines within the
Conservative Party were drawn over the nature of any EU
withdrawal deal. Theresa May had not finalised such a
deal yet, let alone brought it to Parliament. Jacob Rees-
Mogg warned her against being another Robert Peel. In
the week following this article May tried, at Chequers, to
reach accord on the Government's position. David Davis
and Boris Johnson then resigned.

3 July 2018

On 1 November 1845, Sir Robert Peel gathered his Cabinet for
an emergency meeting. The atmosphere was sour and ministers
were divided. The Prime Minister, alarmed by the disaster of the
Irish potato blight, believed the Government needed to suspend
the Corn Laws, which kept the price of grain (and thus of bread)
high. A number of his colleagues were unpersuaded.

And, as it turned out, unpersuadable. Senior ministers, led

by Lord Stanley, believed that the Conservative Party had to remain the party of protection, defending the livelihood of landowners and farmers. Peel, however, was convinced that suspension was the only way to help starving people.

In the end, in 1846, he succeeded in repealing the Corn Laws with the votes of the Opposition, but success brought down his government. And it split the Conservative Party. It took decades to recover.

This is the example that Jacob Rees-Mogg likes to use when warning Theresa May that she should adhere to his Brexit purism, as he did in a newspaper article this week. The fate of Peel awaits her and her party should she make a break for it.

It's rather an interesting historical parallel, actually. Worth dwelling on.

The first point is that Peel was, of course, right. The policy of protectionism was a disaster and its abandonment was essential. Even Mr Rees-Mogg acknowledges this when he adds, after delivering his history lesson about party splitting, 'at least he [Peel] did so for a policy that worked'.

This acknowledgement produces an interesting tension. He is arguing that Peel should not have threatened party unity even though he did it to save lives and rescue the economy, and even though Mr Rees-Mogg believes he succeeded in these objectives.

As a piece of advice to Mrs May, this is disgraceful. It suggests that she should not hazard party unity even if the alternative would damage the country. Peel was vindicated by history. I think if the Conservative Party now chooses to maintain its unity at the expense of the country's welfare, history's verdict will be damning.

It is troubling that a few months before Brexit happens, the Government cannot agree its own policy on customs and is being urged to carry on pretending it can implement plans which are not negotiable or practical even if they could be negotiated. To decide that the most urgent priority in solving this puzzle is keeping Mr Rees-Mogg on side and preserving Tory unity would be shameful.

There are other ways that the Peel parallel can help us. When he fell from office, he was outnumbered in the parliamentary Conservative Party. When, in May 1846, the Commons backed his Corn Law bill, only 112 Conservative MPs supported Peel, while 222 voted against him.

This is not the situation now. If Mrs May takes a pragmatic position – insisting, for example, on a longer transition period for regulation and customs – she would probably command a majority in the party. Because most of the parliamentary party are pragmatists and moderates.

The threat that Mrs May would be deposed if she defies the hard-Brexit European Reform Group, which Mr Rees-Mogg chairs, is an empty one. If the ERG pushed for a vote of confidence in her, she is more likely to win than lose. Indeed her real danger in those circumstances would be ignoring the example of Peel, failing to take a clear stance, and being removed by both sides of the Brexit row because of a feeling that the party was headless.

There's one more part of the Peel parallel that is instructive. When Mr Rees-Mogg talks of the period out of office following the repeal of the Corn Laws he puts it thus: 'This left the Conservatives out of majority office for twenty-eight years.' The reason for this slightly odd phrasing is that, in fact, the Conservatives enjoyed three spells in office during that period, totalling almost four years, but each time in a minority government.

Less than five years after the fall of Peel, Lord Stanley (by then the Earl of Derby) was invited to form a government. But he realised he couldn't form a protectionist government because there weren't enough talented people willing to serve if it meant new tariffs.

A year later Derby did take office, but only because he accepted there was no future in opposing free trade. His ally, Benjamin Disraeli, was even more emphatic, telling friends that protectionism was as dead as Lazarus, and 'already stinketh'.

So within little more than the lifetime of one modern parliament, the rebels abandoned the position for which they had brought down their prime minister. The burden of Mr Rees-Mogg's story is that it was Peel who split the party. Properly understood, it is Derby and Disraeli who did so, and in pursuit of a foolish dogma that reality eventually forced them to abandon.

In other words, if Mr Rees-Mogg is issuing a warning about the political consequences of a repeat of the Tories' split over the Corn Laws, then he should be issuing the warning to himself and heeding it.

Peel wasn't just right about the Corn Laws, he was also right about the direction of the country. He saw that the future belonged to a rising entrepreneurial middle class and to a growing urban working class. The Conservative Party would not succeed if it only represented the landed gentry and the countryside.

If the Conservative Party now ignores the entreaties of business leaders and risks breaking supply chains, losing jobs, seeing lorries queuing for hours at customs points, and discouraging inward investment, it will be turning its back on the future of the country, on young people, on new urban centres, and on the entrepreneurial middle class.

Peel was right, both morally and politically, to risk party unity over the Corn Laws. Of course he might have done it more sensitively. He might have kept Disraeli on side if he had handled his ambition with greater understanding, and he might not have lost Derby if he had been a little less presidential. Mrs May could hardly be accused of Peel's impatience.

But ultimately Peel had to choose between doing the right thing and keeping everyone on side. This week Mrs May could be faced with the same choice. If it comes to it, she must do as Peel did.

PART FOUR

People

While my Arrow of History lecture argues there are patterns in history, I'm very far from believing that individuals don't matter. A big theme of my columns has always been assessing and analysing people in public life – not just politics, but music, creative arts and the academy.

This section brings some of those columns together.

Walt Disney . . . Defend Disney from his Mickey Mouse critics

As the cartoon rodent reaches 80, we should celebrate his creator – a genius and one of the best arguments for capitalism

19 November 2008

In the summer of 1928 Walter Elias Disney hung a bedroom sheet from his office wall and asked some members of his family in to watch a film. Disney was only 26 years old, but he'd lived quite a tough life. And he was down on his luck. He had been cheated in a business deal, he had no money and he couldn't find anyone to distribute his films.

That June night, however, Walt was exultant. He had his brother Roy man the projector and his small team of animators produce sound synchronised to the action. They had to improvise – banging pencils against a spitoon that served as a gong, for instance. But however amateur the improvisation, the result shone through.

Steamboat Willie would be a hit. It would make Walt Disney. It would save the Walt Disney Company. It would change the world.

Yesterday was the eightieth anniversary of the first public showing of *Steamboat Willie*, the first commercial cartoon with sound, and of the first appearance of Mickey Mouse in American cinema. And I want to defend Walt Disney. I want to proclaim that Walt Disney was one of the great men of our era. That Walt Disney helped to make our world a better place. That Walt Disney was a genius.

It seems a bit odd arguing that Disney needs defending. After all, the man made a mint in his lifetime, and his company is still coining it.

But the reputation of Disney the man hasn't done as well as the accounts of Disney the company. These days the Mickey Mouse critics, who began their assault in the final decade of his life, are winning the battle to define Disney in the public mind. Wasn't he a hard-faced mercenary? Don't they say that he was an anti-Semite? And what of his life's work? Didn't he infantalise America, concrete over its culture, homogenise and pasteurise its art? Wasn't he the prince of the phoney, the king of the cute, the master of the comforting myth? Even Disney's famous signature, said one of his assailants, was a fabrication.

This assault on Disney's reputation is worth taking trouble to rebut. Not just because he deserves his rightful place in history, but also because when Walt is being criticised it is more than Walt that the critics are taking on. The attack on Walt doubles as an attack on the values of main street America, an attack on commercialism, an attack on mass culture and on wholesomeness. All these things and Walt Disney, they go down together if we let 'em.

When Disney had the idea of making the first sound cartoon, he did something very typical. He started badgering Roy to find money for it, to seek out a bank loan. Wearily, Roy complied. That was the pattern of their relationship. Walt would have a wild, innovative, absurdly expensive idea, and Roy would somehow persuade someone to pay for it.

Disney may now be the poster boy of commerce, but in his life he didn't care much for money – save that its absence might prevent him from doing what he wanted to do. His aim was not, as a fabulous recent biography by Neal Gabler makes clear ('he hated money and its acquisition, was wary of materialism'), to be rich. It was to be free. He wanted to live his dreams through his creations, and he drove Roy crazy seeking the resources to make his dreams come true.

The result of this relentless pressure was a stream of innovations. So much of the entertainment we take for granted was invented by Disney. Walt Disney invented the sound cartoon, with *Steamboat Willie*. Walt Disney invented the feature-length cartoon film with *Snow White and the Seven Dwarves*. Walt Disney invented the main techniques of commercial animation. Walt Disney invented entertainment merchandising with his spectacularly successful promotion of Mickey Mouse. Walt Disney invented family television entertainment, capturing more than 50 per cent of the audience for his pioneering *Disney Time* show at a time when there was almost nothing else on. Walt Disney invented the nature documentary. He invented the theme park with Disneyland in California.

Even as he was dying of cancer, Walt pressed on. He wasn't much interested in Disney World in Florida, which opened after he died. Disney World's only appeal to him was to allow a city of tomorrow to be built on the adjacent lot. He wanted an experimental land, a Utopian city, the ultimate symbol of his determination to create his own world. He envisaged houses that were completely self-sufficient, with their own power plants and no need for rubbish collection. This was 1965.

When Disney died the following year, his vision of a city of tomorrow died with him. This is the answer to those who criticise him as a control freak, an obsessive. His determination and drive were good, they served his creativity. Without them, his vision could not be realised.

His drive could make Disney a difficult man. He could be moody and he didn't let arguments go easily. He insisted on being in control. But it is wrong to characterise the 'Uncle Walt' image that the company created for him as entirely a fiction. It wasn't just that he was loved by children. Those who worked with him were devastated when he died. When news of his passing reached the studios, employees stayed for hours, weeping.

Nor was Disney an anti-Semite. This is a pernicious myth. Almost every other Hollywood studio of the time was run by Jews and Disney wasn't. But the Disney brothers employed Jews and their main commercial partner, whom they loved, was a New York Jew running a company of New York Jews.

Why should Disney have attracted critics who describe him as unpleasant and bigoted? It is partly for prosaic reasons. He fought a strike and made an enemy of organised labour. He reciprocated the dislike, becoming a strong Republican in the last twenty years of his life. None of this endeared him to the avant garde.

There was, however, more to it than that. The critics disliked Disney not because they hated his flaws, but because they despised his achievements. He created modern mass entertainment. And that is what his opponents don't like. They think it is plastic, naive, a sin against nature, an insult to creativity.

Walt saw it differently. He was bringing high-quality entertainment to people who had little in their lives, good-quality merchandise in place of tat, brilliantly made films in place of amateur ones, artistic imagination to those who almost never encountered it. He provided capitalism with its best defence – that it can nourish creativity and inspiration.

The brilliance of Snow White, the wit of Mickey Mouse, the overwhelming, stunning commercial vision that produced the theme parks. Walt Disney was a genius.

Hillary Clinton . . . Hillary's flaws have defined the US election

Only someone seen by voters as being as self-righteous and deceitful as Clinton could have struggled so long against someone as bad as Trump

Because my column appears in *The Times* on Wednesdays, it has to be written by early evening on Tuesday (though I usually finish earlier). This is a problem with presidential elections which happen on Tuesdays US time. It means I write without knowing the result and it is read by people who do know it. And I can hardly ignore the topic. This column was written on the day of Donald Trump's election but before the result. I thought it quite likely he'd win and was surprised so few others agreed. And I knew Hillary's weakness would be clear even if she did win. So I wrote about that.

9 November 2016

Let me start with a story. In January 2000 Hillary Clinton, First Lady of the United States of America, appeared on *The*

Late Show and she did well. Laughing it up with the late-night TV host David Letterman she was relaxed and funny.

Then Letterman changed the subject. He was, he said, going to ask her some questions about New York. Since it was already clear she would be a candidate for the Senate for that state, she looked earnest. A mistake might cost her dear.

But she didn't make a mistake. Sometimes she had to grope a little for an answer. Sometimes she pondered and appeared uncertain. But she didn't make any errors. It was pretty impressive stuff. The next day, however, the reason for this straight-A performance became clear. She'd been given the questions in advance. The uncertainty had been an act.

I think this story can help us solve an abiding mystery. Why has this brilliant, experienced, hard-working, politically moderate woman struggled to defeat such an oaf? Donald Trump is a liar, a braggart and a bully. His grasp of the issues is tenuous, his speeches incoherent and his behaviour shocking. Yet the fight between the two of them went all the way to the finishing line.

Writing this article on election day is the right time to ask this question, for I am writing it without knowing the result and you are reading it after you know what happened. This gives me an advantage. Your view is conditioned by the outcome. I reflect only on the contest without the distortions produced by hindsight.

There are four reasons why Mrs Clinton found the contest with Mr Trump so difficult, leaving everyone uncertain until the last minute.

The first is relatively simple. She was the Democratic nominee. And not just any nominee either. She was the candidate of the party establishment.

Political scientists, assessing the race before the candidates were chosen, believed that historical precedent and the state of the economy suggested that this ought to be a Republican year. A big part of their reasoning was that the White House tends to change hands after eight years of one party.

The 'time for a change' mood is strong this year and Mrs Clinton, on the national political stage for almost a quarter of a century, is particularly ill-suited to thrive in such an environment.

The second problem faced by Mrs Clinton has, distressingly, been the fact that she is a woman. From the moment she became First Lady of Arkansas in 1979 Hillary Rodham has been attacked because she is female. During her husband's first term as governor, her decision to work and, in particular, to keep her own name was hugely (and disgracefully) controversial, forcing her in the end to call herself Clinton.

When Mr Clinton reached the White House his reliance on her advice came under sustained attack, an attack that other unelected advisers did not face and that she would not have faced if she had restricted herself to picking wallpaper. It is hard to escape the idea that many men dislike her because they feel threatened by her professional ability. This is also the origin of many of the unflattering descriptions of her character. Vindictive, for instance, or pushy.

Her third problem has been that people are weary of what is often called 'the Clinton circus'. This goes beyond feeling that Mrs Clinton does not represent change. Throughout the campaign she was dogged by a sense among voters that they'd simply had enough of the whole Clinton soap opera. Each new so-called scandal was greeted with a shrug. Voters weren't so much outraged as bored and the boredom is what hurt Hillary. Attacking Donald Trump as a reality-TV star ignores the extent to which voters thought of the Clintons in the same way.

But the most important reason why Mrs Clinton was run to the finishing line by the appalling Mr Trump is because she is so . . . Hillary.

The story with which I began this column was identified as the perfect Hillary Clinton tale by the Republican speech writer and columnist Peggy Noonan in her polemic against Mrs Clinton's 2000 Senate campaign. It remains hard to beat.

Mrs Clinton is extraordinarily professional. She is always well prepared, listens carefully to advice and acts thoughtfully upon it. She has had, even before this election, one of the greatest careers in American political history. And yet lots of people find her hard to trust. They suspect that behind every success on the Letterman show is a political trick. And often they are right.

Trust has been eroded by the fact that she has been embroiled in one scandal after another. It doesn't seem to matter that most of them have been entirely groundless, the ludicrous email pseudo-scandal most of all. The problem is that she has handled them badly. By regarding affairs such as the Whitewater property deal as politically motivated, she has foolishly resisted telling everything she knows, making the problem worse.

In his mostly admiring biography of Mrs Clinton, the Watergate journalist Carl Bernstein suggests that his subject is often self-righteous and defensive. She therefore resists investigation, wonders how anyone can possibly question her rectitude and repeatedly ends up in hot water as some new revelation is made.

Bernstein blames the same traits for errors made by both Clintons in the early days of Bill's presidency. While thrilling congressional leaders with her grasp of the details of healthcare policy, she also managed to antagonise the supporters they needed by appearing high-handed. In the end the reform effort collapsed and Hillary was regarded as responsible.

Mr Trump was badly damaged by his behaviour, but the damage would have been far greater if people had trusted his opponent. Because Donald Trump's flaws are so great, European observers have underestimated the extent to which many Americans think Hillary Clinton's flaws are just as great.

And while this may seem an extraordinary judgment to most people on this side of the Atlantic (and certainly seems so to me) it is impossible to understand the 2016 election without understanding this.

Clement Attlee . . . A review of Citizen Clem: A Biography of Attlee by John Bew

10 September 2016

'Few thought he was even a starter; there are those who thought themselves smarter; but he ended PM, CH and OM; an earl and a knight of the garter.'

Clement Attlee's boastful rhyme, contained in a private letter to his brother, Tom, in 1956, is in every way revealing. A man who rose quietly to enjoy one of the greatest political careers of the twentieth century, a radical comfortable with traditional institutions, and someone whose quiet modesty disguised self-assurance and even self-satisfaction.

Such contradictions deserve a discerning biographer, and in John Bew, Attlee has the man he deserves. He has written with verve and confidence a first-rate life of a man who he correctly argues has been under-appreciated.

The appeal of the Labour Party, during its periods of electoral success, has been its ability to do three things at the same time. To provide practical help to working people and the poor, to offer intellectuals and visionaries a glimpse of a better tomorrow, and to ensure that the broad mass regard it as patriotic and able to be trusted with the nation's security.

Clement Attlee (1883–1967) became Labour's leader almost by accident, he was never secure in the job (even in 1945) or much admired by his party colleagues, he made poor speeches, struck many contemporaries as unimpressive, sometimes grasped hold of quite silly ideas, and often did little more than hold the ring as the chairman of a meeting. Yet more than any figure in the party's history he brought together all the ingredients of Labour success.

As a result, a man who was still called an 'arch-mediocrity' by critics (Michael Foot, in this case, quoting Aneurin Bevan) late in his life, nevertheless lived a triumphant one: compassionate as a social worker, brave as a soldier, loyal and loved as a family man, a rock for his nation in wartime, an architect of extraordinary electoral victory, a builder of a modern welfare society supported by a broad political consensus that he did much to create. What a life and what a man.

By the time Attlee became leader of the Labour Party in 1935, he had worked in the East End of London as a Labour pioneer, but also left the battlefield injured in the First World War. He therefore combined socialist ideals with a deep practical experience of how most people lived and thought. He had a surprising romantic streak, but it was expressed in his liking for poetry and love of country rather than in abstract theories.

He was therefore always interested in practical advances for people such as his constituents in Limehouse, where he was MP from 1922 to 1950, and, while at home discussing socialist ideals, hadn't much time for those intellectuals who he thought had created systems in their heads that missed out human beings.

It is true, as Bew shows, that not having much understanding of economics and occasionally falling prey to naive notions, at times Attlee did advance some fairly alarming and impractical ideas. He was attracted in the 1930s to having politics and the economy put on an emergency footing and run by commissars. He held on for far too long to the idea that a world government would solve the problems of fascism. And he sometimes over-optimistically believed that combatants in a civil war (such as in Palestine or India) might suddenly come to their senses when they experienced the reality of fighting.

Yet, for all of this, he retained a keen sense of what was possible and reasonable, and his career as a man of power shows him capable of distinguishing between foolish ideas and sensible reform, even when the foolish ideas had once been his.

The claim that Attlee was a great figure, as great in some ways as Winston Churchill, rests on two things that Bew, a historian at King's College London, brings out particularly well.

The first is the choice he makes as Labour leader in the last half of the 1930s. Under pressure from figures such as Stafford Cripps and Bevan to create a popular front with communists, he decides that they have drawn the line in the wrong place. The right division is not between capitalism and socialism, it is between democracy and dictatorship.

This decision had huge consequences for Britain. It helped to win the war by uniting Labour behind Churchill. (A fascinating side point here is that Attlee fought and was wounded in Churchill's controversial Dardanelles campaign. Yet he believed in the concept of that campaign, arguing that the failing was in the execution. He thus trusted Churchill and reinforced him against the generals.) And after the war Attlee's decisions led Britain to be strongly Atlanticist, to be cold warriors, and to form Nato. His instincts here could not be more different from those of Jeremy Corbyn.

The second claim to greatness is the record of Attlee's government. Bew's book is particularly strong on his subject's ideas, reading and thinking. The author explains Attlee's strong belief in the idea of citizenship, the notion that we must recognise our rights and our duties. This spurs him on to some of his great achievements – national insurance, the NHS and, the one he was proudest of himself, Indian independence – but it also proved a weakness.

In the immediate aftermath of war, using moral exhortation, planning and appeals to patriotism, rather than competition and incentive, to improve productivity and to avert strikes had some chance of working. Within as little as three years, however, the public had begun to tire of this message. It is right to assert an idea of common citizenship and to be hopeful that the public might find it uplifting. To believe that it would long outlast the war was an example, more serious this time, of Attlee's occasional naivety.

Nevertheless, few prime ministers can look back on a period in office that did so much to fulfil their youthful notions. Bevan's attacks, during the war and in government, on Attlee's gradualism were petulant and sometimes close to bonkers.

It is quite hard to get a grip on Attlee as a man. I could, for example, maybe have done with a bit more on his family life. I have always found it intriguing that while his wife, Violet, used to drive the two of them on the campaign trail for mile upon mile in their little family car, she is said by many to have voted Conservative, even in 1945.

However, by using his correspondence with Tom Attlee, Bew does succeed in getting inside the pipe-smoking, slipper-wearing, moustached major from Stanmore. It shows him strong and self-confident, for all his apparent reticence. Never the showman, Clement Attlee still put on quite a show.

Chuck Berry . . . A political revolutionary

The rock 'n' roll pioneer left a rich legacy but nothing as important as his role in creating today's consumer society

Chuck Berry died on 18 March 2017.

22 March 2017

Charles Edward Anderson Berry was a person of great political importance. Which is a pretty odd statement to make, given that he hardly ever said or did a political thing.

Let me start with this. 'He sort of had this persona of wanting to be Hawaiian, the way his hair was, his shirts. He would say he was part Hawaiian, and in a way he could look Hawaiian. I think that something with his being Hawaiian was knowing that he could be more successful if maybe he wasn't black.'

This observation, by the record executive Marshall Chess, is not the only time one of Chuck Berry's friends commented on what his biographer Bruce Pegg has called the musician's 'racial ambivalence'. Johnnie Johnson, his musical collaborator over many decades, once remarked that Berry 'wanted to be everything . . . but an Afro-American I guess'. When the band were stopped by the New York police, Johnson noted that the singer's driving licence identified him as 'Indian'.

Chuck Berry was the grandson of a slave. He grew up in Missouri, in an area so segregated that the first time he saw a white person was at the age of three. It was a firefighter, and he thought it was merely the heat and fear of the fire that had whitened the man's skin. When, as an established star, he performed in the South, he found it so hard to find somewhere to stay that he took to sleeping in his own car.

So he can hardly be blamed for playing down his racial origins. He did it for commercial reasons – to reach bigger audiences – and for safety. He will have been only too aware of how in 1956 Nat King Cole had been beaten up on stage, in front of the audience in the middle of his show, by members of the Alabama white citizens' council.

Understandable though it was, Berry's reaction wasn't everyone's. His great hits, the zenith of his career, came during the turbulent days of the civil rights movement and urban revolt. As black people and liberals all over the world took up the cause of racial equality and resistance, Berry was silent.

Indeed he died at the age of 90 having written an autobiography and starred in many documentaries, leaving behind (as far as I can tell, and I've looked pretty hard) not a single properly political statement or song. He once said he was pleased to see the first black president elected, played at a concert to encourage the Democrats to stage their convention in his home town, and gave $1,000 to a Democratic leaders victory fund. And that's it.

So why argue that he was an important political figure? It's because of the significance of rock 'n' roll to cultural life and Berry's significance to rock 'n' roll.

Few deny the writer of 'Johnny B. Goode', of 'Memphis, Tennessee' and of 'Roll Over Beethoven' the right to be called one of the great pioneers of rock music. It wasn't just the power and wit of his early records, it was his ability to reach new audiences.

Berry's first hit, 'Maybellene' (the title inspired by a bottle of mascara), crossed over not just from the R&B charts into the pop charts, but from black to white audiences. Before 'Maybellene', most black music only became a hit when recorded as a white cover version. Berry's record was one of the first to outsell its white cover versions.

And then in the South, Berry desegregated his audiences. Not by political statements or any act of conscious resistance. Just by playing. The promoters would allow in black and white fans so long as they were separated by a rope down the centre aisle. And each time, as the rock frenzy grew, the rope would come down and everyone would be dancing together.

Berry wasn't much interested in the political implications of this. He was interested in its financial implications. More record buyers, more money. As guitar hero Bo Diddley once said: 'Chuck Berry is a businessman. I admire him for being a businessman. The name of the game is dollar bills.' His local paper headlined a piece on his film *Chuck Berry: Hail! Hail! Rock 'n' Roll* with the words: 'Hail! Hail! The Bankroll'.

Yet it was because of this, not despite it, that Berry was a liberator. He wanted to sell to everyone. Rock 'n' roll is the fullest expression of consumer culture. Its impact was deep. It reached out to people whatever their race, whatever their class, whatever their gender or sexual orientation. It made posh accents seem ridiculous and inherited social distinctions seem bizarre. It was – it is – entirely democratic.

It breaks down national borders too. John Lennon and Paul McCartney lived in a port town, where African-American records came off the boats. Keith Richards first noticed Mick Jagger because Jagger was carrying a rare Chuck Berry record that had to be ordered from Chicago. Then the Beatles and the Rolling Stones went to America and sold back American music to them.

Rock's power isn't that it was the counter-culture, but that it became *the* culture. The only barrier it didn't initially break down was age. There are people whose politics and social attitudes have as their main point of reference sometime before 1958, when Berry cut 'Johnny B. Goode', and those whose reference point is after that.

The generation gap written about in the 1960s didn't repeat itself, as everyone thought it would. Instead it was a single gap, separating the era before rock from the era after it. The people who feared that rock would sweep away customs and barriers and change cultural attitudes were right to fear it.

Sir Tom Stoppard's play *Rock 'n' Roll* tells the (true) story of the attempts by the communist Czechoslovakian government in the mid-1970s to suppress a rock group called the Plastic People of the Universe. They were not avowedly political but the Husák government could see that nevertheless they were.

They couldn't allow the Plastics just to do their thing. They appreciated that unless they imprisoned them and made them cut their hair, there would be no stopping the revolution. Their culminating act of oppression (in Stoppard's drama) is to smash the Western record collection of the play's central character.

Even if Chuck Berry didn't see himself as political, the Czechs could see that he was wrong.

Ted Sorensen and JFK . . . Obama must learn from the real Jack Kennedy

JFK was no liberal: he was successful because he embraced the Centre

This column was written in the week of the death of John Kennedy's famous speechwriter Ted Sorensen. On the day I wrote it, mid-term elections were being held in the US. Although I didn't know the results yet, a big defeat of President Obama's Democrats was expected. And by the time readers saw this piece, that is exactly what had transpired overnight.

3 November 2010

In 1961, at a banquet in California, the defeated presidential candidate, Richard Nixon, spied Ted Sorensen, speechwriter and close adviser to the victorious John F. Kennedy. He wanted to congratulate Sorensen on the new President's inaugural address, which had been widely acclaimed.

'Ted,' said Nixon, 'there is one thing JFK said at his inauguration that I wish I had said.' Sorensen looked pleased. 'You mean that part about "Ask not what your country can do for you"?' he asked. 'No,' replied Nixon. 'I mean that part about "I hereby solemnly swear to uphold . . ."'

Nixon's joke has appeared many times in articles, books and collections of humorous presidential remarks. And it is sufficiently witty to redound to Nixon's credit. Save for this. Nixon didn't say it. Sorensen made it up.

Ted Sorensen was one of the great myth-makers of the modern age. And as the President of the United States wakes up on the morning after the night before, that is something that Barack Obama might care to remember. For if he does not, Mr Obama may find himself shackled by Sorensen's biggest myth.

On Sunday Sorensen, the last of the Kennedy men, died, a little more than a year after the passing of JFK's youngest brother Edward. The last and one of the greatest. There was all Ted Sorensen did for the President in his lifetime, the words he wrote, the advice he gave. And there was something else. The Kennedy myth he helped to create.

From the moment, late in November 1963, when the speechwriter ran out on to the South Lawn of the White House to give JFK some papers as he walked out to the helicopter ride that began his trip to Dallas, to the moment of his own death nearly half a century later, Sorensen dedicated his life to the service of his president as faithfully as he had when Kennedy was alive. He burnished JFK's reputation as a great president.

But he also, subtly and importantly, changed Kennedy in those years, so that the myth and the man became different things. He did not do this deliberately, for I think he was an honourable man; he may not even have done it consciously, despite his intellectual brilliance, but I think he did it nonetheless. Kennedy the myth was Sorensen's ideal, a liberal hero, while Kennedy the man was not.

In his memoir, *Counselor*, Sorensen recalls playing a game of touch football with the Kennedy brothers in the early years, the years when JFK was in the Senate. It was a fake game, a photo op for a magazine, but the writer found himself sprawling in the mud in his one good 'Senate suit', victim of an unsports-manlike shove from Bobby. 'I took that as an indication of how he felt about me,' Sorensen said. Why the animosity? It was because Bobby distrusted the liberalism of the tall Nebraskan, a liberalism alien to the more conservative Kennedy family.

'I am not a liberal at all,' said JFK shortly after Sorensen joined him. 'I'm not comfortable with those people.' And liberals weren't comfortable with him, with his dubious father or with his links to the communist-baiting Joe McCarthy. Sorensen became his emissary to the left of the party, soothing its doubts, seeking out endorsements to counter the openly expressed hostility of that liberal icon Eleanor Roosevelt.

Over the years, as JFK eyed and then won the presidency, this distance closed a little. But Kennedy never became a liberal. He was, strongly, a centrist. He was a Cold War warrior, a fiscal conservative, a tax cutter, a pragmatist, cautious and legalistic on civil liberties, a believer in American military strength and spreading freedom abroad through muscular diplomacy. Neither Kennedy's greatest moment (the Cuban missile crisis) nor his worst (the Bay of Pigs fiasco) displays him as a liberal.

Nor do his greatest words. Sorensen, the outstanding political speechwriter of the twentieth century, is credited with writing Kennedy's inaugural address, with its fine phrases. But in his very worthwhile book *Ask Not*, the historian Thurston Clarke demonstrates that it is all more complicated than that.

Many of the phrases had been used by Kennedy before, and the speech's animating idea, the call to make sacrifices, asking what you can do for your country, was Kennedy's own. And the themes of the speech are not liberal ones.

It is a very Cold War inaugural address, tough and uncom-promising. 'Ask not what your country can do for you' is partly a refutation of welfare liberalism, and 'the rights of man come

not from the generosity of the State, but from the hand of God'
is a rejection of communism. When the torch is passed to a
new generation it is with the defence of freedom that the new
generation is tasked.

It was inevitable that the memorable books of the Kennedy
circle would be written by the great creative liberals such as
Sorensen and the court historian Arthur Schlesinger rather than
by the Irish political operators whom JFK also favoured (such
as Kenny O'Donnell who regarded the Peace Corps as a 'kooky
liberal idea' that made him sick). But this has given recall of
the John Kennedy years a certain slant, as have the Senate years
of Ted Kennedy. But Ted Kennedy, the liberal lion, was a
different politician from his brother in very many ways.

Why should Mr Obama recall this now, as he surveys the
mid-term results? It is because, although fifty years have passed
since his election, John Kennedy was the last Northern Democrat
before Mr Obama to win the presidency. JFK's myth might
hold him out as a liberal who won and whose example can be
emulated. But the history of the man says something different.

It is Kennedy's centrism that won in 1960 and the emotion
of the mythical Kennedy, the liberalism of the two Teds, that
has doomed Northern liberals ever since. And will doom
President Obama now, unless he moves from it and embraces
the Centre.

Restless, fearing for their jobs and their livelihoods, anxious
at the prospects of rising taxes, worried about their place in the
world, the American people have turned to the Right. Be guided
by Kennedy the myth rather than Kennedy the man and Mr
Obama too will find himself face down in the mud in his Senate
suit, victim of an unsportsmanlike shove.

Ayn Rand and Karl Marx . . . Beware zealots who lack the human touch

From Ayn Rand on the right to Karl Marx on
the left, politicians should steer clear of gurus
who loathe compromise

8 May 2018

One morning in 1926, a young Russian was leaving a movie studio in Hollywood. She was downcast, having been told by its publicity department that there was no work for her. Then, at the gate, she stopped to let a car go by and fell into conversation with its driver.

This was how Ayn Rand, as Alyssa Rosenbaum called herself on emigrating to America, met the film director Cecil B. DeMille. And the jobs he gave her were her first steps on the road to an extraordinary career as novelist, screenwriter and political guru.

It emerged last week that Sajid Javid, the Home Secretary, twice a year reads aloud the courtroom speech of Howard Roark, hero of Rand's novel *The Fountainhead*.

The same week saw the 200th birthday of Karl Marx. Perhaps,

like me, you celebrated quietly at home, but the shadow chancellor John McDonnell made more of a fuss, telling a conference about Marx's influence on Labour's future while standing in front of a banner of the great man.

In many ways, Marx and Rand are complete opposites. Rand came to the US largely to escape Bolshevism and, through her books, promoted a vision of free people fighting against socialism. Yet, for all that, I think Rand and Marx made a common error. Understanding it can help us make sense of politics.

It is hard to see why anyone would regard Marx's birthday as an occasion to bake a cake and light candles. For all his intelligence, his analysis of capitalism led him to a series of predictions (for example that workers would only be able to earn subsistence wages or that independent producers would be forced into the proletariat) that have all proved wrong.

Every time a country has attempted to follow Marx, it has ended in disaster. His defenders argue that this is not his fault, but it most certainly is. Marx asserted that we can't be free or human until we eradicate private property and the trade of goods. Doing this, however, results in massive state power and incredible economic inefficiency.

Some argue that this criticism is unfair because European social democracy owes a lot to Marx. In 1948, for instance, the Labour Party published a centenary edition of Marx and Engels's *Communist Manifesto*, the introduction to which acknowledged the party's debt. Yet in each case, as Western European parties contemplated moving from some intervention and planning (an idea that preceded Marx) to a proper Marxist view (the abolition of capitalism), they realised that fiasco would follow, and disowned him.

Another defence of Marx is that he didn't prescribe a particular system, so can't be held accountable for the ways his ideas were put into practice. But this is hardly a defence. Indeed, quite the contrary. What it accepts is that Marx wanted (strictly speaking it is what he predicted, but he predicted it because he wanted it) to smash the current system without a clue about what would replace it. To suggest that this absolves him of responsibility for the subsequent disasters is ridiculous.

To the question of what comes after capitalism, Marx provided an airy hand wave. The problem of how to organise society will disappear. Our behaviour is the result of our economic relationships, and so when we stop trading under capitalism we will have complete abundance, no problems distributing goods and the interests of the individual will be the same for everyone.

It is the study of economics and psychology replaced by one of Ali Bongo's magic tricks. It is hard to understand why it has won the allegiance of so many apparently intelligent people.

Set against this, Ayn Rand's novels at least present a concrete idea of the sort of society she is after, even if it is flawed. She supports laissez-faire capitalism.

Rand's books celebrate reason and creativity. Her philosophy, objectivism, argues that the basis for everything is fact, not superstition or emotion. Our duty is to express our own beliefs and wishes as selfishly (which she argues is a good word) as possible. We may regard looking after others as a good but this makes caring a selfish act. Beyond that we should never have to sacrifice ourselves.

The passion of her belief in reason and knowledge makes her novels occasionally inspiring. I must admit I find them quite strange and contrived, but in one poll of literary influence, Rand's *Atlas Shrugged* came second only to the Bible. It isn't hard to see what Javid gets from reading Roark's speech. It is a hymn to inventiveness and to sticking to one's principles.

Yet here's the problem. Rand suggests that from each individual pursuing their own interests without compromise comes the greater good. Individual interest and the public interest will harmonise (completely; this is well beyond Adam Smith's observations). Rand says this can happen with capitalism, Marx believes this will happen only after capitalism. This is the same error. A rudimentary understanding of human nature tells you there will always be conflict.

Let me give you an example. Javid amusingly said he reads Roark's speech to himself having read it once to his wife who told him not to do it again. Now Rand would argue that if you wanted to read the book out loud to someone you must do so, to fulfil your vision and to be true to your essence. But what if your partner's vision is that she didn't want to listen to it again? She has to be true to that. Rand's answer would be that in that case you shouldn't be together. Which is ludicrous: nobody would be with anybody based on that logic.

This is what eventually happened to Rand. She felt that if someone preferred Strauss to Rachmaninov they couldn't be in her circle. She had an affair with her 'intellectual heir', both of them telling their spouses that it made objective sense for the two greatest brains to be together. Then when her lover had an affair with someone else she expelled him and his wife for behaviour 'grossly contradictory to objectivist morality'.

The common error of Rand and Marx was to fail to understand that individual interests, ideas and values clash and always will. It is the job of politics, sometimes acting through the state, to come up with compromises that allow us to live together in some degree of peace and harmony.

The moderates and placaters, the negotiators and split-the-difference people, may not be amongst Rand's heroes or Marx's irresistible forces, but we do at least grasp human nature.

Gordon Brown . . . The problem all along, Mr Brown, was you

Gordon Brown's self-pitying memoirs persist with
the delusion that he was cheated out of greatness
by Tony Blair

My favourite tribute of all time was innocently given by
the Labour politician Jim Murphy to Gordon Brown on
his retirement. 'We owe him a huge debt.'

8 November 2017

When someone publishes their memoirs it is a moment for
historical reflection, for the making of judgments and the placing
of cards on the table. Yesterday Gordon Brown published *My
Life, Our Times*. So, allow me.

That row, Mr Brown, that you had with Tony Blair? The one
that split Labour modernisers and hampered the government
for more than a decade? The one that drove out of politics some
of its best people? The one that fatally weakened the centre and
right of the party until the left was able to take over? That row
was your fault.

It wasn't Tony Blair's fault and it wasn't six of one and half a dozen of the other. It wasn't understandable in the circumstances or just one of those things. It wasn't tittle-tattle or irrelevant. It was all you, and it was all unnecessary and it all mattered.

Let's deal with the nub of the point. Tony Blair did not trick you out of the leadership when John Smith died in 1994. In your book you say: 'I had no doubt I could and would win.' If this statement is true, it is delusional.

Every serious historical account – except yours – agrees that the momentum was with Mr Blair. A BBC poll of Labour members before your withdrawal from the leadership contest indicated 47 per cent support for him, with 15 per cent for John Prescott and only 11 per cent for you. And the row you were having over spending promises with the unions back then means that they wouldn't have come to your rescue either. So if you had challenged Mr Blair you are one of the very few people, now or then, who thinks you would have been the victor.

If indeed you did think that. But did you? Really? Surely if you did, you would have gone ahead and stood, wouldn't you?

It is probably true, as you write, that during your exchanges Mr Blair said all sorts of emollient words about giving you control and standing down in a second term. But does it occur to you that his motive might not have been to steal your birthright but merely to try to stop you heavying him? Or he might have seen you were a bit down and wanted to pep you up? You can get quite cross, you know you can, and the whole thing was probably quite socially awkward. He was always weak when it came to dealing with you.

So he didn't owe you anything. He became the candidate because your associates in the modernising camp and beyond thought he would be more attractive to voters. And they were right.

In any case, your suggestion that Mr Blair's broken promise about standing down destroyed a perfectly good partnership doesn't survive reading any other participant's memoir or diary.

From the beginning of his leadership you behaved extraordinarily badly. Sulking in meetings, swearing down the phone, exploding either about or to Mr Blair's advisers, engaging in an absurd feud with Peter Mandelson that led to his downfall. If Mr Blair had ever intended standing down, and wasn't just trying to be nice, has it struck you that by the time you were actually in a second term, all these tantrums might have put him off?

He probably drew the conclusion that however clever, studious and socially committed you were, and however formidable you were at the dispatch box as chancellor, you were not temperamentally suited to being prime minister. And again he would have been right.

In the opening section of your book, you accept this up to a point. You argue, essentially, that Abraham Lincoln and Clement Attlee didn't have to put up with constant demands to give their views on soap operas and pop stars, talk about their feelings, or let the cameras in to film the family having Sunday lunch. And they didn't have to use social media. Perhaps, you seem to be saying, you might have done better in their day when you didn't have to blogpost on Faceogram or whatever it is these young people get up to.

Well, it does matter whether a political figure can communicate with voters using the techniques of the day. And if you weren't willing to do that – felt these nonsenses were beneath you – then you shouldn't have hounded Tony Blair until you made him quit. You had a perfectly good political partner willing to be filmed eating cornflakes or whatever, and you insisted you didn't need him or any of his people. But in any case, the idea that Twitter was your big problem is absurd. It wasn't 140 characters that led to your downfall, it was one character: yours.

Having spent years trying to lever out Mr Blair on the ostensible grounds that you stood for a different kind of modernisation, when you finally succeeded you hadn't the foggiest idea what that new and distinct agenda was. And people sensed that.

You regret your inability to persuade voters at the 2010 election that we should have gone on increasing public spending but reject entirely the thought that this might not have been a good idea.

More important than this is that a combination of burning intensity, excessive focus, extreme partisanship, a tendency to feel sorry for yourself and frequent moments of seeming paranoia are not qualities any of us want in a national leader.

You had the ability to demonstrate intellectual grip, and showed it during the banking crisis, but that's not enough when weighed in the balance with everything else.

Your method of ruling through fear and your desire to crush any opponent – real or imagined – destroyed Tony Blair's government and then ate your own. Alan Milburn, Ruth Kelly, David Miliband, James Purnell: these people were your allies, or should have been, for goodness sake. Yet you feuded with them, humiliated them or chased them out of politics altogether.

And when you'd gone, having scorched the landscape, no wonder there was nothing left except Jeremy Corbyn and John McDonnell. Oh, and Tom Watson of course. There will always be him.

Just before you became prime minister, a few days before you took possession of No. 10, I had lunch with Philip Gould, the great Labour pollster and a lovely man who only wanted the best for you. And he told me he had his fingers crossed. 'Gordon knows he will have to change now.' The moment he said that, I realised it would be a fiasco, the whole thing. Because people don't change.

So I should have known that in your memoirs, as in Downing Street, you'd just plough on, giving us the same old stuff on you and your row with Blair. But all I'm saying is that even if people buy your book, I don't think you'll find many who will buy your version of the past.

Millicent Fawcett . . . The Fawcett statue will be a true landmark

When the suffrage leader takes her place in Parliament Square it will put right a part of our history we have got wrong

On 24 April 2018 a statue was unveiled of the suffragist Millicent Fawcett. I'd first canvassed the idea of such a monument in *The Times* in 2015, and then helped persuade the Government to site it in Parliament Square and finance it. This column was written after the statue got the go-ahead.

4 April 2017

'So here's my proposal. In 2018, the centenary of votes for women, why not have a statue of Millicent Fawcett in Parliament Square?'

At around the time that I finished my column with those words, in October 2015, the feminist leader Caroline Criado-Perez went on a run through central London.

She'd finished her successful campaign to get Jane Austen on the £10 note and wasn't looking to start another one. But then, as she ran past Parliament Square, she noticed something. There were eleven statues commemorating significant figures in our political history. And they were all of men. Right there outside Parliament. All men.

She realised, even before she finished her run, that she had to do something. How we tell our national story matters. Who we choose to celebrate matters. In a democracy everyone has to feel that they can make a difference and in making this clear, symbols matter.

So before long we united our efforts and, together with Sam Smethers of the Fawcett Society, set out to make the case for a statue of Britain's greatest suffrage leader, Dame Millicent Garrett Fawcett, in Parliament Square. And so it came to pass. The mayor of London offered his support and this weekend the Prime Minister and the communities secretary announced government backing. Next year, there Mrs Fawcett will be. I believe that this statue will be a political landmark.

Let me tell you why. This year it is the 140th anniversary of the day when someone didn't steal Millicent Fawcett's purse. Sure, the thief took it from her at Waterloo station. He was caught and charged. It's just that Millicent Fawcett's purse did not belong to Millicent Fawcett.

She may have been a bestselling author, carrying money she earned herself, in a wallet she bought herself, but legally it didn't belong to her. She was a married woman and her property was all her husband's. The thief was charged with stealing the property of Henry Fawcett. Millicent commented: 'I felt as if I had been charged with theft myself.'

What sort of law was it that meant that her purse and even her writing didn't belong to her? In her husband's will, he had to bequeath her the copyright of her own book. What sort of law was it? A law passed by men, for men. Millicent Fawcett devoted her life to righting this wrong. She saw the struggle for women's votes through from its first moments to its final success. She helped John Stuart Mill collect signatures for his famous petition in 1866, when she was, aged 19, still deemed too young to sign it herself. And she was still a leader of the movement in 1928 when, the year before her death, equal votes for women was finally conceded.

Mrs Fawcett saw with great clarity what Martin Luther King also saw: that no political victory was as important as winning the vote. All her other campaigns – against sexual abuse and white slavery, for university degrees for women, for equal pay, against oppressive divorce laws, for property rights – could be advanced if first she won the great campaign for the vote.

Emmeline Pankhurst and her daughters are remembered for their campaign of law breaking that caught the imagination, publicised the cause, but ultimately probably delayed votes for women as male politicians used their violence as an excuse for delay.

It was Millicent Fawcett who carried on when the suffragette campaign fizzled out, as it was bound to. She always regarded the Pankhursts as her allies, but their violence as an error. A constitutional campaign of protest would be larger, more durable and more successful. And she was right.

So the Fawcett statue will be a celebration of one of the greatest democratic campaigns ever fought. It will mark the progress made by the supreme cause of women's equality, and point the way to further progress. It will tell the story of one of the most important social changes in human history, the modern recognition after thousands of years that men and women must have the same rights. It will put right a part of our history we have been getting wrong, and tell the story of the suffrage campaign correctly for the first time. It will tell schoolchildren and students, tourists and citizens the story of a hero they have never heard of before.

A woman who was an economic liberal but who understood that it was a faulty liberalism that failed to assign individual rights to all of its citizens. How could one have a modern market economy if married women could not own their own property?

How could one have a modern society if people like her sister Elizabeth Garrett Anderson, the first woman to qualify as a doctor, were not regarded as proper citizens?

A woman who never gave up and never gave in. It was Millicent Fawcett who persuaded Sir Hubert Parry to provide music for Blake's poem 'Jerusalem' to serve as the women voters' hymn: 'I will not cease from mental fight, Nor shall my sword sleep in my hand, Till we have built Jerusalem, In England's green and pleasant land.'

If Millicent Fawcett takes her rightful place in our national story, then so do the many thousands of women who won the vote with her, legally, peacefully but with determination and imagination. And every girl and every woman who wants to improve the life of their fellow citizens can see the possibilities more clearly as they make their way in public life.

In Parliament Square we will also be erecting a monument that says to all who visit Britain and all who want to live here that we have decided that equality for women is one of the great British values, and the insistence upon it one of the things that – however imperfect we are at it – makes us British.

The statue will also stand as a reminder of the value of politics and of its nature.

There's an oddity about the people whose lives we mark in Parliament Square: they clashed with each other. Churchill with Gandhi and Gandhi with Smuts, Peel with Disraeli and Derby with Palmerston. Millicent Fawcett diverged from Disraeli, and battled with Churchill and (for some of the time) Lloyd George. Politics is like that; there's no one right answer. She saw that and coped with it and showed what politics can do. When people say politics doesn't matter we can say: here is Millicent Fawcett. She gave her life for the vote.

Robert McNamara . . . From the fog of war come three hard truths

The fate of the Ford executive who ran the
Vietnam War is a lesson to those who would
bring business people into politics

Robert McNamara died on 6 July 2009.

8 July 2009

'It was a glittering time. They literally swept into office, ready, moving, generating their style, their confidence – they were going to get America moving again. There was a sense that these were brilliant men, men of force, not cruel, not harsh, but men who acted rather than waited.'

In his stunning book *The Best and the Brightest*, David Halberstam captures the glamour, the drive, the elan of the men who came to Washington to help John F. Kennedy to usher in a new era. And of these men none was brighter or better than Robert S. McNamara.

When you see those playful photos of JFK in Camelot with his little children, there are always determined men there, too, with their short hair, and white shirts with thin ties and their jackets discarded. McNamara, Kennedy's man at the Pentagon, was their emblem.

When Bob McNamara was in first grade, his teacher set a monthly test and the class was seated so as to reflect the result. McNamara rarely lost his grip on the front-left seat. And even the Kennedy men, dazzled as they were by their own brilliance, were ready to acknowledge that McNamara had something special. While they were slowly adjusting to their new power, the new Secretary of Defence was ready on day one, full of plans, ideas and top people he had already found and hired.

On Monday Robert McNamara died. He was 93, but he was still a recognisable modern archetype. He was the first person outside the Ford family to rise to become president of the Ford Motor Company and the ideal everyone is still mooning after: the business genius, independent-minded man, with an impressive career in proper enterprise, actually making things. The expert brought in to carry out executive functions, replacing political fixers with cool-headed management science, crossing out incompetence with a stroke of his propelling pencil, conquering party prejudice with an overhead projector.

So what happened to brilliant, bright Robert McNamara teaches a lesson to all those who talk of governments of all the talents. In fact, he teaches more than one lesson to Gordon Brown and David Cameron, who are both keen on bringing business talent into politics.

McNamara wasn't a failure. It is more complicated than that. In many ways his management of the Pentagon was everything you might hope for from a company president. The instincts he used to save Ford – with his championing of the cheap, functional, stripped down and wonderfully lucrative Ford Falcon – he brought to the Defence Department. He streamlined its management, asserted civilian control, reformed procurement practice and reshaped nuclear doctrine. He was able in later years to show off the calendar that JFK gave to his close advisers. The President had the crucial days of the Cuban Missile Crisis picked out in silver as a thanks for McNamara's cool advice.

It would all be remembered as a great success, were it not for one thing. The Vietnam War.

There was a time when the Vietnam War had another name. It was called McNamara's War. Indeed, there was a time when this self-confident man embraced the label. 'I must say,' he proclaimed, 'I don't object at all to its being called McNamara's War.' The Defence Secretary didn't start the conflict but he prosecuted it with – enthusiasm isn't quite the right word – vigour. He pressed for escalation. He ordered up tables to calculate the most efficient way to pulverise the enemy.

But that time passed. McNamara began to have doubts. And although he kept his counsel for more than two decades, he finally admitted his doubts in public. He wrote a book on the Vietnam error, broke down as he talked of the mistakes and starred in a documentary – *The Fog of War* – in which he outlined the lessons he had learnt.

Yet there were three lessons he did not include, for even at the end, even as he blinked into the camera for that documentary, McNamara was not a man given to self-examination.

The first lesson is this: that men of action want to act. They are paid to act, they are brought into government to act. From his very first visit to Vietnam, McNamara could have learnt – if he wanted to – how difficult things were. But he was an executive type and he wasn't about to tell the boss that he couldn't get the job done. So doubt was excluded. The facts were altered to suit the theory.

The second lesson is that men brought into government because of their independence don't stay like that. They form allegiances, they join gangs, they have political love affairs. McNamara certainly did.

Lyndon Johnson fell head over heels for his Defence Secretary and his feelings were reciprocated. LBJ saw McNamara as *his*. The Camelot man who had taken up with the Texan. And McNamara's prosecution of LBJ's Vietnam policy was a symbol of his loyalty. But heartbreak awaited. For McNamara was still a friend of Bobby Kennedy. He gave Kennedy secret documents about the war, and the two men fed each other's doubts. The tug of love nearly ended in nervous breakdown for the rational Ford man.

Jeff Shesol's book *Mutual Contempt* – a history of the hatred between LBJ and Robert Kennedy – records Kennedy's attempts to get McNamara to speak out against the war and Johnson. He sat with him for hours. But he failed. McNamara could not, never did, resolve the conflict of loyalties. He stayed silent on the war until almost everyone else in both gangs was dead. And even then he exonerated LBJ.

The final lesson is that men don't just become prisoners of their allies. They also become prisoners of their errors. Halberstam's book presents Vietnam as a tragedy for the best and the brightest. They never declared war at all, just followed one act with another as logic took over from common sense. Send advisers, protect the advisers, attack is the best form of defence, use bombs to attack, have a ground war to support the air war. Deeper and deeper they sank.

And however independent they may have started off, soon these men became owners of an error they couldn't admit to. It is actually quite impressive that McNamara ever did, even years later, even in a fairly limited way. But although late is better than never, earlier is better than late.

Enhancing political decisions with independent executive judgment is a worthy aim. The life of Robert McNamara suggests that it is easier wished for than achieved.

Gary Becker . . . The man who won a Nobel Prize for parking

From crime to tuition fees, countless aspects of
our lives are influenced by the late economist

In 2013 the former cabinet minister Chris Huhne had been
sent to prison for evading penalty points for speeding. The
story was once again in the news in May 2014 when costs
were imposed on him for the case. In the same week, the
Nobel economist Gary Becker died.

14 May 2014

Why did Chris Huhne need to go to jail for dodging his penalty
points for speeding? After all, as he constantly points out,
hundreds of thousands of people have done this without giving
it a second thought. Yet Mr Huhne would find his sentence
less baffling if he reflected upon what happened the day that
Gary Becker was late. And in the days after the death of the
great professor, I think that's worth doing.

A little more than forty years ago, Becker was driving to the
oral exam of a student when he realised that he wasn't going

to get there in time. Not only that, but he would have to park the car and there were parking restrictions all around the building in which the exam was taking place. Finding a car park would take ages and then he would have to walk.

So here is what he did. He parked in a forbidden area, dashed to the meeting, made it on time and on his way won the Nobel Prize for Economics.

The decision about where to park had, in the end, been relatively simple. The fines for parking outside the building were modest and, more importantly, they were unreliable. In other words, he might park in the restricted area and not get a ticket. Against this was the certain cost of the car park and the professional cost of being late for an important engagement. It seemed to him that the benefit of the parking violation over legal parking was clear.

As he left the car behind, he began to reflect on what he had done. And to wonder whether others weren't doing it too. The standard theory of criminal behaviour at the time was that criminals were mentally ill or social victims. Becker, however, realised that the decision he had made to break the law had been entirely rational. Those who break the law balance the costs and the benefits of doing it.

From this insight came Becker's influential analysis of crime, one of the ways he transformed economics and one of the reasons he became a Nobel laureate. When his death was announced last week, Gary Becker was hailed as one of the most significant social scientists of his generation, at least the equal of giants such as Milton Friedman, with whom he worked at the University of Chicago. When awarding him the Presidential Medal of Freedom, George W. Bush described Becker as 'without question one of the most influential economists of the last hundred years'.

Becker's contribution was to use the traditional tools of economics – the analysis of supply and demand, the working of incentives, the weighing of costs and benefits – and, for the first time, apply it to social policy.

Take, for instance, Chris Huhne and his penalty points. The former cabinet minister thinks that he was sent to jail *despite* the fact that so many others commit the same crime and get away with it. In fact, a Becker-style analysis suggests that he was sent to jail precisely *because* so many others commit the same crime and get away with it.

If a crime is very hard to detect, the incentive to commit it is greater. The benefit of the crime outweighs the cost. As a result, you have to make the penalty greater so that, taken together, the punishment and the risk of punishment make transgression too costly to be worthwhile.

Becker's work was very influential on sentencing policy and prevention of crime. Yet more influential still was his impact on the field of economics. Instead of being a study merely of how money moves around, it became a study of how people behave.

One of his most famous pieces of work concerned racial discrimination in the American South. He showed that you could measure the preference for discrimination of employers by looking at how far they were willing to hire less productive workers merely because they were white.

He also developed and popularised the idea of human capital, now a common term but very controversial when Becker first used it. The professor argued that education could be seen as an economic decision in which the long-term benefit of a better job could offset the short-term cost.

It is impossible now to debate student-tuition fees, for instance, without reference to Becker's ideas. Given that students increase their earning power as a result of a university education, but also that there is a social benefit, who should pay for it? And would tuition fees put off poorer students?

Becker would not have been surprised (as others have been)

that the people most willing to pay tuition fees have proved to be the least well-off, and those least likely to pay have been the middle class. The cost is the same for both groups but the least well-off gain a greater benefit because they have less to fall back on without higher education.

During his life Becker was often accused of treating human beings as factors of production and of being purely self-interested. Yet this is a complete misunderstanding. The real significance of Becker's work is the opposite.

Becker won the Nobel prize because he demonstrated the way in which economics was about more than money. Understanding people's incentives, and structuring social institutions in response to them, does not mean that people's incentives are purely selfish.

People might have a preference for altruism, for example, or for community living. A market-based system takes these preferences into account. It's quite wrong to equate markets with narrow economic selfishness.

This is relevant to the current debate on free schools or the NHS. Allowing competition and choice is not preferring self-interest over public spirit. It is simply structuring the system in line with people's preferences, and these preferences may be charitable.

Becker's work also shows why non-market systems struggle. People calculate the trade-off between costs and benefits. If the system gets in the way of their preferences, they work around it. That's why tourists used to swap their jeans for hard currency behind the Iron Curtain. Then the punishments get more severe to deter such defiance of the law.

The world has lost one of its great thinkers. Fortunately we still have the power of his thought.

Winston Churchill . . . The wartime leader was a great man, but a racist nonetheless

The celebrated prime minister had such great strengths, but that does not mean we should ignore that he was a lifelong white supremacist

12 February 2019

If it wasn't for Sir Winston Churchill, I wouldn't be alive. This isn't a romantic statement. I think that a cold, hard view of my family's history and his history reveals it to be true.

In May 1940 there were others who understood better than him the chances of Britain being able to withstand Nazi Germany, but few with his appreciation of what was at stake, of what surrender or peace terms might mean. He insisted on resistance and defeated the strong lobby that sought a deal with Hitler. Had he not done so, things would have been very different.

So the best historical accounts support the claim that Churchill was indispensable to victory, that his behaviour at this critical moment saved European liberty and democracy. And if this is true, then he saved my family too. If Britain had sued for peace in 1940, I don't think my parents would still have been alive by 1945.

Which is why, with some trepidation, I add this. When Churchill's modern critics, such as the Green Party MSP Ross Greer, say that he was a white supremacist, they are right.

Churchill justified British imperialism as being for the good of the 'primitive' and 'subject races'. Perhaps his clearest statement came in 1937 when he said: 'I do not admit, for instance, that a great wrong has been done to the Red Indians of America, or the black people of Australia. I do not admit that a wrong has been done to those people by the fact that a stronger race, a higher-grade race, or, at any rate, a more worldly wise race, to put it that way, has come in and taken their place.'

And he was also a supporter of eugenics, supporting the segregation of 'feeble-minded' people and showing an interest in the possibility of sterilisation lest the breeding of 'unfit' people pose 'a very terrible danger to the race'.

So to call him a white supremacist is nothing but the truth. And it is never a good idea to deny the truth. To insist that for Churchill to be a great man he must never have thought or done anything bad is to insist that the world is divided into good and bad people and you can only be one or the other.

It is also to insist that great progressive acts – and saving Europe in 1940 was surely one of the greatest – can only be carried out by progressive people. Yet Lord Shaftesbury supported the factory acts while opposing the Great Reform Bill, Asquith was a great liberal who opposed votes for women, and Christabel Pankhurst had a soft spot for Mussolini.

New histories of the American revolution are commendably frank about the Founding Fathers' attitude to slavery. In his biography of George Washington, Ron Chernow correctly devotes a lot of space to his subject's ownership of slaves.

Washington was still a great man but his slaveholding was an abomination. And a large part of him knew it too. To leave it out in order to deify the first president doesn't just fail to portray Washington with all his flaws, it renders much of the early politics of the United States (and arguably its current politics) incomprehensible.

Similarly, to talk only of Churchill as a hero, though hero he was, while ignoring his attitudes to empire and race, is bad history both of the man and of Britain.

It is common to respond to Churchill's critics by saying that it is anachronistic to apply modern standards to a politician who first entered Parliament during the reign of Queen Victoria. Yet while his attitudes may have been more common, they were by no means universal. Indeed, Churchill's diehard views on Indian independence made him a dissident in his own party and separated him from more liberal Conservatives who later became allies on appeasement.

Duff Cooper, the cabinet minister who resigned over the Munich agreement with Hitler, wrote years later that he regarded Churchill's determination to block any move towards dominion status for India as 'the most unfortunate event that occurred between the two wars'.

Churchill's early warnings on the rise of Germany were ignored largely because his position on the empire had made his judgment suspect. So his racial ideas (by race he often meant people or national characteristics) are a vital part of his history. Indeed his confidence in ultimate victory in 1940 came partly from his mystical belief in the superiority of the British 'race' over the Prussians who had once been a 'barbarous tribe'. At the same time this outlook may have led him to underestimate the power of Japan, which seized Singapore in 1942 after the largest surrender of British-led troops in history.

Acknowledging the truth of Churchill's views allows one to deal with the more outlandish idea that he was a 'mass murderer', a charge that often accompanies criticism of his racial views. Historians still debate whether his attitude to the Bengal famine of 1943–44 was callous or whether, even though the Allies were desperately stretched, he did what he could and that his actions saved lives. But the idea that he was a mass murderer, either in Bengal or in the Middle East where he ordered gas to be used, is a wild one.

A proper and rigorous account of Churchill's life reveals him to be a flawed person with erratic judgment, but his greatness remains intact. And no one need fear acknowledging the truth. But there is something else at play, something beyond Churchill. It is hard for one generation not to be irritated when its ideas and assumptions are challenged by the new generation. We think we have done our best to reach an enlightened view of the world and it can be annoying to have our heroes and values questioned.

This irritation is a feeling profoundly to be resisted. Because questioning values and re-examining our heroes is how we make progress and how we learn. Even if Churchill's views were not merely standard for his age and background but actually universal that would not exempt them from criticism. Indeed, it would make the need for criticism more urgent. We learn something when we appreciate that among those common views were attitudes that were powerful, shaped the modern world and were wrong.

To make progress through robust debate among free people and never to be afraid to say what needs saying – that was the real meaning of the victory Churchill won.

Muhammad Ali . . . The boxer could sting like an extremist

The champion was capable of great humanity, but
he couldn't see that racial integration was a goal
worth striving for

This column after the death of the famous boxer
produced an email to the paper from the wonderful chat
show host Michael Parkinson who conducted iconic
interviews with Ali.

He very kindly said he was a fan of the column in
general and had particularly enjoyed this one. 'I read Daniel
Finkelstein's piece in *The Times* and it underscored my
belief that in our sorrow at the death of the great athlete
we should not attempt to deify a man who, like all of us,
is a valuable human being . . . Tell Daniel I agree with
every word he has written and I can attest to the fact that
in the unlikely event of any one of my interviews with
Ali being repeated at the present time he would have been
arrested as he left the studio for making racist remarks. No,
he wasn't perfect but as an athlete and an entertainer he
gave us lasting memories.'

Everything in Moderation

8 June 2016

Mr Yacub was born 6,600 years ago, had an unusually large cranium and was seriously bad news. So bad, indeed, that he was exiled, together with 59,999 followers, to the island of Patmos in the Aegean. It was here that he launched his plan to kill off his fellow black men and create a white 'devil race'.

With thin blood, weak bones, small brains and 'incapable of righteousness' the blue-eyed devils nevertheless eventually became dominant. They imported slaves from Africa and force-fed them swine.

Soon, however, a wheel-shaped, half-mile-wide spacecraft will come to redeem mankind. The mother plane, piloted by the finest black men using psychic power, will first drop leaflets telling the righteous where to hide. Then a hundred planes will leave the mother and bomb Earth until only the righteous are left. After 1,000 years, Earth will be cool enough for the black man to build a new civilisation.

So, in any case, goes the teaching of Elijah Muhammad, leader of the Nation of Islam and messenger of the incarnation of Allah. And it was to this doctrine that the new heavyweight boxing champion of the world, Cassius Clay, announced himself a convert the day after he stopped Sonny Liston before the seventh round.

In the week in which the genius – the dazzling wit, the brilliant sportsmanship, the sheer beauty – of the Greatest is being justly lauded, it is worth spending a few moments considering what the man believed.

The problem with the Nation of Islam was not just that its doctrine was eccentric. Most religious doctrine advances intellectually challenging accounts of history. The problem was that it was an unpleasant cult.

Within days of joining in 1964, Clay found himself in a tug of war between Elijah Muhammad and Malcolm X, a minister of the Nation and its best-known public figure. Malcolm refused to bow his knee to the leader, who he knew was preaching sexual morality while impregnating his secretaries. Elijah was determined to end this insubordination. Both wanted control of Clay, the new African-American hero.

Elijah Muhammad won. He renamed Clay Muhammad Ali and demanded and received fealty. Ali cut off Malcolm X, once his close friend, without a further word. Within a year Malcolm had been gunned down by other members of the cult determined to end his insurrection. Ali said nothing. And when other dissidents were beaten almost to death, Ali claimed he had hardly known them.

As well as being a violent sect, the Nation of Islam was also racist. When Ali declared his conversion, the only white politician to lend him support was the leading segregationist Senator Richard Russell of Georgia. He shared the Nation's dislike of integration. The Nation kept in touch with the Ku Klux Klan, discussing their common vision of a racially divided America.

Indeed, Ali addressed a Klan rally and was cheered as he told them that black women and white men should not marry. 'Bluebirds with bluebirds, pigeons with pigeons, eagles with eagles,' he said. It is disturbing to watch Ali's famous appearances on Michael Parkinson's BBC chat show and see him, on more than one programme, repeat his Klan attack on interracial marriage, employing virtually the same words.

The Nation of Islam was contemptuous of Dr Martin Luther King and the civil rights movement, regarding it as a pathetic, unmanly attempt to win approval from white people. Ali reacted strongly to Floyd Patterson's support for integration and the former champ's (admittedly pompous) claim to be fighting Ali to stand against the bigotry of the Nation. Ali dubbed him the 'Black White Hope' and turned up at Patterson's training camp before their bout with a bag of lettuce, calling Patterson a rabbit and shouting: 'You're nothing but an Uncle Tom negro, a white man's negro, a yellow negro.'

Patterson eventually forgave this but Ali's later opponent Joe Frazier never got over being called an ignorant Tom and the champion of the 'white power structure'.

The Nation's attitude to women also left a great deal to be desired. Ali had four wives and many other lovers. But he divorced his first spouse because she wouldn't dress as the Nation told her to. Ali told the divorce court that Sonji's desire to wear lipstick and a knee-length dress was 'lust to the eye and embarrassing to me'. He was asked by an interviewer: 'What if a Muslim woman wants to go out with non-Muslim blacks – or white men for that matter?' Ali replied: 'Then she dies. Kill her too.' The interview was with *Playboy* magazine.

It is hard to escape the idea that Ali, although capable of great consideration and humanity, attached himself to some very bad people and said and did some pretty bad things. But there is one thing missing from this account. And that is understanding.

There is a revealing tale in David Remnick's *King of the World*, one of the best books about Ali. He records an African-American member of Ali's entourage leaving the champ's bus to get some food in a southern restaurant. Ali tells him not to but he disobeys. In the restaurant, service is refused, even to the pugilist himself. And Ali is furious.

He is furious not with the restaurant but with his aide. He is the Greatest. He is King of the World. He isn't going to plead to be served. If white men don't want integration, he isn't going to go down on all fours and ask for it.

As the African-American essayist James Baldwin put it in 1962: 'The negro's past [was one] of rope, fire, torture, castration, infanticide, rape; death and humiliation; fear by day and night, fear as deep as the marrow of the bone; doubt that he was worthy of life, since everyone around him denied it; sorrow for his women, for his kinfolk, for his children, who needed his protection, and whom he could not protect.'

I'm afraid one must deprecate Ali's views but to fail to understand his position, his refusal to ask for integration with those who didn't want to integrate with him, is to demonstrate a lack of imagination.

As the British government prepares to set out its own strategy on Muslim integration, Ali's story teaches how easy it is to be taken in by people who preach and practise segregation and extremism. Perhaps, though, it also teaches that it is hard to get people to integrate with us if we don't show that we want to integrate with them.

John Major . . . They didn't listen to him then. They are now

Far from being hapless, John Major was a tough, skilful, underrated leader. His party ignores him again at its peril

Since leaving office, the reputation of my old boss Sir John Major has risen with every year. In the run-up to the 2015 election, Sir John made a measured speech supporting a referendum on EU membership and warning that it might be lost unless the EU took the threat seriously.

19 November 2014

At the party conference that followed his defeat in 1997, John Major made a brief appearance to thank the faithful. Just before he went on, he showed me the remarks he planned to make.

I noticed a line in them in which he accepted onto his own shoulders all the blame for the defeat. Naively, I told him that he might want to look again at the wording because if he said that, it would produce a loud 'No!' from the audience. He gave me one of his smiles and quietly said: 'I know.'

Sir John Major isn't quite who you think he is. The nice things you believe about him are right. He is courteous and kind, solicitous (a little touch on the arm, the questions about the family, the handwritten notes), he cares about other people, he is moderate and intelligent. Seventeen years after I stopped working for him, I remain loyal to him and combative on his behalf, because he is that sort of person.

Yet he is also, to an extent not sufficiently understood, very clear in what he thinks, mischievous, tough and politically savvy. He is a proper pro, in other words.

Last week the former Prime Minister made a speech in Berlin on Europe that demonstrated all these qualities – the ones you knew about and the ones, perhaps, you didn't.

It was a superbly crafted effort. It made a well judged emotional appeal to his German audience to help Britain in its efforts to reform the EU, it made clear Sir John's own support for membership and his positive feelings about immigrant communities, and while profoundly helpful to the current Prime Minister it never appeared a contrived effort just to be that. As my son would put it – 'skills!'

Which raises some questions. Sir John's ability is very obvious now. It's not just this speech. A very experienced political journalist said to me yesterday: 'Major is playing the ex-prime minister to perfection.' Yet he is not doing this with a political knack that he has just discovered. So given this, why was his coverage when in office often so bad? And are there lessons that can be learnt from it?

Before I answer this, let's pause for a second on the doorstep of the old Conservative Central Office in Smith Square.

There I was on 2 May 1997, in the small hours, waiting for my friend and leader to return from his constituency after one of the greatest political defeats in a hundred years. I always think of it as raining, though I know it can't have been. It was a miserable moment, and shocking, and Sir John and Norma showed greater fortitude than most of us.

You can't hope to revisit the arguments that were lost in that campaign and expect to win them. No matter how many times you replay the video of that night, the result will be the same at the end of it. We will all still be standing on the doorstep, defeated.

There were good reasons why the Conservative Party was turned out of office – reasons for which everyone in it bears some responsibility. So it is not my intention to argue with the verdict. I merely want to use what we know now to help us understand the past better and to see what it can tell us about the present.

The first point is that it is obvious that the strong media view of Sir John as grey and even out of his depth is quite wrong. This should have been clear at the time. After all, this was someone who largely through force of personality had managed in 1992, very much against the odds, to win an election victory as impressive as it was surprising.

Instead, every story about him was turned into one about the 'hapless' prime minister. A visit to a racing car factory, for instance, would be portrayed as a fiasco because there were no wheels on the automobiles (like the Tory campaign, geddit?). As if God arranges metaphors and as if nothing must be allowed to escape the confines of the simple narrative.

Something similar is happening now to Ed Miliband. I do not wish to see Mr Miliband as prime minister. I have profound political disagreements with him. Yet I wince when he does simple, human and innocuous things (eating a sandwich, putting a couple of coins in a beggar's proffered cup, misspelling a word on Twitter), and these are linked together into a narrative about his leadership.

Part of the reason for Sir John's grey image was the suggestion that his politics were grey. There was an idea that because Sir John was a moderate, his 'prosaic' ideas could not match up to the big ideas of Margaret Thatcher.

Yet he won in 1992 – something Mrs Thatcher would not have done – precisely because there is a lot to be said for small, grounded, moderate ideas. He offered safety and reassurance, which are attractive and valuable and altogether underrated by political observers who prefer excitement and vision.

And then there is the central point. John Major was not a weak politician, pushed here and there by people with stronger positions. He has strong and coherent views. Every one of his advisers will tell you that he can be epically stubborn.

His weakness was in his position. The right simply became unmanageable, refusing to accept his authority as leader even after he had put it to the test in a second leadership contest.

They helped to destroy his government from the inside. People then developed their own ideas on how to win the general election and their own campaign strategies that they were insistent upon implementing unilaterally if necessary.

On election day everyone lost, whether they were with Sir John or against him. Those who had indicated their willingness to treat with the Referendum Party or who courted the Eurosceptic press did just as badly as anyone. The self-indulgence yielded nothing but electoral disaster.

It is by no means obvious that the party has learnt this lesson. Some Tories may try to repeat this nonsense all over again.

And that can only produce one outcome.

Nelson Mandela . . . Rising above victimhood

Mandela understood that saying 'it's tough being me' is self-destructive

Nelson Mandela died on 5 December 2013.

11 December 2013

Bill Clinton has a favourite Nelson Mandela story. Of course he does. The details change a little each time he relates it, but the thrust is the same. In 1998, after a visit to Robben Island, the American asked his fellow president this: 'When you were walking to freedom, didn't you hate them again?'

And Mandela replied with what Clinton calls 'wonderful candour': 'Of course I felt old anger rising up again, and fear. After all, I had not been free in twenty-seven years. But I knew that, when I drove away from the gate, if I continued to hate them, they would still have me. I wanted to be free, and so I let it go.'

These last few days have seen plenty of attempts to analyse Mandela, and the dominant points fall into two groups. There are those who stress his resistance, and those that stress his forgiveness. Clinton's story, I believe, reveals a bigger truth – that Mandela's forgiveness and resistance belonged together. That his forgiveness was a tool of his resistance.

Nelson Mandela rejected the greatest of human temptations. He refused to see himself as a victim, even though he was one. He realised that this status, the one most of us reach for first in any dispute, was enfeebling.

A consistent feature of his stories of defiance in jail and magnanimity upon release is his determination to be in control of the situation, to engage on his own terms. He did this even when, physically, this was virtually impossible.

It is the emerging science of human cooperation that shows how great Mandela's achievement is, by explaining why we desire to cast ourselves as the victim.

The work of Robert Trivers and others investigates why we cooperate with those who do not share our genes, and finds the answer in reciprocity – you help other people because you hope they will help you. This makes cooperation a good evolutionary survival strategy.

On one condition. We must be sure that we are not deceived by those who take our favours and do not return them. And we take a lot of trouble to ensure that this doesn't happen. We have developed all sorts of ways of recording the favours we have done to ensure that they are reciprocated – the importance of reciprocity is a plausible explanation for the origins of counting and writing.

One tool we use to help us to avoid deception is to cast ourselves as the victim, to establish the claim that we have done our bit, but justice has not been done to us. And to make this claim even more potent we become deeply convinced of it; our professions of victimhood seem more genuine because we have allowed it to become part of our identity.

Matthew Taylor of the Royal Society of Arts suggests convincingly that inside almost all of us is the thought that 'it's really tough being me' and we use this to excuse ourselves for lapses of behaviour. There are examples of this in public argument (self-pity is a strong part of the psychology of the Police Federation, for instance) and in private behaviour (people excuse themselves over-eating because they have had a hard day).

Casting yourself as the victim has power in any political argument, of course, and it is fascinating to watch people trade blows, desperate to grasp hold of victim status. A classic example is provided in the debate about political correctness, with one side arguing that they are the victims of prejudicial comments while the other believes they are the victims of the oppressive 'PC brigade'.

Yet whatever apparent power and temptation lie with the adoption of the identity of victimhood it is ultimately destructive. The African-American writer Shelby Steele argues that black leaders such as Al Sharpton and Jesse Jackson have sought to use victim status as a sort of political currency and that it has been a failure for everyone but the leaders themselves.

Steele accuses Jackson and Sharpton of seizing on every controversy – the shooting in Miami of young Trayvon Martin, for instance – as another example of white racist oppression that required them, as leaders, to be appeased, perhaps by the allocation of public or corporate funds, certainly by the allocation of political leverage and attention.

This approach enriched the leaders while impoverishing the African-American community. In his powerful book *The Content of Our Character*, Steele suggests that the development of an African-American middle class in America has been hindered by the destructive view that being poor and a victim was an essential part of real blackness.

The triumph of Barack Obama has been his rejection of the political strategy of exploiting white guilt in favour of one that Steele sees as offering white people a chance of redemption. It empowers the whole African-American community by casting it as capable of success rather than inevitably doomed by racism.

What is important here is not just the rejection of victimhood, but its rejection in a situation where it is perfectly justified. African-Americans have an absolute right to victim status, but Steele argues that those who claim it are wrong to do so, for their own sake.

In *Fear No Evil*, his prison memoir, the Soviet dissident Natan Sharansky explains how he survived his years in the punishment cells by solving logic puzzles in a book by the mathematician Martin Gardner that he had somehow obtained, and then playing similar mental games with his captors. He would guess who their witnesses were then pretend to have leaked information, toying with his KGB interrogators so that they ended up giving him information rather than the other way around.

The idea was always to remain on top. He knew that his life depended on this rejection of victimhood, on inner strength, on the belief, even in circumstances where it was almost impossible to believe, that one has the power to control one's life.

This Mandela understood too. He resisted because he would not let his captors control him. He forgave for the same reason. He was a victim of oppression who triumphed not just over his oppressors but over the very idea of being a victim.

Margaret Thatcher . . . It wasn't her that divided us

In the twenty years before her time in office, the nation endured far more conflict than in the twenty years after it

Margaret Thatcher died on 8 April 2013.

10 April 2013

In the dying days of the Heath administration, Sir William Armstrong, the head of the Civil Service and the Prime Minister's closest adviser, lay on the floor of the waiting room in 10 Downing Street, waving his arms wildly and babbling about Armageddon.

Sir William was using the room because he thought it the one place that wasn't bugged. He was, said a witness, talking in a way that was 'really quite mad'. A few days later he was sent for enforced rest at Lord Rothschild's villa in Barbados.

In the months leading up to Sir William's breakdown, the miners had begun their campaign for a 35 per cent pay increase on top of the large settlement that they had won only two years earlier, in defiance of the Government's pay policy and despite special concessions offered only to them. The Prime Minister had announced that industry would be confined to a three-day working week in order to conserve energy. The miners' response was to go on strike.

Yesterday's coverage of the death of Margaret Thatcher contained a great deal of comment about how divisive she was. It is obviously ridiculous to respond to someone saying 'I found her divisive' by saying 'Well, I didn't'. And in any case, it's not as if I can't see what they are driving at.

In my personal encounters, I found her formidable, impressive but hard to engage with. She would argue with some minor detail of what you had said until you had almost forgotten the point you were originally trying to make. And as I worked for John Major, and still feel personally and politically warm towards him, I thought I might say on his behalf (without asking him and in order that he need not say it) that her behaviour towards her successor was sub-optimal.

So I appreciate that she could be difficult and her way of approaching a political argument could scarcely be more different from mine. But the idea that the fault for the great division in British politics in the 1980s lay with her? No. Sorry, but no. Or perhaps that should be no, no, no.

By the time she became prime minister, the Government of Britain had begun to crack under the strain. Sir William's breakdown is part historical event, part metaphor.

Margaret Thatcher's promise on the doorstep of No. 10 – 'where there is discord, may we bring harmony' – was last night being intercut on the television news with footage of the miners' strike of 1984 to suggest that the opposite occurred. But this ignores the reason why she used these words. She made the promise – the words seemed the right ones to use – because when she took office Britain was already divided; there was already discord.

Inflationary economic policy, designed to produce full employment, had handed the trade unions great power.

Government needed them in order to try to control prices. And the behaviour of the Left, granted this power, was unconscionable. They made demand after demand, becoming increasingly difficult to deal with. The results were strikes, demonstrations, crises and hyperinflation.

Since the time of Harold Macmillan – with the exception of a short but unsuccessful burst of activity by Ted Heath – governments had sought to achieve harmony by conciliating the unions. But this had been a miserable failure.

Margaret Thatcher tried to end discord by defeating those causing it. She ended inflationary finance, ceased conciliation and then waited until the unions, led into battle by Arthur Scargill's miners, had overreached themselves and were defeated. Many people felt, and still feel, a burning anger at this but I argue that it worked. In the twenty years after Mrs Thatcher, Britain was less discordant and more harmonious than in the twenty years before her.

The politics of the Thatcher years were divisive but they couldn't be anything else. The Left wanted policies that were simply impractical and unacceptable. They could not be conceded, no matter how angry it made the unions that their demands were denied.

I was a member of the centrist Social Democratic Party during the miners' strike and argued then, as I do now, that the Government might have done more to help those in pit villages find alternative work. But this was not what the fight was about, nor what the miners asked for. They argued that there was no such thing as an uneconomic pit and that we should use deep-mined British coal, however difficult or expensive to extract.

Such a demand was impossible to yield to. Margaret Thatcher was not being divisive by refusing to yield to it. Yesterday Dave Hopper, general secretary of the Durham Miners' Association, said that the former Prime Minister's death on his birthday made it 'one of the best birthdays I have ever had'.

What sort of human being says something like that? The sort she was right to resist and we should be pleased was defeated. And the sort who takes all the blame for the brave miners he took down with him.

On the front page of the *Guardian* yesterday Mrs Thatcher was accused of sending 'Bobby Sands to an Irish hero's grave without a blink'. But Sands was not a hero and she didn't send him to his grave. He starved himself to death. The Government rightly didn't give in to his demands to be considered a political prisoner with extraordinary privileges, and he starved himself to death.

Was this a dreadful, tragic, chilling moment? Yes. But does it mean that it was Mrs Thatcher who divided politics? Only if one prefers the alternative, which was to surrender to something that should not be surrendered to. Bobby Sands divided politics.

Is this all just history? A few days ago, the MP Tom Watson published (I promise you that he did) the following on Twitter: 'Bad man @george_osborne: Booooooooo Booooooooo Booooooooo #booGideon.' Mr Watson is 46 years old. And a member of the Shadow Cabinet.

The Left's approach to the fiscal crisis has been inarticulate rage of this sort coupled with hyperbole and menace and threats of general strikes. Every reduction in spending has been resisted, the attacks invariably intemperate. And the thrust of the rhetoric, without irony, is that by cutting unaffordable welfare, and arguing for those cuts, it is Mr Osborne who is being divisive, bringing discord where there was harmony.

But the lesson of the Thatcher years is that what broke the harmony is borrowing more than we can afford, that what causes discord is unreasonably demanding that welfare be left untouched when it cannot conceivably be left untouched, and that what seems in the short run to be divisive may, in the long run, be the only way of restoring social stability.

Margaret Thatcher . . . The last prime minister of the Second World War

Margaret Thatcher's world view was formed by the fight against Hitler. Now her generation has finally left the stage

This column appeared on the day of Lady Thatcher's funeral.

17 April 2013

Margaret Thatcher did not like holidays. She was pleased, therefore, to learn that the German Chancellor, Helmut Kohl, was having his vacation close to hers. Good. She could get some work done.

Chancellor Kohl was not happy to be interrupted. Especially by her. But he felt he had no alternative but to agree to see the British Prime Minister. All right, he said, let's have a holiday meeting, and he turned up in his hiking shorts. She, of course, was in full battledress complete with capacious handbag.

After enough small talk to make Herr Kohl feel he had done his diplomatic duty, Mrs Thatcher said something like 'Right, let's get started' and reached into her bag and pulled out a stack of papers. The Chancellor went slightly pale and mumbled that, erm, he was awfully sorry but he had another important meeting scheduled.

So it was that Mrs Thatcher was left wandering – more of a sort of brisk trot really – with her advisers around a small holiday village at a total loose end. And so it was that her advisers spotted Helmut Kohl sitting all by himself in a cafe consuming a large cake.

The dreadful relationship between these two giants of politics, Kohl and Thatcher, can partly be explained by differences in temperament and partly by differences in ideology (while both were on the right, Chancellor Kohl would often emphasise in his speeches that he was a Christian democrat and not a conservative). But the best way of understanding it is the way to understand so much about Margaret Thatcher. The explanation is generational. This story that seems to be about holidays and cake is really about the Second World War.

Today, with gun carriage and muffled bells, Britain marks the passing of a generation. And Baroness Thatcher's funeral can perhaps, even by those who cannot reconcile themselves to her, be celebrated like that as a moment of national importance.

Mrs Thatcher was the last in a long procession of prime ministers who were born before the Second World War began, experienced it as an adult and allowed it to shape their politics. Churchill, Attlee, Churchill again, Eden, Macmillan, Douglas-Home, Wilson, Heath, Wilson again, Callaghan; the line ends with her.

Born in 1925, a wartime volunteer, a student contemporary of returning soldiers, politically active as early as 1935, married to an army captain ten years older who was mentioned twice in dispatches, Mrs Thatcher was, unlike those who came after her, a product of the fight against Hitler. In her memoirs she explains that it was infrequently understood how deeply the war had affected people like her.

The political battle that came to a head in the 1980s was,

above all else, about how to understand the lessons taught by the war. Did it teach, as so many believed, that the state must summon up the spirit of collective endeavour in peace and that planning was the future? Or that there was something special about the British people, as she believed, who must resist the sort of collectivism that produced fascism and Stalinism?

The socialist politician and economist Douglas Jay is famous for his extraordinary statement that 'the gentleman in Whitehall really does know better what is good for people than the people know themselves'. Less well known is that he preceded this with the words 'housewives as a whole cannot be trusted to buy all the right things'.

Immediately after the war, the Conservative Party rallied the housewife against the gentleman in Whitehall, became the party of the consumer against the party of the rationer and the producer. Margaret Thatcher's personal style, her clothes, her way of talking about the economy of the nation as if it was a household budget, are best seen as part of this.

Mrs Thatcher's role as the Iron Lady in the Cold War also resulted from her view of the battle against Hitler. She saw herself, quite explicitly, as avoiding the mistake of the Munich Agreement. In fact, more than that, she saw herself as eradicating the stain it had left. In 1990 when she addressed the Czechoslovak Federal Assembly, at last free again, she told members how she felt we had failed them and remembered 1938 with shame.

Margaret Thatcher and Helmut Kohl came from the same generation, old enough to experience the war, but with no experience of fighting in it. This meant that both saw the balance of power in Europe as the very greatest of issues. But it also produced two very different attitudes. For Kohl, the most important task in politics was to heal the scars of his youth. Germany should be reunited itself and should then create a united Europe in which Germany would be bound, unable once again to dominate or threaten the continent.

Mrs Thatcher also wanted to heal the scars of her youth – by never allowing Germany to assert itself, reunite or create a strong European federation in which it dominated.

After Mrs Thatcher fell – in fact, come to think of it, perhaps it was even the cause of her fall – the terms of reference in politics changed. The baby boomers took over: John Major, born in 1943, was at its very starting edge. The framework was set by the social revolution of the 1960s and the economic revolution of the 1980s (Mrs Thatcher's multiple election victories and the failure of socialism having settled the argument).

Many of the disputes that absorbed Mrs Thatcher's generation – should homosexuality be legal? Should the Government try to set supermarket prices? – now seem bizarre and the language and style antiquated. They are settled, over, done.

So today we are paying tribute to more than just a person, someone who was remarkable, and angular, and magnificent and difficult and even (to some, if not to me) terrible. We are paying tribute to an age and those who dominated it.

To those who fought the war or lived through it and came to create the peace.

I was recently 50 years old and on my birthday I reflected that all the luck that had deserted my parents and my grandparents in their youth had fallen to me. For I have lived my whole life in this great country, in the peace and stability that it offers its citizens.

And today I will think not just of Margaret Thatcher but of all those great prime ministers in that line, all of them in that extraordinary war generation. And, even though it is a Christian service and I am not a Christian, I will find myself, quietly, saying a prayer of thanks.

Brian Epstein . . . and the triumph of capitalism

It was his commercial flair that turned four musicians into a global phenomenon

This column appeared on the day that the entire Beatles back catalogue was reissued in digitally remastered form.

9 September 2009

When Brian Epstein died of an overdose of sleeping pills in the summer of 1967, he was only 32 years old. He was buried in Liverpool at the Long Lane Jewish Cemetery, mourned over by his doting mother Queenie. The Beatles, the group that Epstein had made famous, had to stay away. There would have been too many members of the press and too many fans. The rabbi told the congregation that 'Brian Epstein was a symbol of the malaise of our generation'.

It was an incredibly insensitive remark. Who says such a thing at the funeral of a 32-year-old? It was also very wrong. But it did reflect one faint glimmer of understanding. Epstein was indeed a symbol of his generation. And I think understanding that helps to understand both the Beatles and the 1960s. If you write the history of the 1960s with a bigger role in it for Brian Epstein, you write a different history of the 1960s and see the present differently.

In 1965, when the Beatles received the MBE, George Harrison quipped that the letters stood for 'Mr Brian Epstein'. But there hadn't been an insignia for the group's manager and his early death meant that there never would be one. It is easy to see why Harold Wilson hadn't added him to the list. He was just a suit, after all, not the talent.

Yet without Epstein there wouldn't have been the Beatles. Not as we know them, anyway. It is as simple as that.

When the lads were playing their lunchtime concerts at the Cavern Club in 1961 they were a fabulously tight and talented rock 'n' roll band. But that's all they were until Epstein offered to be their manager. It was only then that they properly became the Beatles.

He was the owner of a large local record store and Harry Epstein's boy, son of a wealthy businessman. And easily the most impressive person who had ever offered to be involved with them. Epstein transformed the Beatles into a professional showbusiness act. He put them in suits, protected their image, added theatrical touches to their stage shows, made sure they turned up on time.

Epstein had taste, an artistic feel. Although Queenie never accepted it, her son was gay, with an attraction to rough trade, and in love with his group, passionately so in John Lennon's case. His attempt to disguise his sexuality from his mother, which culminated in an absurd plan to marry the singer Alma Cogan, led him to breakdown and contributed to his death. But it also meant he understood the sexual power of the Beatles; he shared more than a little bit of the fan's hysteria. He helped the group to exploit it.

The Beatles weren't his only client. He had a knack for finding new talent – Cilla Black, for one – which rarely failed him. (Though it did once. When he was taken to see the young unknown Paul Simon in a dingy folk club, he rejected him. 'He's a bit small and Jewish looking,' he remarked.) Epstein acts spearheaded the British invasion of the United States and helped London to obtain its swinging reputation.

Some of his early business deals were a disaster, it has to be admitted. He basically gave away the publishing rights of the Beatles' songs and lost millions with a naive merchandising deal. Paul McCartney, surveying the damage years later, remarked that Epstein 'looked to his dad for business advice, and his dad knew how to run a furniture store in Liverpool'.

But Epstein's insistence on controlling the quality of the products associated with the Beatles name was a masterstroke. It is possible to argue that the group's entire success has rested upon this. And that it remains, even now, the central plank of the Beatles' commercial strategy and an important reason that they have attained iconic status.

Appreciating the role of Epstein allows one to appreciate that the Beatles are as much a triumph of commerce as of art. They were not merely brilliant musicians fusing avant-garde influences with rhythm-and-blues music. They were a showbiz act managed by an inspired entrepreneur. They weren't simply class rebels against the Establishment, they were the brilliant product of capitalist enterprise, the early pioneers of globalisation.

Money normally enters the Beatles story only as a reason for their demise. When Epstein died, the group famously began to argue about management and contracts and cash. Born out of music, killed by money, that's the usual story.

However, Tony Bramwell provides a different account. Bramwell was friends with all the group, present when Paul met John; he was Brian Epstein's right-hand man, fixing gigs for Jimi Hendrix and mixing drinks with the Rolling Stones; and was still there when Phil Spector produced *Let It Be*. In his recent book *Magical Mystery Tours* (a wonderful insider memoir) Bramwell argues that it was penal tax rates that helped to destroy the group's cohesion.

First told to give away vast amounts to avoid tax bills – which they did in a series of madcap ventures, offering money to any old person who dropped by with a demo tape – then told they had to make £120,000 in order to keep just £10,000. Soon their finances were in chaos and their energy sapped, as nutters beseiged Apple HQ pressing tapes on them. They also ran a clothes shop as a tax dodge.

Bramwell blames Harold Wilson, the Prime Minister, directly. 'There were enough new regulations and red tape to tie up free enterprise for years . . . One minute Swinging London was like a giant theme park, the envy of the world, then they – Wilson and his gang – closed it down. It was as if they went out and stamped on it.'

The reason why the influence of the 1960s endures is because it was the dawn of modern consumer capitalism. It was this culture – of commerce and consumption – rather than the counter-culture that made the era and now shapes our time. And of this era, Brian Epstein was a symbol.

David Bowie . . . Rock's great rebel owed it all to capitalism

David Bowie showed us that, far from being polar opposites, Western consumerism and creativity go hand-in-hand

David Bowie died on 10 January 2016. When this article (which continues the argument I made over Brian Epstein) appeared, I received the following email from Laurence Myers:

In 1970 I signed David Bowie for management to my company Gem Management, and for records to my production company Gem Productions, which issued Hunky Dory and Ziggy Stardust through a distribution deal I made with RCA Records. My personal Hunky Dory and Ziggy gold discs are on the wall above my desk as I write.

David's motivation was commercial success and he crafted his art to please his audience. I am not knocking this; in addition to my belief in his unique talent, it is one of the reasons I risked a considerable sum of my own money to help develop him. The world is littered with unsuccessful talented artists who refused to 'sell out'. I am

not knocking them either, other than those who are bitter
in their belief that the music industry conspired against
them. David admired a clichéd sign on my desk saying
'Art for art's sake. Money for fucks sake'.

13 January 2016

In 1998, David Bowie completed the famous Proust question-
naire, first filled out by the novelist and since completed by
dozens of artists and writers – Allen Ginsberg, Hedy Lamarr,
Gore Vidal and so on.

Bowie's answers were characteristic. Often witty ('Which
living person do you most admire?' 'Elvis'), always interesting
('What is your idea of perfect happiness?' 'Reading'), sometimes
self-consciously clever to the point of pretentiousness but not
quite beyond ('What is your current state of mind?' 'Pregnant?').

The most revealing, however, was in his response to the
question 'Who are your heroes in real life?' Proust had cited
Émile Boutroux, the nineteenth-century historian of philosophy.
Bowie replied, truthfully and insightfully: 'The consumer'.

David Bowie – undoubtedly one of the artistic geniuses of
the past fifty years – was the great producer and the great
product of consumer capitalism. The man who understood its
possibilities, knew what people would take and would buy, saw
just how far he could push things. He was always on the lookout
for the next look, always seeking the hit of another pop hit.
He was the man who sold the world.

He was subversive because capitalism is subversive, over-
turning the status quo, restless, and profoundly democratic. He
knew that the taste of every teenager with enough money to
buy a 45rpm single could define art, challenge received wisdom
and force big corporations and the Establishment to do their
bidding.

The Richard Curtis film *The Boat That Rocked* provides a fine example of the conventional view of rock and its relationship to society. It portrays the effort of the stuffy Establishment to prevent pirate radio. It begins by telling the audience how little rock music was allowed on the BBC in the mid-1960s and pushes the fallacy that pirate pop was being stamped on because it was rebellious.

In fact the restrictions on pop music were the result of the insistence by the Musicians' Union that radio should not play too much recorded music, because it takes work away from live musicians. And the campaign to close pirate radio was a state initiative, supported by Tony Benn, to prevent commercial enterprises from challenging the Government's broadcasting monopoly. The resistance of the unions and the state monopolists was futile.

Commerce is and always has been the engine of rock music. And rock was never the counter-culture, it was the culture. It didn't rebel against the postwar era, it created it.

On Monday there were many references to David Bowie's appearance on *Top of the Pops* singing 'Starman' for the first time, a wonderful song, wonderfully performed. People talked about how that moment changed their lives and of the challenge it represented. Yet the *Top of the Pops* performance was not in fact 'Starman''s TV debut. That came three weeks earlier on the children's teatime television show *Lift Off with Ayshea*, appearing after a puppet owl called Ollie Beak.

Ziggy Stardust is a brilliant artistic creation and a challenge to conventional ideas of sexuality. But its creator primarily saw it as a way to score another teen hit that would hand him the initiative as he duked it out with Marc Bolan to be the biggest star with teen consumers.

His early career saw him picking up and discarding managers, record companies and musical styles as he sought to break through. His first two famous releases were both novelty singles – 'The Laughing Gnome' and 'Space Oddity', released to take advantage of the hype surrounding the moon landing (although the Americans belatedly realised that the song portrayed a space calamity and edited it to almost nothing by removing anything negative about Major Tom's journey).

His songs are scrutinised for their hidden meanings, and sometimes yield them, but when Bowie recorded 'The Bewlay Brothers' for his *Hunky Dory* album he quietly said to the producer: 'Don't listen to the words, they don't mean anything. I've just written them for the American market, they like this kind of thing.'

Bowie liberated the mind and trampled on convention, and is therefore a kind of political hero. But his political references were often embarrassing. Not many fans (me among them) wish to dwell on his statement that 'Britain could benefit from a fascist leader. After all, fascism is really nationalism.' Or his assertion that 'Hitler was the first pop star'. Or the open fascination with Nazi images that inspired him during his Berlin phase. All of which he later acknowledged was 'ghastly stuff'.

Even his bisexuality he later dismissed as a pose, complaining about the commercial damage the image had done him in America.

Rock music is often said to be inspired by a desire to leave the dreary suburbs. But when Bowie first made it big, he used the money to move to a large house in Beckenham, just as in their time the Beatles bought mock-Tudor homes in Weybridge. Rock music was their route to the suburbs, not from them.

John Lennon spent his last few years baking bread and looking after his son. Bowie gave up drugs, didn't drink, read *The Times* and took his daughter to school. When asked why he needed so much money he said that part of the reason was that 'being working class, I feel there's never enough to leave my family'.

So Bowie was a revolutionary not because of his desire to lead a social movement, but because of his eye for the main chance. He wanted to be a star and if a brave new world was created, it was a by-product. He was possible because in a consumer capitalist society nobody can ultimately stop anybody doing anything. He understood this better than almost all his contemporaries.

His commercial instinct, like his musical one, was always ahead of others. In the 1990s he grasped what the internet would mean to consumer taste, making the artist follow the audience rather than vice versa. And his famous bond deal on the rights to his music blazed a trail that others followed.

To say that David Bowie created a product – himself – and then recreated it to suit changing tastes is not to belittle him. It is simply to argue that pop, with Bowie at its head, saw that consumerism isn't base and philistine. It can be the ally of artistic endeavour. Commerce, liberty and art, arm-in-arm. That was the great David Bowie.

William Hague . . .
His two faces are the two
faces of Toryism

Cameron's reshuffle and Hague's retirement
expose the tension between partisan, traditional
Conservatism and its pragmatic, open-minded
opposite

Preparing for the 2015 general election David Cameron
reshuffled his Cabinet in the summer of 2014. Controversially, Michael Gove was moved from the Education
Department to become chief whip. And William Hague,
another old boss of mine, stepped down from the Foreign
Office and announced that he would spend a year
campaigning for a new Tory term and then leave politics.

16 July 2014

In an idle moment years ago in an Indian restaurant near
Catterick garrison, I was eating a curry with the Tory leadership
team when someone mentioned a date far in the future. 'A
Monday,' responded William Hague casually.

'A what?' I asked incredulously. 'A Monday,' he repeated. So

I began to test him. 26 March 2044? 'A Friday.' 14 October 2031? 'A Tuesday.' I checked. He was correct. So I congratulated him and said: 'Just one more thing, William. Brilliant though the ability you have demonstrated might be, I want you to make me a promise. Never ever, ever do that trick in public. We're in enough trouble as it is.'

So we never talked about it again. I suppose it's all right to reveal it now.

I can't pretend to a neutral view of William Hague. I worked for him throughout his leadership, spending hours every day in his office. He became a friend. Despite four difficult years and hundreds of meetings, I can't think of a single anecdote that would make you think less of him as a person. I admire and like him hugely.

I suppose one appreciates most in others what one is least capable of oneself. In his case it is his eerie calmness under almost any amount of pressure. This is linked both to (an entirely justified) confidence in his own intellectual abilities and a well-developed sense of humour, which prevents him taking either himself or difficult situations more seriously than they merit. My main memory of working for him will be the laughing.

My perfect William Hague story? George Osborne, in the opposition leader's office, holding up the front page of a newspaper in which William was pictured, sitting next to Jacques Chirac. 'Did you ever imagine,' George said, 'that one day, here you would be, on the front page of the *Financial Times*, sitting next to the president of France?' William gave him a puzzled look and replied: 'Of course I did, you idiot.'

Yet while proximity may rob me of critical distance, it has a compensating advantage. It means that I have spent a great deal of time thinking about the topic of William Hague. Perhaps you will let me share the proceeds of that thinking with you. I think it has broader relevance to the Tory party and to this reshuffle.

I have always felt that there are two William Hagues. One is the Rotherham William Hague. The Yorkshire Conservative politician, brilliant parliamentary debater, partisan party man, political hobbyist still fighting the municipal socialism of the 1970s.

This Hague is at home with the nostalgia of the Conservative Party, loves party conferences and wants them always to be in Blackpool. This Hague is a parliamentary and political traditionalist, can't resist a robust political joke and is at one with the Tory activists he addressed when he was 16.

This is the Hague who gets out of London whenever he can, trying never to spend a weekend there. The populist 'right-wing' Hague who said of his policy document that 'if *The Common Sense Revolution* could walk and talk, it would look like Ann Widdecombe'.

Then there is the other William Hague, the Hague with a first from Oxford, who worked for the blue-riband management consultant McKinsey and went to INSEAD, one of the world's top business schools. The INSEAD Hague is a cool pragmatist, so reliant on intellect rather than emotion that his team disguised its extent, as I did with his date trick.

This Hague is ministerially minded, a problem solver who was thought a model boss by civil servants. He is moderate and recognises the electoral case for Conservative change. The common-sense revolution of this Hague looks like Angelina Jolie.

The tension between those two Hagues was there throughout his leadership and will never be completely resolved. The past four years have belonged to INSEAD Hague. I suspect that in the next year we will see more of Rotherham Hague, as he stomps the country, attacking Ed Miliband, cheering up 'the troops'.

It is not, however, a tension confined to him. One reason Hague has been such a successful party figure is that he reflects its ambiguity so well.

To some extent, of course, the tension between INSEAD and Rotherham Hague is present in all politicians as they oscillate between being warriors and managers. Michael Gove is a good example. The most courteous (very), evidence-based, clearest-thinking manager on the one hand, a pugnacious (very) political street fighter on the other. It has clearly been determined that it would be better to use his pugnacity in a party role, sensing that it wasn't an advantage at Education. This is a disappointing conclusion and a disappointing outcome.

There is also the Tory tension between its traditions and the modern world. This, too, is unresolved. Those who look for a consistent ideological theme in the reshuffle will struggle. The changes represent a generational shift but don't really alter the political composition.

An interesting example of the tension is provided by Nicky Morgan, the new education secretary, who in some ways is a textbook moderniser – warning against Conservatives talking 'about what we hate' all the time, floating the idea of all-women shortlists. Yet at the same time, she voted against same-sex marriage.

Similarly Philip Hammond, the new foreign secretary, is a traditional Tory figure with strong views, yet has been promoted mainly because he is a pragmatic, safe manager.

The truth is that this tension will never be removed, because it is there deep in Conservatism. David Willetts, now departing but one of the best ministers of the past four years and among the most influential Tories of the past two decades, has long argued that there are two strands to Tory thinking.

There is the open, free-market, international Conservatism – INSEAD Toryism if you like – and there is a Rotherham Conservatism, protective of traditions and the nation state and existing institutions. They are both part of the Tory identity and always will be. Yet they are sometimes uneasy bedfellows.

And so we roll on to election day, 7 May 2015. A Thursday.

Luciana Berger . . . Her exit was a distressing sight

For all her bravery and grace, it is profoundly
upsetting that a Jewish woman has been hounded
out of the Labour Party

On 18 February 2019 a number of Labour MPs announced
they were leaving the party to form an independent group.
Prominent among them was Luciana Berger.

20 February 2019

I cried. Now, I admit I cry easily. I tear up when friends tell
me they are going to have a baby. I welled up when I saw Ringo
Starr join Paul McCartney on stage.

But this time it was different. When I watched Luciana Berger
deliver her speech resigning from the Labour Party I cried because
of its integrity and bravery and grace. And I cried because in
my entire adult life what happened yesterday is one of the lowest,
most dispiriting political moments for British Jews. I cried
because I despair at what has happened. I cried because I don't
think it is over.

There is so much to say about the creation of a new political
grouping. So much about its profound effect on Labour. So

much about the challenge to Tory moderates. So much about Brexit and about the history of the SDP and about, well anyway, so much. Yet every time I think about all these sophisticated points I find myself struggling to see beyond one simple one.

Yesterday, in modern Britain, a young woman was driven out of Britain's biggest progressive party by people who hate Jews and by other people who won't do anything about it. Set against that, so much else just seems blah.

I attend meetings of the Jewish community where we discuss the problem and what to do about it. The room is full of dynamic people used to getting things done. There's plenty of strength there and determination and brains too. Yet we all feel numb.

How did this happen? How can we stop it? There's not a person in the room without relatives who have been killed or exiled by anti-Semites. So there isn't just numbness. There is fear. When I came home from the last one, I just shook my head rather than explaining what we talked about. I didn't want to bring it into the house.

What really set me off when I watched Luciana speak was when she started by accidentally referring to herself as a Labour MP. It was something she had done at hundreds of meetings and it just slipped out. That little mistake spoke to the years she has spent campaigning for the party, her years of comrade-ship and devotion to the cause. It spoke of her ambition, which surely she had, and has probably had since she was in college, to be a minister in a Labour government serving the cause. She has the talent for that and more.

And now it's over. She won't get back in for Liverpool Wavertree, I suppose. She may not be able to get back into Parliament at all, even if her venture soars. So what we saw was raw courage as well, I think, as utter despair.

I found that very moving. She couldn't stay any more in a party where her own constituency chairman appears on a crackpot conspiracy-theory talk show claiming the Rothschilds finance neo-liberalism while internet viewers watch anti-Semitic images pass across the screen. And nobody does a thing about it.

John McDonnell said yesterday that his party needs to have 'a mammoth, massive listening exercise'. Well OK. Let's start with this. There's plenty more, but here's a couple of things.

Mr McDonnell is president of the Labour Representation Committee. It's very much his baby and he has been involved in it from the beginning. Within the last fortnight, he was reappointed to his post. Along with him, a group of officers were elected that include Jackie Walker, who will be responsible for the LRC's work on ethnic minorities.

Ms Walker is one of the leading voices on the left who argue that complaints about anti-Semitism are a Zionist-inspired witch-hunt concocted to protect dissident Labour MPs from criticism. 'Look at Luciana Berger – they think they are untouchable. And they're right,' she told the LRC conference earlier this month.

She has stepped up this campaign ever since she ran into trouble for calling Jews 'chief financiers' of the slave trade. This slur is an invention of the Nation of Islam, the political vehicle of Louis Farrakhan, one of America's leading anti-Semites. If John McDonnell wants to listen, he can listen to this: tell Jackie Walker that either she goes as a board member of the LRC or you will go as president. Serve with her in charge of 'equalities' and all your words are meaningless.

And if he wants to listen, he can also ask Jeremy Corbyn why he hasn't had a meeting with Luciana Berger since 2017.

Last March the Jewish community held a rally in Parliament Square at which Luciana spoke. There were quite a few speeches but I particularly remember hers because it was eloquent and had moral force. And because it finished with an appeal I thought touchingly ridiculous. She urged us all to join the Labour Party.

We were all standing outside with banners and loudspeakers protesting against the way Jew-hatred had grown inside Labour and the leadership was doing nothing about it. It wasn't the most propitious moment for a membership drive, let me put it that way. As she spoke, a friend of mine turned to me and said, 'I might just do it, right now I reckon they'd give me a good rate.'

Yet Luciana was still fighting. She still wanted to make it work. She probably knew deep down that it wouldn't work but she hadn't given up. How, in these circumstances, and given all the things that were happening, could the leader of the party have failed to meet her?

On *Newsnight* on Monday, the shadow education secretary Angela Rayner said that Jeremy Corbyn had 'reached out' to Luciana. How? By ESP? I think what Angela Rayner meant is that she'd like to believe that Mr Corbyn had reached out to Luciana, because that is the sort of person she imagines that he is. Never mind that in fact he didn't, because he isn't.

So if you are going to listen, John McDonnell, then you have to accept that Mr Corbyn has been part of the problem. That he has repeatedly met anti-Semites and provided succour for them, and that he has done nothing remotely sufficient to tackle the problem.

There has been a fair deal of talk since Monday about the SDP and whether it was a success. We can debate that for ever but in one respect the SDP's success was undeniable. Joining meant that its members didn't have to stand up for things they thought unconscionable, or promote as potential prime ministers people they thought unfit for office.

That is Luciana's position now. And I am happy for her freedom, truly I am. But as a Jew it was a desperate day.

Donald Trump . . . and the pastor who propelled him to the top

A belief in positive thinking is key to the tycoon's business success and explains the breadth of his appeal to voters

Donald Trump won the United States presidential election held on 8 November 2016.

16 November 2016

There have been three great influences on the professional life of Donald J. Trump, president-elect of the United States of America.

The first was his father, Fred Trump, the man he followed into the property business. Fred was Donald's bank, lending him money and guaranteeing his loans, his network, providing vital political contacts and a name that opened doors, and his spur. The desire to outdo his dad drove Trump to become a builder of Manhattan towers rather than suburban homes.

The second was his lawyer. Trump met Roy Cohn in a nightclub and engaged him to fight a lawsuit accusing the Trumps of racial discrimination. Cohn became much more. He had been Joe McCarthy's aide, the man whose antics had inspired the famous rebuke to the Senator by army counsel Joseph Welch: 'Have you no sense of decency, sir?' And he had since become attorney for mafia bosses such as 'Fat Tony' Salerno and Carmine 'The Cigar' Galante.

Cohn became Trump's shield but also his tutor. He taught the property developer how attack can be the best form of defence and how to use publicity as a weapon. He passed on his 'take no prisoners' approach to his client.

And then there was the third influence. Norman Vincent Peale, the pastor of New York's Marble Collegiate Church, the man who officiated at the 1977 wedding of Donald and Ivana.

Most of the analysis of Mr Trump's victory stresses the strong political appeal of his populist message, the weaknesses of Hillary Clinton's candidacy or Mr Trump's misdemeanours. And each of these is worthy of study. Yet it is important not to ignore another factor in his victory – his attraction as a candidate and a person. And to understand that, it's worth learning a bit more about Peale.

Norman Vincent Peale was no ordinary pastor. He was an exceptional orator, a gifted community leader and, most important of all, a bestselling author. In 1952 he published a book called *The Power of Positive Thinking,* which sold millions of copies. It also launched the positive-thinking movement with its motivational speakers, its role in business morale conferences and its shelves of self-help books.

Positive thinking has become one of the most influential modern ideas, particularly in America. It is hugely popular and many find it deeply convincing. The first chapter of Peale's bestseller is called 'Believe in Yourself' and begins like this: 'Believe in yourself! Have faith in your abilities! Without a humble but reasonable confidence in your own powers you cannot be successful or happy.'

Positive thinkers accompany this belief with another. You can make things happen by wanting them to happen. You can change things by believing strongly enough in change. If change does not happen it just means that you didn't believe it enough. Or in the words of Doug Cox, a motivational speaker and Trump favourite, hired to gee up the crowd at his birthday party: 'We are never given a dream . . . without the power to make that dream come true.'

Peale is, along with Fred, the only person Donald Trump openly calls a mentor (since Cohn was disbarred shortly before dying of Aids-related illness after years spent opposing homosexuality, the president-elect is more sparing in his references to him). In his campaign book *Crippled America*, Trump writes that after hearing Peale speak, 'I would literally leave that church feeling like I could listen to another three sermons.'

Peale, he said, 'would install a very positive feeling about God that also made me feel positive about myself'. As Trump put it in the early 1980s: 'The mind can overcome any obstacle. I never think of the negative.' The business career, the politics and even the boasting (Trump overlooked the requirement to be humble) all bear the imprint of Peale and of the positive-thinking movement.

'There is nobody like me. Nobody.' Who on earth would say something like that? Let alone write it down in a campaign book. The answer is someone who believes that saying it makes it come true. Someone who thinks that you have to believe in yourself in order to be happy and successful.

Ditto: 'I'm rich. I mean, I'm really rich. I've earned more money than even I thought I would – and I've had some pretty big dreams.' Positive thinking teaches that you can believe yourself rich.

Mr Trump now talks of how everyone will be so, so proud, of how things are going to be just beautiful and of how, for instance, Britain is a 'very, very special place' for him. He puts things like this because positive thinkers believe that the superlatives help make it happen.

You can see this thinking in his policy platform too. He is just going to make things happen. He will get rid of illegal immigrants by deporting them and building a wall (he is good at construction); he will solve the healthcare problem by locking the experts in a room until they have a solution; he will create jobs; he will destroy Isis; he will get a better trade deal out of China; he will stop Iran building nuclear weapons.

There is very little on how he will do any of this. Mainly it is because there is nobody like me (nobody). With enough imagination, imagination becomes reality.

The trouble is that it doesn't. Positive thinkers are simply wrong to argue that the mind can overcome any obstacle. We often have dreams without the power to make the dreams come true. It is utter nonsense to suggest otherwise.

In *Trump Revealed*, Michael Kranish and Marc Fisher tell the tale of their subject's investment in casinos in Atlantic City. When critics questioned whether there was a market, he brushed them off. The critics weren't thinking big enough. These would be 'monster' properties, he'd made a 'fantastic deal', he said. The casino business went bankrupt. All the positive thoughts in the world couldn't save it.

Donald Trump started teasing people that he would run for president before 2000. And from the moment he did, he was a strong candidate. He was one of the top ten most admired Americans in Gallup polling and he led presidential polls when people were asked. He is a star. Almost a cartoon of success and dynamism. Why not the presidency? It's just that few people believed either he or the voters were serious about it. It turned out they both were.

The idea that a positive-thinking chief executive type can dream America and the world out of its problems may be flawed but it is very seductive, quite apart from the political attractions of Trump's nationalism.

And I suppose Trump's positive thinking does have this to be said for it. He said: 'I'm going to be president.' And now he is.

Theresa May . . . and how history will see her

Everything depends on how her successor does now

This article was written on the day Mrs May announced she would be leaving office in July.

25 May 2019

Theresa May's premiership has ended in failure. Nobody can seriously argue with this conclusion however well disposed they are to her. No historian, however revisionist, is likely to revise that.

She set herself the task of delivering Brexit smoothly and on time and she hasn't. She committed herself to an ambitious attempt to take the problems of those just about managing and she hasn't been able to make much headway. She sees herself as someone who profoundly understands the Conservative Party, yet she has been deserted by its members and its voters.

Much more open to debate will be the reasons for that failure. There are two broad and conflicting accounts.

The first is damning. She was in above her head. Elected because all the more suitable candidates eliminated themselves, she never had quite what it takes to be prime minister.

Extremely reserved, what some people interpreted as a tough-minded self-discipline was in fact a crippling lack of self-belief. As a result she was dominated by her own political advisers and incapable of building strong relations with her parliamentary colleagues. It was impossible to know what, or even if, she was thinking.

She became, by default, the choice of everyone as leader and that quickly turned into being the leader of no one. Her decision to dispose of George Osborne and announce that Brexit meant Brexit cut her off from her more natural supporters in the centre and left of the party. Yet she couldn't see that the right would never trust her. She ended politically friendless and that was her fault.

Having promised MPs she would not call an election she then called one and more or less lost it. MPs would have forgiven the first of these let-downs if it hadn't been for the more-or-less-lost-it bit.

The election setback was entirely her fault, the result of wooden performances and a disastrous manifesto that she approved.

The moment she lost her majority it was obvious that any deal she struck with the EU would have a hard time getting through Parliament. Yet for two long years she ploughed ahead without regard to how to assemble a majority for any deal either in the Commons or outside.

And every day she showed her greatest failing – a total lack of political imagination. The cunning of a Wilson, the emotional appeal of a Blair, it was all beyond her. So she kept on keeping on until keeping on became impossible. And then she stopped.

There is, however, a more generous assessment that could be made.

Like any politician Mrs May has weaknesses as well as strengths. She certainly keeps her views to herself, while not cold she is undoubtedly shy and while not friendless she lacks a following of her own.

Yet being self-contained and letting others do the talking can be a big advantage in politics. It's absurd to suggest that she became prime minister by accident. Nobody becomes prime minister by accident. Staying above faction and maintaining extraordinary self-discipline are political skills. She demonstrated these skills while others did not. That's why she reached No. 10.

While it is easy now to argue that she should not have announced red lines and shouldn't have said that Brexit meant Brexit what other alternative was there? There wasn't any other tenable response to the referendum result, certainly not for a Tory leader.

And calling the election was a smart move. Everyone agreed that at the time. In fact, it is the answer to those who accuse Mrs May of being incapable of creativity and surprise and incapable of assessing her own position realistically. She saw that she needed a bigger majority and struck out boldly to get one.

Not even a generous account, not even her own account, will be able to describe her election performance as a triumph. But she managed to stay on the horse, while other riders would have come off.

In that period she has shown three characteristics of leadership that are highly praiseworthy. She has been realistic, adapting her plans to accommodate European and parliamentary realities. She has been tough, keeping on going even when the problems seem overwhelming and the job thankless. And she has shown a sense of duty, being willing to endure humiliation and attack to do what she feels is the right thing for the country.

Yes, it has ended in failure. But that is because the country is deeply split, her party is deeply split and the parliamentary situation deteriorated from forbiddingly difficult to completely impossible. Relentlessness, her chosen political weapon, did not work in the end, but it wasn't a stupid choice.

So which of these accounts will ultimately dominate what is said about Theresa May by historians? It all depends on how her successors fare.

The Tory party is almost certainly going to test the idea that there was an alternative to Mrs May's approach. Rally Leave voters and Conservative MPs, seek a new deal from the EU and use a genuine determination to leave with no deal as a way of wringing concessions on the issue of the backstop.

If this fails, challenge Parliament to accept no deal and hold an election if they baulk. Pit a no-deal Conservative Party against a Labour Party offering a second referendum.

Should this fail, or should her successor stumble while trying it, Theresa May's own failings may seem more understandable and the judgment of them might be less harsh. Similarly should Remainers force a second referendum and lose it, they may repent of the decision not to have accepted the deal she negotiated. And her own resistance to the idea may look more sage than stubborn.

The May premiership is not a period in the political history of Britain that very many people will look back on with great affection. It has been a period of stalemate and frustration and division. But it's too early to be sure what the judgment will be of her own role in this. Was it her fault? Or did she do her best in very trying circumstances?

Jeremy Thorpe . . .
The extraordinary story
of a fantasist

The former Liberal leader believed he was a man
of destiny. He was also a showman who loved
celebrity

This appeared as a review of Michael Bloch's biography of
Mr Thorpe, which was published not long after the former
Liberal leader died on 4 December 2014.

20 December 2014

Andrew Newton had a plan for doing away with Norman Scott.
He was going to meet him at the Royal Garden Hotel in
Kensington and kill him with a chisel hidden in a bunch of
flowers before escaping. This was an obviously ridiculous scheme.
How could he possibly have thought it would work?

Yet it was probably a better idea than Jeremy Thorpe's suggestion to his friends that Scott be taken close to the entrance of
a disused tin mine and then dropped in. And the course Newton
eventually took – to take Scott and a faulty gun out onto the
moor and shoot Scott's dog – wasn't much of an improvement.

The series of events that landed one of Britain's leading politicians in the dock at the Old Bailey, standing trial for conspiracy to murder, are scarcely credible. The story is simultaneously shocking, hilarious and moving. It ensures that Michael Bloch's new biography of the former Liberal leader is never less than riveting. I spent much of the time with my mouth open, even though I know the essentials of the story.

Bloch's account is convincing and simple. How Thorpe got himself emotionally and, almost certainly, sexually entangled with the very unstable Scott, a stable boy in 1961. How the latter developed the delusion that Thorpe had ruined his life and pursued him for sixteen years, blackmailing him. How Thorpe involved his friends in paying off Scott until it all became too much.

And how, between the two 1974 elections, they finally launched a plot to silence him for good. It is still not clear whether the idea was to murder Scott or simply frighten him off. This uncertainty is one of the main reasons for Thorpe's acquittal. Bloch, though, offers a plausible theory. The plotters were incompetent and new to murder. They were nervous about what they were doing. They launched a course of action that might have led to Scott's death but were not absolutely determined upon it.

What makes this biography a triumph – which it absolutely is – is the way that Bloch weaves the Scott story into a proper political and personal account of Thorpe's life. He describes a man who was a brilliant showman, a wit and a fabulous mimic. He was wonderful company, a great charmer. He was also politically principled and transformed the prospects of his party with a combination of charisma and clever positioning.

At the same time Thorpe was a chancer. Shallow, a risk taker, a liar and always playing the clown. He was also – and in this he was similar to Scott – something of a fantasist.

He was a superb television presenter, rivalling his Oxford

contemporary Robin Day. This would have been a much better career for him. Yet it would not have satisfied his feeling that he was a man of destiny. Thorpe believed, wrongly, that he was the heir to a long-dormant peerage which one day he would claim back. He also, as a student, told everyone he intended to marry Princess Margaret and to become prime minister.

Despite the fact that these ambitions were mutually exclusive, he took them all seriously, continuing to do so in adulthood. When the princess announced her engagement to Tony Armstrong-Jones, Thorpe was visibly upset, telling a friend that it was a shame since he had intended 'to marry the one and seduce the other'. He took his future wife past Downing Street and told her that one day this would be their home.

Reconciling his position as a serious figure and his rich fantasy life was hard work and Thorpe was often unscrupulous in how he went about it. Although also brilliant at it. He raised a fortune for the Liberals and spent a fortune too on hovercrafts and helicopters and closed-circuit television that they couldn't afford. His relationship with party donors was sometimes questionable and his accounting for their donations even more often so.

A central feature of his trial concerned the way that he asked one party donor to send him money in cash via the Channel Islands, money that was almost certainly used to pay Newton. He then (unsuccessfully) asked the donors to lie about it to the police.

The biggest tension in his life, of course, was his active homosexuality which, at the time, was incompatible with a political career. The fact that a man had to keep being gay a secret is outrageous and a personal tragedy for Thorpe. The fact that Scott was in a position to blackmail the Liberal leader was entirely the result of social conventions that now appear entirely wrong. Bloch might have made more of this point.

In general, though, the biographer is sympathetic to his

subject. By the time Newton takes the unbelievably tiresome, dreadful Scott out onto the moor, the reader is almost tempted to offer to share the driving. The book is unblinking in its portrayal of Thorpe but you understand his actions while at the same time thinking them both appalling and more than a little mad.

While all this is going on, the book provides a history of the Liberal Party as it seeks to revive after its post-war collapse. Thorpe's triumphs in North Devon, the seat he won from the Tories in 1959, are well covered. Some of this is strictly for political aficionados (though, done with economy and verve, it isn't boring), but the central event of Thorpe's political life is of wider interest.

After the first 1974 election, Thorpe found himself in a position both powerful and awkward. Edward Heath sought his support to remain in office, offering him a full coalition deal. Bloch shows how messy and poorly thought out the discussions were, with neither party ready to have them. Nick Clegg – so much better prepared – emerges with credit from the present period.

After the trial Thorpe was finished, despite his acquittal. And rightly so. His behaviour had been disgraceful, the lies epic. He was only 50 years old when he threw his cushions from the dock in triumph and lived another thirty-five years, dying this month, a period Bloch is able to cover in just twelve pages without missing out anything of importance. Yet it is hard not to like Thorpe or be charmed by him. At least on paper.

The hidden gay life, the blackmail, the fraud, the raffish and unsuitable friends, the family suicides, the payoffs, the lies, the secret letters, the bizarre murder plots, the fantasy lives, the celebrity world, the story of Jeremy Thorpe is one of the most extraordinary political tales of the twentieth century. And in Michael Bloch it has found a worthy chronicler.

George Martin . . . From the Goons to the Beatles

George Martin, the subject of a new Arena documentary, knew the Beatles not as stars but as brilliantly talented friends

One of the best assignments I have ever been given by *The Times* was to interview the Beatles' producer Sir George Martin. After it appeared he sent me this email: 'Thank you so much for your beautiful piece in *The Times*. Made us all feel good, and I guess because you really managed to get under my skin. I'll never have a better one!' I'm prouder of that than of any of the journalistic awards I've won.

15 April 2011

'I found it rather absurd that I was inducted into the Rock and Roll Hall of Fame.'

Mmm. Now let's see. I am talking with George Martin, the man who gave the Beatles their first recording contract when no one else would have them; the man whose production genius lifted their music; who produced (in *Sgt Pepper's Lonely Hearts Club Band*) what is still regarded by many as the finest pop album ever; who changed the way people recorded and even listened to rock music. No, on balance I'd have to disagree. It wasn't absurd to induct him into the Rock and Roll Hall of Fame.

But as I sit with the 85-year-old in the lounge of his London apartment and talk about his career, which is the subject of a new *Arena* documentary on Easter Monday, I slowly begin to grasp why he said it. It wasn't false modesty, because there is nothing false about him. It was an insight into how he sees himself, and how he has always worked.

When, in the early 1960s, the Beatles were turned down by record label after record label, they became increasingly desperate. They weren't to know that it was a tremendous piece of good fortune. Because repeated rejection made them turn to their last hope, a tiny label called Parlophone, headed by a young executive called George Martin. And here they found not just someone to take them on but someone who understood them as they, at the time, didn't understand themselves.

And the reason for this was partly that he wasn't a rock 'n' roll man. In fact he still isn't. Classically trained (at the Guildhall School of Music and Drama) and a producer of many classical records, when Martin listens to music these days it is to the great composers. 'Bach, Debussy, Ravel, Fauré. Even Tchaikovsky. Mainly the syrupy stuff,' he adds with a laugh. And he doesn't really understand the distinctions others make between different categories of music. Fashions change, but the fundamentals don't. 'There's only two kinds of music. Good and bad.'

He also hasn't lived a rock 'n' roll life.

When I arrive at his flat – furnished simply and with orthodox oil paintings – I am greeted by his wife Judy, to whom he is clearly devoted and whom he met at Parlophone in 1950 and married forty-five years ago. He even suggests that he could have ended up in a different career altogether. His family were not musical (his father was a carpenter from North London) and entirely lacked the connections to aid his professional life. But a piece of good fortune (he was overheard playing on the piano at the end of a Forces concert) brought him to the attention of Sidney Harrison, a Guildhall professor who helped him get a musical education and then put him up for a job with EMI. That said, his talent was clearly innate. 'At the age of 5,' he says, 'if I heard a new song on the radio, I could go and play it on the piano. Just natural. It was my language.'

But what first produced the bond between the four lads from Liverpool and the upright man with his tie and his war service ('I might have stayed in the Navy. I was very keen on the Fleet Air Arm. I'd be a retired Admiral now') wasn't music at all. It was comedy. Martin wasn't sure the Beatles were all that good. But they made him laugh, he found them funny. And they were in awe of his work as a comedy producer.

Because before the Beatles, came the Goons. In the 1950s, seeking to make his way in the record industry, Martin hit upon comedy. 'I was mining a seam that people hadn't dug out yet. Parlophone was a dying label and I knew I had to do something radical to make it work. I turned to comedy. My first comedy record was with Peter Ustinov and then Peter Sellers and then Spike [Milligan] and Bernard Cribbins and Charlie Drake and Rolf Harris.

'The Goons were lovely people. Spike was as mad as a hatter, of course, but he had this streak of genius of doing the unexpected and Peter was a great foil because he had all the voices that one could think of . . . And Harry [Secombe] was a great buffoon.'

The relationship became so close that in 1962, in the same month as the Beatles' first recording session with him, Martin served as Milligan's best man. 'At his second marriage,' he chuckles. 'His first wife was a lovely woman but they just didn't get on. She couldn't stand him in the end, because he must have been desperately difficult to live with.

'In those days there was no internet but you could send telegrams to people. If you sent a telegram you could phone it, and a little man with a pill-box hat would cycle up to the house and hand over a brown paper envelope and the person would open it and read the message. So one day, Spike was in his bedroom sulking away and his wife was getting on with the kids and so on, and suddenly there was a knock at the door and there was this telegraph boy with a message. She opened it up and it said: "I'd like one boiled egg, a slice of bacon and a cup of coffee for breakfast. Thank you very much. I'm upstairs. Spike." How maddening. Can you imagine? So they divorced.'

At around this time, the work with Sellers, which had produced two successful albums (*The Best of Sellers* and *Songs for Swinging Sellers*), was coming to an end. 'When Peter became a film star he started getting worried that maybe our records weren't as funny as they used to be. He was a perfectionist. And he was like this on film as well. He would fret like mad. So it became more difficult to get him to approve the scripts that I was providing for him. He would say: "Is it funny? Is it going to be good enough?" That kind of thing. But we never rowed.'

Martin was looking for something else. Recording 'Nellie the Elephant' or 'Right, Said Fred' with Bernard Cribbins or 'Sun Arise' with Rolf Harris depended commercially on the novelty of the piece to work. Parlophone needed something more reliable to produce an income. Enter, the Beatles.

Nowadays the arrival of the Beatles is thought of as a social watershed, a leap across a generational divide. But it didn't seem like that to Martin at the time. 'I recognise now, looking back, there was quite a dividing line – perhaps more a comma – marking the difference between the 1950s and 1960s. But there was no distinction for me. My work was continuous, I didn't see any change in it. I was still recording comedy people when I was recording the Beatles. I was still recording the orchestral stuff and Shirley Bassey.'

He takes this view at least partly, I think, because of his resolute refusal to take himself too seriously. Regarding his own work as a watershed would seem pompous.

His comments about the Rock and Roll Hall of Fame reflect his strong sense of humour (he sees a lot of things, and probably, in a gentle way, people, as somewhat absurd) and his way of coping with his own fame. He worked with revolutionary acts over two decades but says only: 'I never really thought about it. Well, you don't. You know what you've got to do. You see someone you like, think they are worth recording and go and make a record. It's not a big deal.'

He lifts the same raised eyebrow when asked about the obsessional, extraordinary worship the Beatles still attract, the endless examination and discussion. 'You see, I can't be rational about this, because the Beatles aren't the Beatles to me as they are to someone on the street. You ask them what they think of the Beatles and they say: "Oh, they are fantastic." The Beatles are four people I knew very well, and two of them are still living. And they are my friends. So it's not this big icon that everybody talks about.

'I still find it difficult to believe that they are probably the finest rock band we've ever had, or the most famous, or whatever. They are certainly very talented people and they've caused a tremendous effect on young people in this country and the world, in fact. But I can't look at them like that. I look at them like I might look at you and say: "Daniel Finkelstein, what do you play by the way?" You're a person, you're not a thing.'

So the iconography of the Beatles is a bit odd to you, I ask. The iconic status? 'Well, I didn't give them the iconic status.' He laughs. 'And they laugh about it too. How else can you deal with it? If you're Paul McCartney how can you deal with it? You can only deal with it by shrugging your shoulders and saying let's get on with the show and let's do another one. That's it really.'

I wonder if he feels a little the same, because he has iconic status too. 'Yeah, but I'm not an icon like they are. They are the biggest thing ever. No. I don't want to be any more famous than I am. Would you like to be Paul McCartney? I wouldn't. That's the last thing I would like. It's like being Prince William.'

But his ability to remain completely grounded doesn't lead him to underestimate their achievement altogether. He may regard it as just work, but he knows the Beatles' work was very good. He knows that 'their music was special. When I first met them I wasn't convinced that they were able to write a good song. But now, looking back on history, the catalogue of songs that they have conceived is fantastic. I think we recorded well over 200 titles and of those probably 60 per cent were great songs. I mean not just a pass-by thing, but really great. And I would have given my eye teeth to have written even one of them.'

I am unable to resist asking the most clichéd of all Beatles questions. 'Do you have a favourite song?' He grimaces slightly: 'Not really, no. People ask me this all the time.' But when I promise to tell him mine if he tells me his, the characteristic Martin humour and courtesy triumph and he relents. I say 'Here, There and Everywhere' and he replies: 'Well now, if I ever give an answer, I take it into Paul and John's territory. If it's Paul, I say "Here, There and Everywhere" and if it's John, "Strawberry Fields Forever."'

His pride also comes out when he tells me about John Lennon's comment that he would like to have rerecorded everything that the Beatles ever did. 'I said to him: "I can't believe that, John. Think of all we've done and you want to rerecord everything?" "Yeah, everything." And I said: "What about 'Strawberry Fields?'" And he looked at me, pulled down his glasses, and said: "Especially 'Strawberry Fields'." Which I was very disappointed with, really. If he felt that way about it, he should have recorded the bloody thing himself.'

Towards the end of the Beatles' recording career, Lennon and George Harrison took the tapes of *Let It Be* and asked the 'Wall of Sound' producer Phil Spector to work on them. When Martin heard that, despite working on the originals, he was to be left off the album credit, he suggested the cover read: 'Produced by George Martin, overproduced by Phil Spector.'

His analysis of Spector – recently jailed for murder – turned out to be shrewd. 'You mention the words Phil Spector and it fills me with grief. He's an idiot, really. I thought he was a genius when I first heard "You've Lost That Loving Feeling" and all the other stuff he did with the Ronettes, and so on. But he's crazy. John worked with him and he came to me, complaining: "That guy's crazy." And I said: "Look who's talking." He said: "You think I'm crazy? You should see Spector." Spector would come into the studio like a Mexican bandit, bands of cartridges criss-crossed over his chest, guns in each holster and he would fire guns in the studio.'

Even a little of such behaviour is unacceptable to Martin. Perhaps because he is the real deal – you can't get much bigger in rock music than to have discovered, guided and produced the Beatles – he finds ill-mannered celebrity high jinks contemptible, 'a blot on the escutcheon'.

And when I ask about *The X Factor*, he replies: 'I think it's awful. There's so much sort of envious competition, there's so much looking for freaks, and I hate the put-downs by the critics, the people on the panel. Particularly Simon Cowell. So unnecessarily rude to people . . . I do like manners.'

So he avoids grandstanding, keeps out of politics ('There are so many idiots in Parliament but I don't have time to go and sort it out') and confines himself to traditional charities.

One of these is Deafness Research UK. At 85, Martin is losing his hearing. We sit close to each other at the dining table so that he can pick up what I'm saying. Rather ridiculously, I ask him if he finds this frustrating. 'Yes, of course. One of my best friends was Tony Hart, the artist. We knew each other for forty to fifty years, lovely man. And he had a stroke. After the stroke he became crippled. And he found that he couldn't hold a pencil or a pen or a paintbrush. So he couldn't do what he had done all his life. I say: "God's got a funny sense of humour. He takes things away from people if they're enjoying them too much."'

But Martin can still do some work. His schedule is still remarkably busy. He showed me a choral piece on his Apple Mac that he was working on, and we talked about his visit to Las Vegas for the fifth anniversary of the Beatles' *Love* show.

He'd spent three years working on the show, remixing the Beatles' music into a single stunning ninety-minute piece of music. 'I often wonder how John would have handled the *Love* work. Paul and Ringo and Yoko and Olivia thought it was great. I'm not sure whether John would have liked it.' I suspect a large part of why Martin liked it himself had to do with working on it with his son Giles, which had been a very happy experience.

'We have a similar sense of humour, and we love each other, it's as simple as that. And love is terribly important. Love and laughter are the keys to life.'

PART FIVE

Pastimes

On the day that the Iraq war started my friends all imagined I would be busy at the paper. And so I was. Writing an article on whether Bolton Wanderers versus Blackburn Rovers should properly be considered a derby match.

The paper is full of so much more than politics and social affairs and you get a chance to write about other things you follow or love to do.

Hours not to reason why (or how I'm pushed for Times)

If the Diet Coke doesn't get me I should live
until my eighties, but that isn't that long

23 March 2005

I absolutely can't. And I am baffled that you can. Let me take
you through my calculations.

I am 42 now and I reckon I'm good for another thirty-eight
years. This might, of course, prove hopelessly optimistic. My
wife thinks it will. Whenever she sees me head for the fridge,
she expresses the fear that at a young age she will be the world's
first recorded Diet Coke widow.

Considering that she is a doctor, she is a little vague over
exactly how the Diet Coke will kill me. Ring-pull finger, perhaps.
Or there was that Sue Townsend novel where the guy chokes
on a bottle during a car accident. I've had to promise that when
I'm driving I'll only drink from a can.

Let's assume the fizzy drink doesn't get me. It is a reasonable
guess that I will die on 21 March 2043 at about 2pm. This will
be a convenient moment. I'll have had lunch and there won't
be anything on TV yet.

So I have 332,880 hours left.

I'll spend 129,818 of these hours either in bed or in the bathroom. And given my working week and the amount of time I spend in the car or Tube travelling to and from the office, I'll use up a further 91,080 hours earning a living, even if I retire at a reasonable age in order to stand outside the Post Office with a shopping trolley on wheels.

It will take me 25,483 hours and ten minutes to prepare breakfast, lunch and dinner. This, incidentally, proves that Jamie Oliver is wrong. You may add two years to your life by eating only carefully prepared meals, but you will spend almost all of it chopping onions.

As a result of these meals I will occupy 10,402 hours washing up, plus a further fifty-six hours complaining that we've run out of Brillo pads and, of course, there will be the time I spend buying Brillo pads (0 minutes). And naturally I'll need to go to the supermarket. This would normally take, let's say, one hour a week. However, I now use the internet to save time. I shop for 45 minutes online and then use 45 minutes to go the supermarket because I asked them to bring lemon drizzle cake and they brought some lemons and an umbrella instead.

I have set aside 21,170 hours for reading. I should spend it on improving books but will instead use at least half of it reading Robert Crampton's column in *The Times* magazine.

I will need time to buy *Dark Side of the Moon* by Pink Floyd, because *The Eye* said I had to. Then I'll listen to it once, remember that I hated it, and try selling it on eBay. A man in Arizona will pay me £2.78 and it will cost me £2.79 to post it to him. Twenty years later I will do this a second time.

Once I've watched television, gone out for dinner, looked after the children, lost and found my mobile phone, been 'held in a queue' on the telephone for 1,898 hours, shouted at the *Today* programme, looked for parking places, opened three letters a day asking me to join the 'Porcelain Figurine of the Month Club' and offering me a free leatherette-bound copy of *The Wind in the Willows* if I do, explained to my mother that I still don't like cauliflower soup, written a book, listened a sufficient number of times to 'God Only Knows' by the Beach Boys, backed the car gently into a tree and gone to synagogue, I'll have only 5,003 hours left to live.

I will also have to buy thirteen new computers and install the software on each of them, spending at least a week each time calling up the company that sold it to me to ask what 'Error message 413b' means and why every time I try to print something it says 'hardware device not detected'.

Even though they should be able to see that I'm dying, friends will still ask me to join their committees (3,952 hours), and take part in quiz supper evenings because they think I'm going to be good at them even though my team always comes fourth having played a joker on the geography round and scored zero (532 hours). I will also go through a phase of reading the *New Statesman* in order to discover what the Left is thinking (2 minutes).

So you see, by the time I've done all this I will have less than an hour of my life left and I'll need at least thirty minutes to reply to annoying emails accusing me of double-counting.

I think I've proven my point.

I haven't got time to start doing Sudoku.

Football's ridiculous. And unfair. But it's such fun

The money sloshing around the sport is part of
what makes it so compelling. 'Financial fair play'?
Nonsense

23 May 2012

It was almost 11 o'clock on Saturday night, well past his bedtime, and my middle son, my nine-year-old, was still up. Worse, he was running round the lounge, jumping up and down and shouting at the top of his voice.

This is not behaviour I would normally condone. But I would have felt a hypocrite telling him off, given that at the time I was running faster, jumping higher and shouting louder. It's not every night that Chelsea win the Champions League.

I can't really explain to you where my liking of football comes from. I don't come from a footballing family. My father's hobby – I am not making this up – was studying the history of the Rabbinical School of Warsaw. While this need not logically have excluded cogitation on whether the 160-goal midfielder Matt Le Tissier was right to have spent his entire career at Southampton, in practice it did.

My elder brother preferred offbeat sports – coxless rowing,

triathlons and that Japanese, or is it Thai, thing they do in parks. So while he was an inspiration for much else, he was only able to be indulgent of my football obsession. I must therefore, I suppose, have picked it up from my schoolfriends. I have always slightly feared that being a fan is an indication that I succumb too easily to peer pressure.

In any case, I imagined that as I got older the whole fan thing would fade. Not a bit of it. Oddly, as the years have gone by, it has got stronger. You may have picked up the paper on Monday and wondered why on earth an adult would want a twenty-page special Chelsea edition of *The Game*. My only problem with it was, why not twenty-eight pages?

The big question, I suppose, is: 'Why?' It can't be about identity. True, I wouldn't dream of being a fan of anyone other than Chelsea. When I was seven, I was taken to a game at Stamford Bridge by a friend whose dad had a shop nearby. I have supported them ever since and so I suppose it is part of who I am. But as a North West London Jew, Tory and think-tank wonk, I am hardly in need of extra pieces of identity. On the identity front I am only outbid by Sammy Davis Jr (African-American, Jew, one eye, member of Frank Sinatra's Rat Pack).

Nor do I invest football with some great intellectual or cultural properties that it doesn't possess in the hope of persuading you that its place in national life, or even my own, might somehow justify the investment of all that time and energy. I am very interested in analysing the game rigorously because it enhances my enjoyment, but my attachment to it is so unintellectual as to be almost witless.

Over the weekend there was a fuss because John Terry, the Chelsea captain, had collected the cup wearing full kit, including shin-pads, despite the fact that he had arrived wearing a suit, having been banned from the match. I have been explaining to friends that not only do I not care about this, but as he was the captain of my team, having just won the Champions League,

I would have been perfectly content for Terry to have collected the cup wearing *only* shin-pads.

If you are wondering if I realise how ridiculous this sounds, then let me reassure you. Of course I do. But I provide the same explanation as the Watergate conspirator G. Gordon Liddy when asked how he could bear to put his hand over a naked flame until his flesh burned: 'The trick is not caring.'

I don't care where Chelsea's money comes from as long as there is plenty of it. I don't care if Didier Drogba rolls around on the floor without really being injured as long as (eventually and please take your time, Didier) he gets up and scores. I don't care that Chelsea footballers are paid a lot of money. Pay them more is what I say. Especially Frank Lampard. I don't feel embarrassed to use 'we' when talking about winning the cup, even though my own contribution, particularly away to Barcelona, was modest. I happily, and without unduly feeling it absurd, accept congratulations from my friends on Chelsea's latest trophy acquisition.

In other words, it is precisely the ridiculous, sweep-everything-away, argue-for-an-hour-about-nothingness of football that makes me love it.

I don't read much fiction. Who needs it when you have soccer? A football match is for me a great work of fiction, one in which the ending is impossible to predict. On the stage or in a book, you can usually work out where it's going even if the author has been very careful. Football never ceases to surprise. If Drogba had equalised in the last minute of *Swann's Way* I might have gone on to read the rest of Proust.

The idiosyncrasies, the unfairness, the rabbit out of the hat, they are football. What else is it? A Russian billionaire comes along in the middle of the night and buys a club for a pound. A sheikh turns up and takes over a club that used to belong to the exiled Prime Minister of Thailand and a couple of years later they win the title. What tremendous fun. What's not to love about that? Who wants logic? Or rigour?

So I can't be doing with people who want to iron it all out. UEFA, the European government of football (and everything that description would lead you to expect), is introducing some new rules to ensure what it calls 'financial fair play'. The idea is that you wouldn't be able to waltz in and put your millions into a club; all the money that a team spends has to come from its income from football. This removes some unfairness but, like all such well-meant schemes, won't really work. It will make the game more unequal (as the big clubs grow their income and the little guys can't catch up) and more predictable. And what's the point of that?

In any case, the big money hasn't spoilt football; it has improved it. Better players have come from abroad, improving standards all round. And there is always the chance that your club could be next in the money. In the years before big-money football, Liverpool won the title seven years in a row and there wasn't a sheikh in sight to save us from them.

More important still, the rules might impede Chelsea, which I am against, whatever the other arguments. People ask me if I didn't prefer the purity of the old days. Well, I have sat in the stands before Roman Abramovich came along and we were in Division Two and the manager was sitting all by himself in an empty bit of the stand as we lost again.

Saturday was better.

Hamilton musical makes a Founding Father a hero of our time

The Broadway hit reminds us there's nothing new about political rows over federal superstates and the economy

When this article appeared, some readers objected to the fact that key roles in the Hamilton musical were taken by members of ethnic minorities when the people they were portraying were white. I defended the artistic statement pointing out that, yes, George Washington was not really African American, but it was equally true that when Alexander Hamilton first proposed federal assumption of state debt he didn't do it in song.

19 December 2017

Though he died before he was 50, Alexander Hamilton led an extraordinary life. An immigrant to America, he became a military hero of the revolution; right-hand man to George Washington; founder of the two-party system; first Secretary of the Treasury; creator of the currency and banking system; biggest influence in four presidential elections; and the subject of America's first sex scandal.

All before being shot dead in a duel at the age of 47 by the vice-president.

Despite his turbulent life and undoubted importance, when his widow Elizabeth Schuyler Hamilton died more than fifty years later she was still waiting for the first proper biography of her hero. Hamilton had been forgotten by his friends and traduced by his enemies. When Aaron Burr shot Alexander he didn't merely kill him, he erased him.

But in the twenty-first century Hamilton has enjoyed a revival. From being the least-known Founding Father he has become one of the best known. It's all because of two works: the first was Ron Chernow's *Alexander Hamilton*, one of the best political biographies of the past thirty years.

One of the people who bought it was a musician called Lin-Manuel Miranda. Reading it by the pool on holiday, he wondered how he could turn it into a hip-hop concept album. This unlikely thought developed into the hit musical *Hamilton*, a fitting memorial to its inspired and inspiring subject. It has its first night in London tomorrow, and the scramble for tickets is as fierce as it has been everywhere it's been staged.

Hamilton would have adored all the fuss. He was a man of monumental ambition and self-regard who, as the biography and musical show, cared more about his legacy than his life. He lived in order to be remembered.

One of the things that caught Miranda's imagination was that, as Chernow put it, Hamilton 'embodied an enduring archetype: the obscure immigrant who comes to America, recreates himself, and succeeds despite a lack of proper birth and breeding'. In the musical, the insurgency of immigrants is symbolised by an ethnically diverse cast. An African American played George Washington on Broadway, despite the first president having been a slave owner. But there is much more that makes *Hamilton* a show for our times. Miranda has made a song-and-dance routine about the founding of modern capitalism.

The political heart of Hamilton's story is his battle with Thomas Jefferson, until recently the far better known Founding Father. Hamilton wanted the new American republic to be a capitalist state, and was fiercely resisted by Jefferson and his allies. And even though he died as a result of one of the arguments he provoked, he nonetheless prevailed.

The three big battles the two men fought dominate today's politics. The first is the battle over capitalism. Hamilton believed that America needed to become a prosperous, trading economy. This contrasted with Jefferson's belief that a market economy would destroy the purity of revolutionary society. He argued for a simple, communal, rural life.

Hamilton was contemptuous of this green vision. He pointed out that Jefferson lived in luxury and that the rural idyll of his landed estates was only made possible by slavery, which Hamilton saw as an abomination. He realised that if America was not a capitalist country, it would be forever a slave-owning one.

The second battle is over the merits of populist, direct democracy as opposed to representative bodies like Parliament. Jefferson romanticised the war of independence against Britain and had a fair deal of sympathy for direct action and the French Revolution. Hamilton feared disorder and mob rule. Hamilton's allies promoted the power of the courts as a check on popular fervour and emphasised the power of the president to use his own judgment instead of blindly following public opinion.

Jefferson and his allies accused Hamilton of being a secret monarchist, in league with the English to undermine the revolution. They suggested (ludicrously) that Washington, under Hamilton's malign influence, fancied himself King of America. Ultimately Justice Marshall's Supreme Court settled this argument in Hamilton's favour.

The third battle is between federalism and local sovereignty.

Jefferson wanted America to be a loose collection of states, each sovereign over its own territory. Hamilton was certain the states could only be strong together and persuaded Washington to agree. As an activist or as a minister, Hamilton sought to strengthen federal bonds. It's hard not to see our debate between Remainers and Leavers reflected in Hamilton and Jefferson's respective positions.

The most important political act of Hamilton's life came when, as Treasury Secretary, he sought to create the basis for a single federal currency and central bank by promising Congress that the Government would assume all the country's debts. The Jeffersonians, under James Madison, controlled Congress and blocked the move.

Finally, Jefferson hosted a dinner for Madison and Hamilton and a deal was struck. It is wonderfully portrayed on stage by Miranda in the song 'The Room Where It Happens'. They agree that the US capital will be in the South, on the Potomac, where Virginians might reasonably expect to hold sway and where slaves could be brought without fear that the Government would free them. In return, Hamilton, who had wanted a capital in the North, got his way on assumption of the national debt.

At first Jefferson laughed at Hamilton for accepting something so abstract in return for giving way on the location of the capital. But Jefferson came to see the deal as the biggest error of his life. Assumption allowed the creation of a strong federal currency, and that made federalism irreversible.

If Hamilton had lost his political battles, America would not have emerged as the engine of modern prosperity or the arsenal of liberty. There is good reason, therefore, to regard him as one of the most consequential political figures of the modern age.

In Ron Chernow and Lin-Manuel Miranda, Eliza has at last found narrators worthy of her husband's achievements. And while *Hamilton* is in London, make sure to be in the room where it happens.

Whose finger on the off switch?

Those responsible for violent or sexually explicit film and TV must exercise their judgment occasionally and not leave it all up to me

25 May 2004

Life is full of little mysteries. There's Harold Pinter's inflated reputation, for instance. And all those people who travel for miles to a site of natural beauty and then eat their picnics in the car park.

As mysteries go, however, neither of these can hold a candle to hotel television. Why is it that when I return to a hotel room late at night, I then sit up for at least two hours watching absolute rubbish on television? Films badly dubbed from the original Belgian, sports matches with rules I don't understand, detective mysteries where I've missed the crucial clues. Why don't I just go to sleep?

It was while staying in a hotel room above a pub in Yorkshire a few years ago that I stumbled across Denise Van Outen's television programme *Something for the Weekend*. I must have missed the item on Einstein's theory of relativity. I tuned in just as Ms Van Outen was encouraging her guests to imitate the look on their partner's face when they were ejaculating. The best imitation won some sort of prize (not being forced to return next week, for instance).

The following day I mentioned this programme to a number of people who, not having been staying in a hotel, had been unfortunate enough to miss it. I said that I couldn't believe that such a gross, insulting, sexually explicit item was being shown on mainstream television.

There are a number of perfectly appropriate responses to my complaint. 'It sounds pretty funny to me', or 'It's all harmless fun', or 'Stop being ridiculous, you great fool' would have all been reasonable ripostes, although not ones I would have accepted.

Instead I invariably received one of two replies. The first was 'There is an off switch, you know', the second was 'Well, I don't believe in censorship'. The first of these statements is undeniably true, the second probably isn't (if Denise Van Outen had been putting out racist propaganda my interlocutors would have all wanted to censor it). But whatever their veracity, they are non sequiturs.

I didn't say I was physically incapable of turning off the television or that I wanted *Something for the Weekend* to be banned. I just said I couldn't believe it was being shown on mainstream television.

Whatever my friends' intent, their use of these non sequiturs has an impact. It relieves those who make and screen such vacuous offensive material from responsibility for their output. Putting out the show is their civil right and watching it is my fault.

At no point does anyone question the taste or judgment of the mature adults earning big salaries and holding prestigious posts in large organisations who screened this programme, or the many, many others which are far, far worse. I don't think they should be banned but I don't think they should be able to hide their behaviour behind the fact that they have a right to it. I have an off switch, but so have they.

In the last week the British press has been pouring scorn on the American media for bleeping out the swear words in *Prime Suspect* and for the way US critics got heated about Janet Jackson baring her breast on the Super Bowl programme and Bono cursing at the Golden Globe award ceremony. I've read some of this stuff with disbelief. We now think swearing on television and breast-baring are so sophisticated that only hick Americans could object, do we?

Last week Quentin Tarantino arrived at the Cannes Film Festival to show *Kill Bill: Vol 2*. He announced that he would like to shoot the most violent film ever made. 'Violence is fun, man,' he said. The pendulum has swung so far that I feel a bit of an idiot pointing out that it isn't.

The normal excuse used by middle-aged men with children who make money out of filming people having their skull repeatedly slammed in a door is that they are only responding to public taste. But this excuse won't do. To start with, it is a version of the Nuremberg defence – 'I was only obeying [the public's] orders'. It is also untrue. The fortunes of Hollywood are closely tied with the production of family movies. If economics was the only consideration, studios would be making more children's films. And, as the critic Michael Medved points out, no one ever left a cinema saying that they liked the film but didn't think there was enough swearing.

A few weeks ago Michael Moore, the left-wing film-maker, had a clash with the Disney Corporation which decided not to screen his new anti-Bush film. Moore, who on Sunday won the Palme d'Or at Cannes, accused it of censorship. It was, of course, guilty of nothing of the sort. It was just using the off switch. Moore should be able to understand this since he is forever, quite rightly, holding company employees, say in tobacco firms or firearms manufacturers, responsible for their output.

The correct criticism of Disney (which is not above violent and sexually explicit films) and of the thousands of other producers of films and television programmes, is not that they exercised their judgment just this once and decided there was something they would rather not be associated with. It is that they almost never do.

Fidget in the office to beat the fat

Move while you're working and fight obesity and heart disease. Is a desk treadmill the answer? A *Times* writer tries one out

1 April 2014

Of one thing I am now confident. When Oscar Wilde wrote *The Ballad of Reading Gaol* he got off the treadmill first.

I understand the case for a treadmill desk. I can write the advert: Lose weight as you work! Put an end to those 'My office life is too sedentary' blues! Add hours to your working day and years to your life!

The case is particularly strong for me. I like the office chair. I enjoy the House of Lords because I can sit in it without running or standing for office. Yet I know all this sitting down is not good for me. So, as I say, I see the case.

Allow me to put the counter-case.

The first and most important part of it is this: it's impossible to concentrate on what you are doing. You will look great and feel great as you are dismissed for incompetence.

Trying to get started on my football-statistics column, 'The Fink Tank', while walking on the treadmill proved inordinately difficult. The urge to stop the thing or get off while I thought of an opening line was almost irresistible.

'The Fink Tank' involves mastering spreadsheets and understanding the implications for Manchester United's Champions League prospects of a Monte Carlo simulation. It is, even at the best of times, fiddly, and it is easy to make a mistake. The treadmill made the thing virtually impossible.

Lyndon Johnson once said of Gerald Ford that the latter was so stupid that 'he couldn't walk and chew gum at the same time'. After an afternoon on the desk treadmill, my sympathies are entirely with Ford. It was very hard to do anything – open mail, consult a book, even drink a can of Diet Coke – while simultaneously walking at the same speed as the treadmill.

When I'd finished writing, I started to prepare for the coming week. I called an adviser to the Prime Minister to get his view on some polling. I don't think he noticed what I was doing. I can't, however, be sure, because I can't remember anything he said. Nor did I write it down, because it was hard to take notes and keep going. I'm going to have to phone him again.

So although the idea of the desk treadmill is that you can do two important things at once, I think the secret is that you do both badly.

Along with the distraction of treadmilling is the danger.

Treadmilling? Yes. Walking, you see, isn't an adequate verb. When you are walking you can vary your pace, stop, take in your surroundings. With a treadmill you have to keep going or fall off.

It only takes a moment of hesitation, greeting someone as they walk by for instance, and you start to slide back alarmingly. I hadn't been on the thing long when I decided to slow it down. This was to avoid an accident, rather than because I couldn't stand the pace. It struck me that the optimal speed was stationary.

I had taken off my shoes, because someone told me that was

what you were supposed to do, and I kept on catching my toes against the side of the conveyor belt. Yet my toes were the least of it. The big problem was my back.

After about ten minutes of trying to write and treadmill, I began to get quite bad backache. I soon decided that the best posture was to lean over the desk, resting both elbows on it, while moving my legs like the Road Runner being chased by Wile E. Coyote.

The only thing that made me feel more comfortable on the treadmill was getting off it. I was quickly sufficiently dizzy to wish to get back on. This is not a working method for anyone who suffers from motion sickness.

I shouldn't be too unfair. I suspect you could get used to it and would then be able to take advantage of the health benefits without suffering the problems I encountered. I couldn't stand my varifocals when I first got them, and now I can't imagine being without them.

Yet in order to adjust to the desk treadmill, I'd have to use it for a long time. And that, my friends, is not going to happen.

Daniel Finkelstein was using a LifeSpan TR1200 DT7 at £1999.00 including VAT.

Oscars night: can real men get red-carpet ready?

All eyes will be on Brad and George. But can any
man pull off that Hollywood look?

25 February 2012

I have had my fork eased by three-eighths, I've been cut all the
way from the crown, my seat has been scooped out and my
body is now in balance. I've got kick tape on both legs and I
feel fantastic.

It's the award season, and time to get out my evening dress.
I am not going to the actual Oscars, naturally enough. But I
do get invited to plenty of events that are billed as, you know,
'the industry Oscars'. Recently, as compère, I handed someone
their prize for being declared 'Outsourced service provider of
the year'.

So I need black tie. There is, however, something mysterious
about mine. Every time I collect it from the cupboard it has
toothpaste on the lapel. I don't understand why this is since I
never brush my teeth while wearing the jacket. But there is no
point arguing with the facts.

As a result, one of two things happens when I am invited to
a dinner-jacket event. I turn up wearing bow tie, black jacket

and Macleans or I forget the suit and have to rush to Moss Bros at the last minute and rent whatever is in stock. It is time to get a proper, crisp, good-looking new suit and then leave it hanging in the office.

Unfortunately, proper, crisp and good-looking are slightly outside my range as a dresser. I am, I'm afraid, the Messi of messy (football joke, ask someone). Bill Gates has been described as an inky-fingered genius. I just got the inky fingers. When Mrs Foot protested that the donkey jacket her husband wore to the Cenotaph was 'brand new' I was sympathetic. If I were ever on the red carpet, I would have one of those discs marked 'Miss' pinned to my jacket, so as to save newspaper graphics departments the trouble.

A professional is definitely required. And fortunately, one is at hand in the form of Jeremy Hackett, the founder of the classy men's outfitter that bears his name. The company had just been the official menswear stylist for the Baftas. It had dressed Stephen Fry (big man, super nice apparently, weight fluctuates, looked fantastic on the night), Cuba Gooding Jr (who made the Burgundy jacket work), Jim Broadbent and that good-looking guy in *Great Expectations*. And now it was my turn. Somewhat Lower Expectations.

'Formal dress is not fancy dress,' declares Jeremy, prescribing a restrained classic look for me. And he explains that the details – cufflinks, studs, shoes – are crucial. 'It's all about detail and fit.' At this point he looks at my shoes, which were last polished during the coalition negotiations in 2010. He is a lovely, civilised man, Jeremy, who doesn't give away much. But he couldn't disguise a pained look. 'You'd better borrow a pair from us,' he says.

There are all sorts of materials I could have, apparently. And different weights of cloth. Graham Simpkins, Hackett head of tailoring, takes me through the choices. Hopsack, barathea, mohair, they'd all work fine. He says the mohair will give me a traditional, clean look and I reply that clean sounds good. This would have been the moment to ask about the toothpaste, I suppose, but I let it slide and now it will forever be a mystery.

Since an 8oz suit is too lightweight and doesn't have enough structure, and a 12oz might be too heavy and hot, we settle on 9oz. Single breasted, peaked lapel, mohair 9, the decision is made.

Now the shirt. I ask if I should tuck the wings of my dress shirt outside or inside the bow tie. The answer, it appears, is neither. Jeremy tactfully guides me to a normal dress shirt and doesn't demur when I joke that the wing collar is a 'stupid idea I got off *Brideshead Revisited* twenty-five years ago'.

So far, so simple. Time for fitting and I try on the trousers. They have buttons on the fly. 'Black tie is a military look,' Graham explains, leaving me to struggle. If so, I am surprised we weren't stuck in the toilet doing up our trousers when Hitler invaded.

Graham gives me a quick once over. We are going to cut the jacket from the crown (the shoulders) he says, shorten the jacket to balance your body, let out the waist and, I swear he said this, ease the fork in your trousers. Then we'll put kick tape in to prevent fraying.

And so he did. I must say, it looks pretty good. Even I can't ruin it. I am working on it, though.

Thank you for your highly original idea . . .

I spend far too long replying to emails. Perhaps
some standardised replies might save time and
trouble

31 December 2014

The break over Christmas and New Year has given me the
opportunity to reflect upon my work and consider how I might
do things more efficiently. And the more I thought about it,
the more I realised how much time I spend on individual replies
to emails. Surely it must be possible to develop a system for
responding?

The American journalist H. L. Mencken used to answer all
argumentative correspondence with a letter that read: 'Dear Sir
or Madam, You may be right. Sincerely yours, H. L. Mencken.'

This is obviously excellent but I think I will need a number
of standard replies to cover the most common emails I receive.
Here are the ones I have produced so far:

- Thank you for your email. I would be happy to help you
  with your PhD on 'Idiots who have given the Conservative
  Party electorally disastrous advice'. Please thank your

supervisor for thinking of me. Since you need only four hours of my time, we must fit in a meeting. It might be difficult in the next twelve months, as it is election year, but I will make every effort to organise it. It would certainly be easier for me if I didn't need to visit you in Sheffield.

- Thank you for the intriguing assertions that you made about Zionism. It is only someone as perceptive as you who realises what we are up to. I do hope it is nothing that I said that let you in on the secret.

- Thank you for your email and the accompanying parcel containing the first draft of your novel. I was happy to pay the postage. You certainly seem to have enjoyed writing it and I am confident it is an idea that will not have been thought up by anyone else. I am deeply flattered to be asked to provide a foreword. I regret that for complicated contractual reasons I will not be able to oblige, but thank you so much for asking.

- Thank you for your email. I am certain that gay people will be grateful that you are praying for them.

- Thank you for your email. I do apologise if you felt that my column was an insult to UKIP and its members. I was surprised to hear that, since my topic was the chance of Queens Park Rangers being relegated from the Premier League. Nevertheless I am sorry to have offended you, however inadvertently. When considering my predictions for the outcome of the next election I will certainly take into account your optimism about UKIP's prospects.

- Thank you for following up our exchange on social media. I looked up your description of me in the dictionary of urban slang and so was not in need of your more detailed exposition, but I am grateful for the trouble that you took.

- Thank you for your email. Your theory is highly original and I am grateful to you for elaborating upon it in such detail. It had never previously occurred to me that such a

simple solution was available to a problem that had hith-
erto seemed to me so complicated.

- Thank you for your email. I do not believe that we are
related and I don't think I have ever met your cousin
Chaim Finkelman. My father was a professor of measurement and control engineering and lived in Hendon, so I
don't think that the fur shop in Bethnal Green that you
visited as a child can have been his.

- Thank you for your email. I am sorry that you feel like
that. Are you sure that you didn't mean to write to Matthew
Parris?

- Thank you for your email and your kind invitation to
speak at your breakfast seminar. I would be happy to oblige,
but unfortunately I will not be in Durham the day after
tomorrow at 7.15 in the morning. In any case, although it
does sound like a most stimulating event, I do not regard
myself as a sufficient expert on the Venezuelan pension
system to be able to provide a different perspective from
that of the eleven people who have already agreed to be
on the panel.

- Thank you for your email with its many attachments. The
divorce from your wife sounds traumatic and I am sorry
that your custody case did not conclude successfully. Your
many years of legal struggle must have been very tough. I
am not entirely sure how I can help, but it was certainly
interesting to read your correspondence with the Pope and
the Lord Chancellor.

- Thank you for your email about the European Union. I
had not, until now, been aware that when we joined, it
was known as the Common Market. I was impressed by
your formidable list of things that would have been better
if we had not joined. Your use of a mixture of capitals and
lower case assisted my understanding no end. I am not
able, I am afraid, to provide current contact details for Ted

Heath. However, if I should bump into him, I will be sure
to tell him that you think he is a liar.
- Thank you for your email with its most interesting suggestion for a regular series of articles in *The Times*. The first
instalment was well written and I will certainly pass it on
to the comment editor who will, I am sure, give it careful
consideration. Do you think it might work better as a
letter to the editor? If you do, you might consider reducing
the piece in length as we rarely publish letters of 4,000
words.

Over the coming days I intend to compose further responses
to people writing about how all MPs live in a bubble, how
members of the House of Lords are spending taxpayers' money
on champagne, how the British public were never consulted
about mass immigration, how footballers are paid too much,
how Gordon Brown sold all our gold for the wrong price, how
I am sorry that my tie did not go with my shirt when I appeared
on *Newsnight* and how it would be very nice if I could provide
some words for the back cover of a new book on tarot cards.

Our sepia-tinted PMs were arrogant and remote

Look back at our 53 former prime ministers and
most would not stand up to the scrutiny of
today's demanding voters

23 August 2016

'Sidmouth, in many ways, was a dull man. He had no wit and
little humour. His private life was decorous to the point of suffo-
cation. His talk was drab and his writing doubly so. A career
devoid of panache and eccentricity; responsible, sober and prosaic;
may fairly be said to lack the more obvious kind of appeal.'

By the time I came across this description of Henry Addington,
Lord Sidmouth, I had been reading about him for hundreds of
pages and had hours of reading still to complete. You might
fairly ask: how did it come to this?

I'll tell you how. About two years ago I happened upon a
blog post by an American who had just completed the self-
imposed task of reading a biography of every US president. I
knew immediately I had to do it too. But not on American
presidents – on British prime ministers. I decided to read at
least one biography of every person who had served as PM.

With the accession of Theresa May, there are now fifty-four

people who have achieved the highest post, with an average time in office of five years and four months each. I have read biographies of thirty-three of them.

This is actually rather a harsh calculation. I've read two volumes of Charles Moore's life of Margaret Thatcher, but can't include her until I've read the third. I've read the memoirs of James Callaghan and Tony Blair but have decided that memoirs don't count. And I don't think you can include the books on David Cameron yet.

There is one problem. Not every prime minister has a proper biography. I finished reading about Sir Robert Walpole only to discover there wasn't one about his successor Spencer Compton. I felt like a Dalek whose plan to conquer the world was frustrated by a staircase. For the time being I've decided to use the *Dictionary of National Biography*.

Other questions to settle include: should I read other books too (definitely yes), do I need to read books on people whose biographies I have already read (no) and do I need to read them in order (also no)?

To read them in order would mean being stuck in the Georgian era for an eternity. On the other hand, picking people at random poses the danger that you read all the most obvious people first. I'm worried about being left with a tail end of also-ran PMs like the Dukes of Grafton and Portland, the Earl of Shelburne and Viscount Goderich.

The project also leaves me at the mercy of the quality and length of the biographies. One might ordinarily decide to skip reading about the Earl of Derby upon discovering that the only modern book on him, by Angus Hawkins, consisted of two huge (although also, as it turns out, excellent) volumes. And it was extraordinary to read a substantial biography of George Grenville that was so dry and political that it failed to note that he was one of only two people whose son also served as prime minister (the other being William Pitt).

Has the whole thing been worthwhile so far? Certainly. To start with, it means that I now know the dates of all the prime minsters from 1721. I couldn't just learn them by rote. Reading the books embedded them in my memory.

Having this grid of dates allows you to place any historical event from then onwards in political context. This proves helpful even when doing something as non-political as visiting the home of Jane Austen (where she lived during the premierships of Spencer Perceval and Lord Liverpool) and understanding what was going on in the world as she was writing. While she was sitting at her little desk Perceval was assassinated and Wellington triumphed at Waterloo.

And there are political examples too. In the lobby of the Houses of Parliament is a statue of Stafford Northcote. Why is this man who never made prime minister in such a prominent place? You can tell from the dates. He died on the Downing Street sofa in 1887 after hearing he was to be removed from the foreign office in a reshuffle. The statue was up in a year. It's a guilt offering.

The most common question I have been asked since starting is: who is my favourite prime minister? This points to the main historical lesson learnt. The answer really is – many of them and none of them. There is no one person who is consistently right or wrong.

Take the Earl of Derby, three times prime minister (1852, 1858 and 1866) although each time only briefly. Moderate, sane, the creator of the modern Conservative Party, right on voting reform, often correct on social reform and then, just as you are getting to like him, spectacularly wrong on votes for Jews and conditions in Ireland.

Was Gladstone a pompous, windy, self-absorbed nutter or a titan of reform and conscience? Both. Was Disraeli a conman, incompetent and a snob or a creative genius and political miracle worker? Both. Was Asquith an inflexible drunk who was besotted with his mistress when he should have been running the country or a transformative figure who modernised Britain? Both. Was Robert Walpole a crook and a chancer or a statesman who kept Britain at peace? Both.

Lloyd George, bounder and opportunist or great radical leader? Bonar Law, unimaginative minnow or great war leader? The Duke of Newcastle, old fool or master of the patronage system? Both, both, both. The idea that there are simple heroes and villains collapses under the weight of evidence.

As does the idea that politicians were so much better in the past. No, they weren't. They were less experienced, less in touch, less broad-minded and less accountable. We are much better served now.

Reading the history of prime ministers walks you along a long line of people who were elected to Parliament in their early twenties, hardly visited their constituencies and had little experience of other social classes. They had no way of gauging public opinion and weren't much interested in doing so, being pretty contemptuous of it.

The idea that we now have politicians who, unlike in the past, do not have experience of 'the real world' is actually the opposite of the truth.

There has been one other lesson I wasn't expecting because it isn't strictly speaking one about prime ministers. What a tragedy it is to read of young people going to die in wars that appear so insignificant to us now that I (ignorantly) did not even realise that they had happened. War with Sweden, for instance, or battles over the Polish succession.

The great heroes of history seem to be those who have won wars. True successes, however, may be those who managed to avoid fighting them. But I may be wrong. I've still got another 21 biographies to go, after all.

PART SIX

Crime and the Law

If I hadn't become embroiled in politics and then become a journalist, I would have quite liked being a lawyer. I very much admire the legal mind and will often read court judgments or lectures by judges because I find the clarity magnificent and the content an intellectual challenge.

As a result justice, both miscarriages of justice and the good working of the legal system, has been a theme of my columns. This section contains just a few examples.

Serial killers and serial errors

I am fascinated not by the grisly act of killers but
by the banal details of their ordinary lives

7 April 2003

My wife thinks that I might be a serial killer. Of course, on
one level she realises I'm not. She knows that not only do I
have an aversion to violence, I'm also hopelessly impractical. If
I bought a shovel and started building a patio, the police would
arrive without being called.

If I am ever responsible for anybody's death, it will be because
they knocked over the pile of books teetering on the edge of
my desk and suffocated underneath a stack of pamphlets about
welfare policy.

Nevertheless, Nicky remains worried. She can't understand
why I keep buying books about murderers. She thinks my
interest in such things is extremely unhealthy and is worried
that I might get some funny ideas.

My fascination, however, is not with the grisly acts of killers,
with their large and terrible crimes. I am riveted by the banal
details of their small, ordinary lives and by the insight that these
awful stories provide into the workings of the minds of killers,
victims and observers alike.

In Brian Masters's book *Killing for Company* there are full and horrible descriptions of the murders carried out by Dennis Nilsen, the man who disposed of bodies in the drains of his house in Muswell Hill. But what I found extraordinary was Nilsen's parallel life as an executive officer at the Kentish Town Job Centre, the way he continued going to work, complaining about petty office slights and applying for promotion, acting as normal while the corpses piled up at his home.

Fifty years ago this week saw the arrest of one of the most notorious of all serial killers – John Reginald Halliday Christie, inhabitant of the ground-floor flat of a tiny, claustrophobic house, 10 Rillington Place.

Christie killed eight people and, when he was eventually apprehended, two bodies were discovered buried in his garden and three in an alcove behind a cupboard. His wife was found underneath the floorboards. But his other two victims were no longer at 10 Rillington Place. They had been found years earlier while Christie's murderous impulses were still a secret. And it was then that he did something which has guaranteed his place in the annals of devilish crime. Christie succeeded in having another man blamed and hanged for their murder.

In 1950 Timothy Evans, a 25-year-old van driver for the Lancaster Food Company with the mental age of a ten-year-old boy, was executed for the crime of killing his baby daughter, having first killed his wife in the house that he shared with Christie.

The latter, posing as an innocent invalid, was the main prosecution witness. Evans blamed Christie but was not believed. This miscarriage of justice stands as one of the strongest arguments against capital punishment, an argument that I, for one, am unable to resist.

There is one more amazing part of the Christie case, one that speaks volumes about human behaviour. It took thirteen years from the discovery of Christie's other crimes for Evans to be given a posthumous pardon. In the meantime, two inquiries continued to maintain that Evans was guilty. Despite Christie confessing to the murder of Mrs Evans, it was concluded that this was 'no ground for thinking that there may have been a miscarriage of justice'.

Now for this to be true, two necrophile stranglers would need to have been operating entirely independently inside one little house at the same time, killing only women, using exactly the same methods, telling the same lies, wrapping the bodies in the same way and hiding them in the same places.

When one was discovered he must have decided, completely coincidentally, to blame his crimes on the one other man in the world secretly committing exactly the same crimes as him. This is, let's agree, unlikely.

Why, then, did such a ridiculous story remain the official version for so long? Because no one wished to believe that they had hanged an innocent man. Accepting that Evans was not guilty was too painful. The political establishment had maintained for too long that the British legal system would never allow such a thing to happen.

Human beings have an incredibly strong attachment to consistency, to being able to show that we never alter our positions, never change our mind. We will bend our stories and the truth, convince ourselves of all kinds of nonsense so we can maintain the comforting illusion that we are consistent. Evans's innocence contradicted a deeply held, oft-stated view, therefore Evans must be guilty.

The value we attach to consistency can be seen every day in countless small ways. The politician attacked for making U-turns or the fuss about the coalition having to change its plan in Iraq.

From Ludovic Kennedy's classic book *10 Rillington Place*, about the injustice done to Timothy Evans, I have learnt that we value consistency too highly, that there is much to be said for the man who does a far more difficult thing: changes his mind.

All that clairvoyant stuff, I don't see it myself

A new law against mediums would not work

11 April 2007

I want to consult you about a proposed change in the law. But before I do, I'd like to ask you a question or two. What would you do if you were genuinely clairvoyant? If you could really tell the future? The possibilities are endless.

You could make a fortune stock-picking and betting on sporting events. You could win the Nobel Peace Prize (by anticipating world crises and advising how they could be avoided), the various Nobel scientific prizes (by demonstrating in a series of controlled experiments that what we thought we knew about the natural world was wrong), and the Nobel Prize for Literature (by copying future masterpieces and passing them off as your own). You could save lives, avert catastrophes, only call restaurants when you knew that there was a table available. What fun you could have.

And who would you speak to if you could genuinely commune with the dead? Your own dearly loved relatives, of course. But perhaps also Jack Ruby, who might clear up a thing or two about why he shot Lee Harvey Oswald. And given all those nice things that Gordon Brown has to say about Adam Smith, I'd love to find out if the feeling was mutual.

Here are some of the things you wouldn't do: advertise on the internet, call yourself a celebrity psychic, appear on daytime TV, rent a table at a Psychic Fair just off Stanmore High Street, take a part-time job in Holland & Barrett while receiving clients at home of an evening, live in a caravan park in Totnes, sell your wares in the classified section of the local paper and stand in front of a group in a half-full village hall saying that you've had a message from someone called John and asking if anyone knows anybody with that name.

I can't help feeling that the slightly tatty nature of the 'psychic' industry is a bit of a giveaway. There was an outlet near my home that appears to have gone out of business. Surely a well-organised clairvoyant would have been able to avoid such a fate.

Claims to be able to speak to the dead and tell fortunes seem so obviously ridiculous that they are easy to make fun of. At least they are to me. But if you share my view, try expressing it to the next intelligent person you meet. There is a good chance you will be rewarded with an anecdote. A friend had a cousin who consulted a medium living in Watford. She was then able to find his long-lost wedding ring. 'There is no way the medium could have known where it was. It was uncanny.' It is pointless telling your friend that it is them who isn't being canny. Trust me, I've tried this. It never ends well.

Psychic readings, tarot sessions, audiences with clairvoyants and telepathists have all become big business. Last April Selfridges began offering sessions with psychics in their basement (again, working in the basement of a department store isn't what I'd do with my special powers, but there's no accounting for taste). The shop wasn't particularly amused when some sceptics presented their receipts at the customer services desk and attempted to get their money back because the future hadn't turned out as well as they'd hoped.

Meanwhile, the Ministry of Defence spent £18,000 on an experiment to see if psychics could identify the contents of a sealed envelope. They couldn't. Bang goes the chance of using them to find Osama bin Laden. The MoD simply replicated the findings of American intelligence agencies, who spent more than $10 million in a decade on psychics before concluding that their guidance was not assisting the identification of targets or sources of danger. We should have known Saddam Hussein had got rid of his WMD – typical Taurus behaviour.

But if the idiocy of this mainstream toying with psychic nonsense doesn't bother you, consider this. Much of it is also, at least in this country, illegal.

No, I didn't know that either. But there is something called the Fraudulent Mediums Act 1951, apparently. This law was introduced to replace the Witchcraft Act of 1735 and makes any person eligible for up to two years in prison who 'with intent to deceive, purports to act as a spiritualistic medium or to exercise any powers of telepathy, clairvoyance or other similar powers'. If you make it clear that you are just an entertainer you are fine, but I looked in vain for such a disclaimer on psychic advertisements.

The reason neither of us has heard of this law is that it is hardly ever used. Between 1980 and 1995, for instance, there were just five prosecutions, all ending in conviction. I could find you five people offending against the Act in five minutes, using that intrepid detective agency – Google.

So now some of my fellow sceptics are petitioning Downing Street (petitions.pm.gov.uk/mediums) for the Act to be revised so that it can be used. I am deeply sympathetic to their cause. The activities of the pyschic industry have victims. Grieving people are being exploited and the naive enticed to part with cash. Falsely suggesting to the bereaved that you are in communication with a dead relative seems to me a terrible thing to do.

But sympathetic as I am, I will not sign the petition. I am not happy seeing a multimillion-pound fraud trundle on, picking the pockets of the vulnerable. It is just that the alternative would be worse, I fear. The appetite among the public for assiduous prosecution approaches zero. The sympathy for Helen Duncan, the old con artist prosecuted under the Witchcraft Act back in the 1940s having earlier been caught regurgitating a cheesecloth undervest and pretending it was ectoplasm, was such that the law had to be changed. Use the new law more frequently and you would have thousands of Duncans on your hands.

I had a friend at university who approached every political problem with the phrase 'a fool and his money are easily parted'. He is right; as I, rather reluctantly, think that the Government is right. It proposes repealing the Fraudulent Mediums Act as part of an EU tidying-up exercise. It claims that a new, more general, commercial practices law will be available for use if necessary. But I think without psychic powers we can foresee that this will be the last we hear of the whole thing.

And probably that's for the best. Probably.

J'accuse: *this man must not languish in jail*

Like Alfred Dreyfus before him, Eddie Gilfoyle is
in prison for a crime he did not commit. He
should go free now

Eddie Gilfoyle is no longer in prison, but scandalously his
clearly unsafe conviction still stands.

7 September 2010

On 9 June 1899, Alfred Dreyfus boarded the cruiser *Sfax* and
began the long journey home to France from captivity on Devil's
Island. He had spent almost five years in prison, almost all of
it in silence, forbidden to speak or be spoken to. And if it hadn't
been for the extraordinary efforts of his brother Mathieu, and
of one honest army investigator, he would surely have died there
in silence too.

Dreyfus was returning because the case against him – that he
was spying for Germany – had now collapsed. His conviction had
been secured by secret documents pointing to his guilt that
had been given directly to his judges and not been shown to him
or his lawyer. Now these documents had been shown as prosecution forgeries, and the forger had killed himself.

The handwriting evidence that convicted him – always dubious, controversial even at his trial – had been utterly discredited. The letter full of French secrets had, it was now obvious, been sent by someone else, and the culprit had fled. There was nothing left of the case against Dreyfus. His innocence had been proven.

Yet two months after his return, a military tribunal found him guilty again. This time with 'extenuating circumstances', whatever they were. The President of France saw this as sufficiently embarrassing that he pardoned Dreyfus. But it was a full six years later before Dreyfus's conviction was finally reversed and he was restored to the army as a major.

This second, entirely ridiculous conviction of Dreyfus is a wonderful example of one of the most striking features of miscarriages of justice. When all the evidence lies in tatters, when the case for quashing the conviction has been clearly made, when no one can any longer properly doubt that an injustice has been done, still the conviction persists.

The tenacity with which the legal system and those responsible for the original case hold to their story and to their insistence that they were not in error is astonishing. Doubt it? Then read the history of the Birmingham Six, or the Guildford Four.

Or read the history of Eddie Gilfoyle. A man who languishes in jail after two failed appeals even though the case against him – one that was, in my view, always hard to credit – has now little left to it.

Eighteen years ago in June, Eddie Gilfoyle's wife Paula was found dead in their garage in the Wirral. She was hanging from a beam, with a ladder behind her. There was no sign of a struggle and she had left an anguished suicide note telling her husband not to blame himself. Merseyside Police who attended the scene were confident it was a suicide, and were, as a result, quite cavalier with the physical evidence.

But over the next few days the police began to think they

had got it wrong. Paula's friends said she had shown no signs of depression and wouldn't have killed herself when she was in the last month of pregnancy. A psychology professor backed up their speculation that Gilfoyle had tricked her into writing a note for a course he was attending. Professor David Canter said that the note showed signs of being faked. So was born the bizarre prosecution theory that Gilfoyle had tricked his wife into writing a suicide note, and had then somehow fooled her into climbing a ladder and had then put a noose round her neck without provoking a struggle.

And this theory carried the day at Eddie Gilfoyle's trial, sending him to jail for life. The more obvious idea, that Paula was disturbed, and that she mounted the ladder herself, failed to persuade the jury.

Why did this story prevail? Three pieces of evidence were absolutely crucial. The first is that it would not have been possible for Paula to ascend the ladder at that stage in her pregnancy. She would then have been too short to throw the rope over the beam. Video of a pregnant policewoman of similar height attempting the feat and failing was used to emphasise the point.

The second thing to count against Eddie was evidence that the time of death would have allowed him to be home from work in time to kill Paula. And finally there was evidence that pregnant women as near to birth as Paula simply don't hang themselves.

Most powerful of all, however, was something that wasn't really proper evidence at all. It was simply Paula's friends saying that they couldn't imagine her killing herself.

Such was the weak, rather unlikely, body of so-called facts that sent Eddie Gilfoyle to prison. It is surprising that it ever resulted in a conviction. But that he should still be in jail now is a scandal.

Just as with the Dreyfus case, the evidence against Gilfoyle has collapsed. Police notes from the scene were not available at the trial. For years, even when this newspaper pushed hard, the police said they couldn't find them. Now they have been found and show the doctor thought the time of death to be a moment when Eddie was still at work.

The video with the pregnant policewoman has been revealed to have employed a different rope, floppier than the real one, and less easy to throw – giving a misleading impression that Paula couldn't have thrown it round the beam.

The – almost quaint – idea that pregnant women don't hang themselves has been shown up as nonsense. And Professor Canter, after years of study, has bravely returned to the case and concluded that the suicide note was definitely written by Paula unaided.

Eddie Gilfoyle is not guilty. Yet still, weeks from his forty-ninth birthday, he languishes in jail. In his fine book, *Why the Dreyfus Affair Matters*, Louis Begley tells how the captain's conviction tore France apart. And he makes a grand comparison to Guantánamo Bay.

The case of Eddie Gilfoyle lacks this political majesty. And I do not make grand comparisons. But in the end Dreyfus was just an innocent man wrongly imprisoned and crying out for justice, and so is Gilfoyle. He is a test of our capacity to admit error and to allow truth to triumph. Where are the legal lions who will free this man?

These bundles of charges pose a real danger

William Roache was cleared, but gathering similar allegations into one prosecution will bring miscarriages of justice

On 6 February 2014, William Roache the *Coronation Street* actor was acquitted of two counts of rape and five of indecent assault. I believed that the case raised important questions about the administration of justice.

12 February 2014

The road to the trials of William Roache begins in 1915 at the breakfast table of Joseph Crossley, the owner of a guest house in Blackpool.

On 2 January of that year, Crossley was reading his newspaper when he came across a story that startled him. It concerned a woman found dead in a bath. An accidental death. A tragedy.

The newspaper told the story of recently married John Lloyd who had nipped out from his lodging house, telling the owner he was off to buy some tomatoes for supper. On returning, Lloyd called out for his wife, but there was no reply. He entered the bathroom and there found his wife, dead in the tub.

What brought Crossley up short was the memory of a death that had taken place in his guest house a year earlier. The deceased was a woman called Alice Smith who had arrived with her new husband George and shortly afterwards had been found dead in the bath. As with the Lloyd case, an inquest had determined it an accidental death. Putting down his paper and picking up his pen, Crossley wrote to the Metropolitan Police informing them of his suspicions.

He was right to be suspicious. George Smith and John Lloyd were the same person. And only three years earlier, using another alias, he had married Bessie Munday. And she too had been found dead in the bath.

What became known as the 'Brides in the Bath Murders' was not only a grisly case, it was also an important legal milestone. It helped to form the precedent for 'similar-fact evidence' to be admitted in court.

George Smith was tried for the murder of Bessie Munday, and it was decided that the circumstances of the deaths of the other two brides should be allowed as evidence. The facts in the other two cases were so strikingly similar it was hard to believe they were mere coincidence. They could be – and were – properly regarded as part of the case against the accused. On 3 August 1915, Smith was hanged in Maidstone Prison.

Now let me explain what all this has got to do with William Roache and why it is of wider importance.

Last May, after the *Coronation Street* star was charged on two counts of rape, a number of women came forward making accusations against him of indecent assault. Save for the fact that the women all accused the same man, the allegations were each rather different. Yet the decision was taken to try them all together. A dangerous decision indeed.

Yet a very common one. It is quite usual to see accusations of sexual abuse tried together, with the defendant contesting perhaps as many as ten or even more allegations at the same time. And it surprises me that we don't have more debate about how problematic this is.

The brilliant cultural historian Richard Webster has traced the story of the admissibility of similar-fact evidence and how it has gradually broadened from its limited beginnings.

As the Brides in the Bath Murders demonstrate, sometimes it is essential to allow a court to consider evidence of other possible crimes. The Makin case, for instance, involved a couple whose foster child was found buried in their garden, having died, so they claimed, of natural causes. Their protestations of innocence in this case might reasonably be said to be undermined by the discovery of twelve other Makin foster children buried in the gardens of their previous homes.

Discovering other dead bodies in identical circumstances may help to support a murder charge. Yet as Webster argues, this does not mean that one allegation of wrongdoing that may or may not have taken place can be used to support another quite different allegation of wrongdoing that may or may not have taken place. Yet we now hardly bat an eyelid when such faulty reasoning is used.

As it was in the Roache case. It was an explicit and implicit part of the case for believing the accusations against William Roache that he was being charged with more than one crime at the same time. Explicit because the prosecution asked the jury whether all the women could really have been lying. Implicit, because clearly the prosecuting authorities felt the weight of making numerous allegations would cover up the weakness of individual cases.

Nazir Afzal, the Chief Crown Prosecutor for North West England, was inappropriately bullish after the acquittal, saying he wasn't shy and that he followed the evidence. Yet one of the charges against Mr Roache had to be dismissed during the trial because the woman concerned said she could only vaguely remember the incident. The only possible explanation for trying the actor on this charge is that, despite the fact that it would not stand up on its own, which the prosecutors must have sensed, it might help to send him down on the overall package of charges.

It is obvious that trying someone for more than one alleged crime at the same time prejudices the jury. Common sense suggests it must. And often it's meant to. Yet this isn't the only danger.

Even when two allegations are strikingly similar, so similar as to support each other, there is the danger of collusion between the accusers. This collusion may not be deliberate. It may, for instance, be the result of the police or the media accidentally passing information as a case is being built.

In the Roache case, everybody in the country, pretty much, was aware of the accusation of rape. So the one similar 'fact' that justified trying the accusations together – the idea (incorrect as it turns out) that Roache was a sexual predator – was one that had been suggested to every viewer of the evening news. The accusers were therefore not independent of each other.

We have finally woken up to the fact that sexual abuse and child abuse have been much more common than we all allowed for. And we have decided to do something about it. Because of the nature of the crime, the abuse can be hard to prove and establishing a pattern of behaviour is important. There are also practical – administrative, financial – problems with trying cases separately.

Yet bundling together different allegations in one case is fraught with danger. There will be miscarriages of justice. Maybe many. William Roache, thankfully, is a wealthy man of good standing who can pay a top QC to fight for his reputation. What about the care worker or the teacher who can't?

On the day of the Roache acquittal, Nazir Afzal said: 'This case was treated like any other.' I'm sure it was. That's what I'm worried about.

We should all be free to choose how we die

Noel Conway wants the right to decide when his
life will end and most of us, including disabled
people, agree with him

18 July 2017

I want, if I may, to try a thought experiment. Imagine it was
already legal to allow terminally ill patients a bit of control over
the way they die. And then answer my question – do you think
anyone would dare try to take that right away?

Imagine that someone like Noel Conway, a man dying a
terrible death, didn't have to petition the court, as he has this
week. Instead, think where we would be if he already had the
ability to seek help to end his life.

Let's say that it was already possible for two doctors to agree to
help someone who was in the last six months of their life, provided
that they could persuade the family division of the high court that
the patient was of sound mind and had made a consistent decision
without duress. Can you imagine such a law being repealed?

Do you think it would really be possible to persuade people
to sacrifice genuine control and rights for a mishmash of vague
rhetoric and guarantees?

It is always hard to make big social changes, particularly when they are unfamiliar and have powerful voices raised against them. But where these changes come after years of thought, offer people rights and dignity that they are desperate to have, and represent settled and broad public will, we rarely regret it.

I believe we have reached this point with assisted dying.

Noel Conway is seeking a simple right, to be allowed to die as he has lived, as a free man. He's not asking to play God, or have anyone else play God. He's just saying that he'd rather not suffer avoidable, and unnecessary, anguish as he dies. It's a right – I'm sorry to put it like this, but it's true – that we wouldn't deny, that we do not deny, to a cat.

He doesn't want to die. He is not choosing to die. He is accepting that he is going to die, and asking for the option of medical help to assist with the means and timing of his death. I think it is unconscionable to say no to him.

Or to me. The right that Noel Conway seeks is one every one of us hopes we would never have to use. But I'd like at least that option if it comes to it. Wouldn't you? You don't have to use it; I can't imagine wanting to use it. But who knows? And at least there would be the choice.

Actually, let me be a little bit more precise. The choice of how to die will be there whatever we decide to do with the law. That's just a matter of medical science. The question is who makes the choice. Am I – or Noel Conway – allowed to make it for myself or will the state make it for me?

It is this question that would make an assisted-dying law so hard to reverse once it was passed. Those proposing reversal would have to argue that we are not capable of exercising this choice even when we can show that we are being consistent and reasonable.

They would ask us to swap a concrete legal and medical procedure for a lottery. Instead of careful consideration and legally clear deliberation, they would offer a return to an arbitrary and disturbing mess. The person who helps you to die might know what they are doing, or they might not. And your loved one might end up in jail or they might not. Suck it and see, why don't you?

They would ask us to go back to a system where we trusted that the doctor would 'know what to do when the time came'. Even though talk of such things is a bit of a myth. Without assisted-dying law, doctors can't and don't (and shouldn't) just assist death.

They would seek to persuade the public that we should return to trips to Switzerland, where people die earlier than they need to, just in case they aren't fit enough to make it later. And where this choice is available only to those who can afford the considerable cost and have a friend willing to accept the risk of being prosecuted, given the virtual certainty of being investigated. A choice for the few, not available to the many.

I don't think any of this would prove a winning case if someone were trying to reverse assisted dying, so why should it now?

I believe that once the law was in force, it would also undermine what has proven one of the most powerful arguments against reform. At least, powerful with me. The moments when I have been forced to pause during the debate on dignity in dying have been when I have been listening to the advocates for disabled people.

Their fear is that provision for assisted dying would demonstrate that we do not value disabled people and are not willing to protect the most vulnerable. I listen to this with respect and concern, but I do not feel I can accept it.

I don't think Noel Conway is awfully impressed by the idea that the current law – which judges him incapable of making a choice for himself, even with safeguards – values disabled people. And ensuring that if anyone wants help with dying, they have to do it without any sanction or regulation is hardly protecting the vulnerable.

Perhaps for these reasons, although opposition to reform is expressed passionately by many disability groups, it is not the opinion of most disabled people. Indeed far from it. Polling by Populus showed 86 per cent of disabled people supported the assisted-dying reform I've been advocating.

And this means that they are broadly in line with the rest of the population. Most MPs believe that their constituents are quite evenly split on assisted dying. And when there is a debate, they find their postbag has as many from one side as from the other. But in fact, their constituents are not evenly split. They overwhelmingly want change. There has been around 80 per cent support for it for thirty years. Public opinion is consistent and clear and stable. And positive.

What holds Parliament back is fear of the unknown. And that is understandable. But this is not the unknown. We have seen what has happened in Oregon, in California, in Switzerland, places where the law allows choice. We know that the fears aren't justified.

I realise that for some, none of these arguments matter. Religious principles make it impossible to contemplate allowing someone to end their life before it ends naturally. But that is a choice for them. I am seeking a choice for me. And for Noel Conway.

Prosecutors don't know how biased they are

Recent scandals show how dangerous the authorities' blinkered approach to justice can be for innocent citizens

The Director of Public Prosecutions responded to a series of trials that collapsed due to failures in the disclosure of evidence by asserting that no one who was innocent would have gone to jail as a result of such mistakes. I found this claim outrageous.

23 January 2018

I wonder whether Alison Saunders, the Director of Public Prosecutions, has heard this story.

It's about Dorothy Martin, who was sure that on 21 December a flood would destroy the world. Aliens from the Planet Clarion told her it would. But she, and other true believers, would be rescued by a flying saucer. People gave up their jobs, sold their houses, joined Ms Martin and waited.

And then? Nothing. No saucer. Eventually the cultists realised that the moment had come and gone. The obvious conclusion was that the whole thing was nonsense. But that wasn't how the cult reacted.

Instead they called the newspapers. Previously averse to publicity, they now proclaimed the word to everyone. They had received another message from Clarion. There wouldn't be a flood because their devotion had saved the world.

There are two things worth knowing about this story. The first is that it was the basis for one of the most famous books in the field of social psychology: *When Prophecy Fails* by Leon Festinger, Henry Riecken and Stanley Schachter. The second is that the 21 December in question was in 1954 and the book was published in 1956.

In other words, we have had more than sixty years to absorb the lessons from Festinger and his colleagues, yet it seems some are still struggling to do so.

Several prosecutions have recently collapsed at the last minute after it emerged that information in the possession of the police, but not disclosed to the defence, cast strong doubt on the complainant's story.

There was the rape charge against Liam Allan, where police failed to disclose evidence that supported his story, and demonstrated that his accuser pestered him for 'casual sex'. There was the case of Oliver Mears, who spent two years on bail accused of rape before evidence emerged that his accuser had lied.

And there was the case of the family doctor Stephen Glascoe, who faced a series of charges, including the alleged rape of a young girl, before they were dropped just before the trial opened. The accusations derived from so-called 'recovered memories'. The accuser claimed the doctor had performed a forced abortion on her, although her accounts appear to have been based on watching *Call the Midwife*.

During the eighteen-month investigation into Dr Glascoe, police developed a close relationship with the woman involved, with one officer exchanging more than 1,000 texts and 500 emails with her.

The DPP has described these failures as 'disappointing and

irritating', stressing the need to get the job done properly. She has added that she is confident that no innocent person has been jailed as the result of such an error.

That response isn't good enough. I'm not suggesting that Mrs Saunders is unconcerned about people who have been unfairly accused. But has she learnt anything from academic research of the past sixty years into how human beings think?

Festinger's work on the cult was the pioneering study in what is now a vast field. It suggests that once we develop a theory, it is very hard to shake. Indeed the stronger the counter-evidence, the harder we work to save our original idea. And the bigger the disaster brought about by being wrong, the harder we work to convince ourselves and others that we are right.

One piece of work on university fraternities showed that the more humiliating the initiation ritual for a fraternity, the more likely students were to value joining it. Who wants to think themselves the idiot who went through all that for nothing?

Understanding this is vital to gaining an insight into the behaviour of police and prosecutors. Police do not behave like Morse on television, piecing the puzzle together, before revealing the improbable killer right at the end. They develop a theory and then build a case.

Our 'confirmation bias' – an elementary part of social psychology – explains how we seek comfort in every piece of evidence that confirms we are right and find a way of excluding anything that suggests we are wrong. Or even turning it around in our heads so that it becomes supportive. How does someone get it wrong after exchanging 1,000 texts with an unreliable complainant? Precisely because they've exchanged 1,000 texts with her.

As a result, police and prosecutors will not wish to disclose evidence that undermines their case and, crucially, may not even appreciate that it does. They may genuinely, but incorrectly, see the new material as irrelevant. That's what confirmation bias does to you.

The failure to disclose crucial evidence to the defence is not just happening in a few cases. A report last summer from HM Inspectorate of Constabulary and HM Crown Prosecution Service Inspectorate suggests that the process is 'routinely poor'.

So I was disappointed that Mrs Saunders suggested that no innocent person was in jail because of it. This would appear to add to the social psychology failure, a failure to think in statistical terms as most social science now does.

Only if the probability of wrongly convicting someone was virtually zero, and there was almost no randomness in results, can it be true that in a vast sample of convictions no one was wrongly imprisoned because of poor disclosure.

Indeed, Mrs Saunders comically misses the point when she suggests that anyone who feels they have been wrongly convicted because of disclosure failures should speak out. They are unlikely to know if there is vital evidence in their favour if they were never told about it.

Still, it's not surprising that she sticks to the untenable theory that nobody has been wrongly jailed as a result of such failure. She is the DPP after all, so she wouldn't want to accept an idea, however compelling, that prosecutions can be wrong. Festinger would understand her.

There needs to be a better internal system for challenging police officers and prosecutors as they become committed to a theory, and some external judgment about what material should be disclosed.

And, given that prosecutors seem to be relying on recovered memories despite all the work that Elizabeth Loftus has done to show how unreliable they are, it might be a good idea if everyone involved had some extra classes in social science.

PART SEVEN

My Times

When I wrote the earliest column that appears in this book Tony Blair was prime minister, and the most recent column to be included was written on the day that Theresa May announced her resignation.

The book therefore covers sixteen years of political news and it isn't possible to include an article about every significant controversy during that period. However, I do want to give a flavour of the big political issues that made the news and prompted me to express a view.

This final section, which begins with Mr Blair's return in 2005, therefore includes columns on some of the major political developments, including the rise and fall of David Cameron, the singular politics of Jeremy Corbyn and, naturally, Brexit.

It's simple, all the new leader has to do is to win over some new voters

The Conservatives are well placed to progress. But only if they learn some home truths

This article appeared on the Saturday after the 2005 general election. Labour had won a third term. The Conservative Party felt it had made progress because it had won a few extra seats. I felt differently. It was going to need a new leader (to replace Michael Howard) and, I was sure, a new position. I got going on the argument immediately. Later I realised the argument I made here wasn't completely right. The problem is correctly identified but you can't separate the personality of the leader from an understanding of the political problem. A leader has to be the solution as well as know the solution.

7 May 2005

Who is going to be the next leader of the Conservative Party? It does not matter in the slightest. And it does not much matter who picks them, either.

Over the next few months there will be plenty of debate about the personal qualities and appeal of different contenders. Yet, apart from establishing basic competence, this beauty element to the contest will be largely beside the point. What counts is whether the winner understands the nature of Thursday's result. If he does not, he is destined to remain leader of the opposition at best. But if he does, a great prize awaits.

Winning seats has a tremendous positive effect on morale. Having waited at dawn in Conservative Party headquarters in 1997 to greet the defeated Prime Minister I had worked for, and having trailed disconsolately around a count as I lost a marginal seat in 2001, I understand well that this result feels very different to the Conservative Party. Friends of mine who lost narrowly last time have woken up this morning as MPs. It would be surprising if they were not happy. Being seen to have made an advance is good, too. I can confirm that it is a relief not to have Alastair Campbell waving his hand in derision an inch from your face, while the media laugh.

So all of this is a plus – just so long as no one makes the mistake of believing that it was a good result. The Conservative Party scored basically the same proportion of the vote as it did last time, and little more than in 1997. It only won more seats because it was helped by three things that may not be repeated next time.

First, Tony Blair's unpopularity with the middle-class Left. Many of them voted Liberal Democrat and helped the Tories in marginals. The Iraq war is primarily responsible for this. By the next election, both Mr Blair and Iraq will be history.

Second, Charles Kennedy is a chump. By positioning the Liberals to the left of Labour, he won unlikely seats from them, but failed on his main battleground in the Tory–Lib Dem marginals. This left vulnerable Tories in place. Either he or someone else in his party might wake up to the idea that this was not wise.

Third, Lynton Crosby, the Tory campaign director, and Gavin Barwell, the campaign organiser, are not chumps. They produced good on-the-ground campaigns that helped the Tories to win some tight fights. Labour's marginal seats campaign was poor. This, too, may be put right by the next election.

So the only way for the Tories to advance next time is to win more votes. The debate about how to do this must begin by facing a few facts.

To start with, the Conservative Party did not lose this election to the UK Independence Party or to the political wing of a free-market think tank. It lost to Mr Blair's Labour Party. The voters that the Tories need to win are those currently inclined to vote for parties of the Left. The temptation of political analysts is to seek complicated explanations for why voters behave as they do. Sometimes, however, the answer is relatively simple.

When Populus, the *Times* pollster, asked voters to place themselves on a ten point left–right spectrum, the average was 5.20, just to the right of centre. When voters placed Labour on the spectrum, the average (5.33) was to the right of the average voter. But the Conservatives, at 6.01, were seen as significantly to the right of the average voter. So the task of the Conservative Party is to move as close, or closer, to the average voter as New Labour.

Gordon Brown might help a little before the next election by moving his party left but, at least at first, that will actually move Labour closer to the average. So the Tories will probably have to do most of the heavy lifting.

As well as shifting general perceptions, the Conservative Party will have to win back its core vote. This may seem an odd observation. But although the Tory share of the vote has stayed the same, the type of people voting for it has been changing. Tory voting has become more downmarket behaviour. One Conservative MP told me last week that 'now when I'm out campaigning and I see a guy with a T-shirt, big muscles and a tattoo, I think, "Oh good, a Tory."'

In 1992, the Conservative share of AB class professionals was 54 per cent, in 1997, 43 per cent, in 2001, 40 per cent, and this time, 35 per cent. Over the same period, the proportion of AB voters in the population has risen from 18 per cent to 24.9 per cent. Disproportionate numbers of these voters live in the marginal seats that the Tories need to win back.

A new Conservative leader will have to understand how the class of people who used to vote Tory has changed, how their values are different from those of their parents, for example, and their lifestyle.

Part of R. A. Butler's reinvention of the Conservative Party after the landslide defeat of 1945 involved appealing to suburban housewives as the party of the consumer. Now the grand-daughters of those housewives are out at work and are not voting Conservative on the way back from the office. A worrying gender gap has opened up, with the Tories doing worse among women. In the past, at least when they have won, they have done better among women than men.

None of this need mean that the party has to abandon its basic beliefs. But it will have to accommodate itself to the views of others and use a more attractive tone of voice. It will also have to develop a smart new policy agenda, using traditional Tory policy tools in new combinations and with different priorities.

The Tories have made essentially the same appeal to voters twice and scored essentially the same number of votes. What is the point in being leader if you are not going to try something different?

Tonies and Phonies

Blame a plate of sandwiches for a choice image of
today's Tory division

The 2005 Conservative Party conference allowed leadership
candidates to pitch to activists. This was the occasion on
which David Cameron, seen as an underdog, suddenly
became the favourite, overtaking David Davis. At a dinner
early in the week, Mr Cameron told a group of newspaper
executives that he was the natural 'heir to Blair'. They
didn't much like it, but it inspired this column written to
appear on the final day of the conference.

5 October 2005

In the spring of 1993 I sat down to lunch. It took me ten years
to digest the contents.

There was nothing wrong with the food, you understand. It
was my guest that I spent all that time chewing over. I was
director of the Social Market Foundation think tank and we
had asked the Shadow Home Secretary in for a chat. We asked
him for dinner, actually, but Tony Blair said that he liked to
go home to his family in the evening and would it be all right
if he came at lunchtime instead?

I'd gathered a mixed group to join us, but as it so happened most of the guests were Conservative-inclined. So as the conversation ranged over the big issues of the day I was mildly surprised that our Labour visitor seemed to agree with almost everything that was being said. The only time he politely dissented was when someone, a *Guardian* journalist, began arguing that burglary didn't matter.

When Mr Blair left, everyone round the table was impressed. I wasn't. I pointed out that all he'd done was assent to every proposition that had been put to him, only occasionally adding remarks that wouldn't offend a centre-right gathering. Come off it, how impressive was that? Didn't he have any views of his own?

And for years that's what I'd say if anyone asked me what Tony Blair was like. Very pleasant, perhaps a bit vanilla, taller than you'd think, and so anxious to please that he agreed with everybody.

After he'd been prime minister for a couple of years my view of the encounter changed slightly. I moved from thinking that the man believed nothing to thinking that he believed everything. Yet believing nothing and believing everything end up being pretty much the same thing, so my shift in view didn't cost me much sleep.

And then, around about the same time as the invasion of Iraq, a new thought occurred to me, this time a much more disturbing one. Within a year or so I became completely convinced of it. Mr Blair didn't assent to everything that the lunch group had said because he believed in nothing or everything. He assented because he shared the views of that centre-right group that I'd invited to lunch.

Why am I prattling on about some sandwiches I ate in 1993, when I am in Blackpool to watch the Conservatives choose a leader? Answer: because the question I've been wrestling with for all these years is what this week by the seaside is really all about.

Last week in Brighton was about Gordon Brown. Blackpool is about Tony Blair.

What, after all, are the Conservative leadership contenders really arguing about? You can't describe one candidate as a wet and another as a dry. Wets and dries divided over the 1981 Howe Budget, no longer a live issue, funnily enough. And, with Ken Clarke's surrender, there isn't a split between Europhiles and Europhobes either. At least, not for the moment. The battle isn't even over willingness to talk about change, since they all do that.

No, the real division in the Conservative Party is over what you think about the Prime Minister. The real division is between Tonies and Phonies.

The bulk of the Conservative Party still thinks of Tony Blair as, in the phrase that Tories used continuously during the 1997 election campaign, Phoney Blair. They think the whole thing, his entire premiership, all his speeches, his basic political position, is an act. Blair believes nothing and he believes everything. His only innovation as a politician has been to copy the popular bits of Conservative policy. It would be madness, argue the Phonies, for the Tory party to allow itself to be diverted by such a man. Soon he will be gone and not long after that forgotten, except perhaps by the writers of textbooks on public relations.

Candidates seen as coming from different wings of the party, Ken Clarke and Liam Fox, are in fact united in the Phoney camp. Both want to offer the party 'raw politics' instead of 'spin'. And the Phoney/Tony split solves the mystery of the identity of David Davis too. Hard man of the right or John Major's loyal follower? Eurosceptic or Maastricht whip? Mr Davis understands that these distinctions don't matter in the current leadership race. He has become leader of the Phonies. His entire argument is that the Tory party should not try to emulate Tony Blair in any way.

For Tonies, this position will not do. They believe (we believe, because I share this view) that Mr Blair has changed politics fundamentally and that Conservatives have to understand this if they are to regain power. Mr Blair has changed the style of politics, but also the substance.

His political position is a real one – he supports a vigorous global free market, reformed public services, tougher policies on law and order and a neoconservative foreign policy. He has found new ways of talking about these ideas that win broad support from Middle England. Pragmatic rather than ideological, responsive rather than unbending, persuasive rather than hectoring, politics will not be the same after Tony Blair.

There are Tonies running for the leadership (David Cameron and Malcolm Rifkind) and plenty in the top echelons of the party – David Willetts, Oliver Letwin, George Osborne, Tim Yeo. Yet this group remains in the minority. The reason? The fear that the moment the Tory party accepts that Tony Blair really means it, there will be nothing left to say.

Yet this fear is baseless. There is plenty that Tonies can say. For reasons that are secret between him and his psychiatrist, Tony Blair decided to campaign for global free markets and public-service reform in a coalition with Frank Dobson and Amicus. Unsurprisingly, it hasn't worked out too well. He has achieved only a fraction of his potential. Realising he really means it doesn't diminish his failure. It simply makes the case for a Conservative alternative stronger by showing that trying to achieve his aims on the Centre Left has proved impossible.

In other words, accepting the truth about Tony Blair wouldn't be the end of proper opposition. It would be the beginning.

The truth behind Cameron's victory: the triumph of the Smith Square set

His experience as a political professional was
central to David Cameron's victory

This article was written on the day of David Cameron's
election as Conservative leader.

7 December 2005

Yesterday was a very good day for anyone who has ever been
employed by a political party.

You see, working for a party can be exhilarating, but there
is a snag. The upside is this – you may get to be present when
history is made, although in my case this mostly consisted of
being in the room when people resigned or were informed of
a fresh political disaster. The downside? Who is going to employ
you when it's all over?

In all the years I spent at Conservative Central Office I never
once saw a job advertisement that read: 'Wanted: Enthusiastic
person who knows just how to frame a difficult question to the
Prime Minister. Essential – a clean driving licence and a freakish

recall for embarrassing things once written in *Tribune* by Margaret Beckett.'

Karl Hess, the chief speechwriter for Barry Goldwater's 1964 presidential campaign, went looking for work after that election was over. He was turned down by every Senator and Congressman he approached. He then applied to become the Senate lift attendant. When he failed to gain even this appointment, he went on a welding course and took a job on the night-shift in a machine shop.

In my own darker moments I saw myself as junior public affairs assistant (the senior adviser being a Labour supporter) to North West Utilities, responsible for dragging old colleagues to partake of canapés with the finance director at party conferences.

So yesterday was a good day. A new career opportunity opened up for party professionals.

In the past few weeks the papers have been full of remarkable facts about David Cameron, yet none of them make him unique as a party leader. He is, apparently, related to the Queen, but if we go back far enough, aren't we all? Even me (Charles II definitely looks Jewish). Mr Cameron is in his thirties, but so was William Hague when he became leader. He likes rock music, but so does Michael Howard.

What marks David Cameron out, the experience that made him as a politician and which none of his predecessors shared, is that he began his career working for the Conservative Research Department (CRD), the Tory party's policymaking and briefing division. This makes him the first leader of any political party ever to have risen from the ranks of its professional employees.

It's not unusual for potential leaders of the Conservative Party to have worked for the CRD. But until now, the CRD's role in leadership contests has been to provide the loser. Since the CRD chairman Rab Butler was first overlooked in 1956, CRD staffers Reggie Maudling, Iain Macleod, Enoch Powell, Douglas

Hurd and Michael Portillo have all had their eyes on the prize but been denied. Two members of Labour's staff have challenged for the leadership of that party – Denis Healey and Peter Shore each ran twice – but they too were defeated.

Now Mr Cameron has won. And his background as a political professional was central to his victory. The new leader's close friends and advisers are known as the Notting Hill set, as if they all first met by bumping into each other outside the Gate cinema. In fact, the place they all met is in Conservative Central Office.

Almost the entire inner circle – George Osborne, Mr Cameron's best friend, Rachel Whetstone, his longtime ally, Steve Hilton, his strategist, Catherine Fall, his aide, Edward Llewellyn, his new chief of staff, and Ed Vaizey, his parliamentary booster – worked together for the CRD. They are the Smith Square set.

And it was their professionalism that helped their old friend to a most improbable victory. At two vital moments in the long leadership campaign – the launch event and the drafting of the conference speech – Mr Cameron's team was simply better organised than its rivals. Only when control of David Davis's drive for the leadership passed from MPs to two able former party staffers – Nick Wood and David Canzini – did Mr Davis stage any sort of recovery, although by then it was far too late.

It was not just organisational ability that gave the Smith Square set the edge. It was also superior understanding of Tony Blair and the way he has changed politics, gained through their work at CRD closely following his rise.

The first time I met Mr Osborne was at the Labour Party conference in 1994, watching Mr Blair announce his intention to abolish Clause Four. He was the CRD observer sent to monitor Labour's new leader. Afterwards, at lunch, Mr Osborne told me that he thought the Tory party would be forced to change deeply to meet the Blair challenge, something very few people indeed understood at that point.

So the election of Mr Cameron marks an important new stage in British politics – the triumph of the political professional. It can be seen on the Labour side too. The political success of the Blair premiership depended greatly on the quality of his staff.

In the Brown era it will go further. The Miliband brothers, for example, will continue their advance. And having created all of Gordon Brown's economic policies, Ed Balls conducts almost all of the Chancellor's interviews now too, leaving Mr Brown only the job of feuding with people.

Is this increased professionalism in politics a good thing? No. It makes politics too inward-looking, robbing it of the experience of others. The triumph of the party staffers has come about because the rules of politics are now so elaborate, the language so obscure, that the 'game' can only be played by those who have spent a lifetime studying it. This is not a healthy development.

The Smith Square set should see one of their tasks as being to open up politics to those who do not share their expertise.

No, no, no. You've got it all wrong. It's Brown that's New Labour, not Blair

Tony Blair has moved on from the formula that brought success

15 November 2006

I want it all back. Every minute of it. The hours, the days, the weeks I've spent listening to people going on about the Blair–Brown relationship. Give it me back, God (or Richard Dawkins, whichever of you is up there), and I promise I'll use the time better this go around.

Granita; New Labour versus old Labour; Gordon's holding out over the single currency; sources say he's furious; they're furious; this month nobody is furious; now they are furious again; will he or won't he; the question is when; he doesn't want to say; apparently he threw a wobbly; that's not what I'm hearing; Alan Johnson; maybe not Alan Johnson. Aaaaaaaaaagh. Shut up, shut up, shut up.

They're on about it again as you read this. The Queen is getting togged up to go to Parliament and read her speech and the airwaves are dominated by Blair–Brown blah. Is the new legislative agenda agreed with the Chancellor? Does it trap him? Yes. No. Who cares?

Look, it is not that this is all unimportant. It's the relationship between the Chancellor and the Prime Minister, for heaven's sake. It's the future of the Government. Of course it's important. It's just that I think we've spent much of the past decade getting it wrong.

The debate about Blair and Brown has centred on this idea: Mr Blair is New Labour while Mr Brown, if not exactly old Labour, has old Labour tendencies. Those who find this formulation too crude describe Mr Brown as being more of a traditionalist or as being more concerned with the party, but these are different words to make basically the same point.

Occasionally someone sticks up for the Chancellor and says that he is New Labour to his fingertips. But then they find it hard to answer the follow-up question – why does he differ from Mr Blair and why doesn't the Prime Minister entirely trust him to keep the party on the right track?

The answer came to me while I was watching Mr Blair make his final party conference speech. (I wasn't as impressed by it as everyone else, by the way, because after saying a lot of things that I agreed with entirely he concluded: 'You take my advice. You don't take it. Your choice. Whatever you do, I'm always with you. Head and heart.' Whatever you do, I am with you? What's that about?)

Just after he'd defended his Iraq policy and just before he lambasted David Cameron, the Prime Minister said this: 'A governing party has confidence, self-belief. It sees the tough decision and thinks it should be taking it. Reaches for responsibility first. Serves by leading . . . The British people will, sometimes, forgive a wrong decision. They won't forgive not deciding.'

And then I realised. The person who is no longer New Labour is Mr Blair. The division between the Prime Minister and his chancellor is not that Mr Brown is in any way old Labour. It is that Mr Brown is New Labour to his fingertips, dogmatically New Labour, the architect of the whole building and still tied to his blueprint. The Prime Minister, meanwhile, has moved on.

The campaign run by the Labour Party between 1994 and 1997 was one of the most innovative and effective in British political history. You establish trust on key Tory issues such as the economy so that you can draw dividing lines with them in the best places; you avoid creating unpopular policies and change the subject on difficult issues; you characterise hard choices as false choices and develop a third way, an unexpected way, of dealing with them (for example, don't raise income tax, don't cut spending, impose a windfall tax); you are not above using what the unkind might call a gimmick as a way of showing you care about an issue. That's the substance.

And the style? You campaign continuously, fight the war round the clock, seeing everything as political, keeping focus, letting nothing go; you aggressively combat every small slight made by every two-bit journalist but schmooze their proprie-tors and editors like crazy; you never answer a question you don't want to answer and relentlessly repeat your soundbites; you expect loyalty and discipline from every party member with you in total control, at the head of a small group at the top.

Is there one part of this that the Chancellor has departed from since 1994? I can't think of one. The world has changed a great deal in the past ten years, but not the Chancellor. He is still plugging away.

His idea of an independent board for the NHS was classic New Labour (not for all that choice stuff, not against all reform, a third way). So was his Veterans Day (we can be trusted on Tory cultural issues). His relations with the press follow the New Labour rulebook exactly.

Now think about the Brown–Blair divide over tuition fees. It was characterised as an old Labour versus New Labour fight. Wrong. The Chancellor was taking the classic New Labour view. He felt that there was no point putting forward an unpopular policy when it wasn't strictly necessary. He turned up to the Cabinet committee meeting where they were dotting the 'i's and crossing the 't's on the policy paper and provoked a stand-up row with Charles Clarke by proposing that they not have a policy at all.

But for Mr Blair this classic New Labour position is no longer enough. The British people 'won't forgive not deciding', remember?

He is fed up with the caution of the classic approach and wants to go farther, faster towards free markets, globalisation and liberal interventionist wars, if only he could get it through the party. He doesn't mind so much being unpopular, it's too late for all that. He can't be bothered chasing down every small negative article and has replaced his aggressive war room with an exasperated shrug. He thinks people are tired of repeating soundbites; he now prefers lengthy exhausting explanations.

We're about to hear the last Blairite Queen's Speech. Then prepare for the return of New Labour.

The best-dressed corpse in the morgue

Of course the Conservative Party has to change

Just before Gordon Brown became prime minister the
Conservatives contrived to have a major row about their
policy on grammar schools. David Willetts, the shadow
education secretary, made a speech presenting new research
on their shortcomings and David Cameron supported him.
Graham Brady, a frontbench spokesman, then resigned.
The real battle, of course, was about how serious the Tories
were about modernisation.

6 June 2007

I was there, actually in the room, for the critical moment in
David Cameron's leadership of the Conservative Party. Which
is pretty good going, because Mr Cameron didn't manage to
make it there himself.

In his defence, the whole thing took place thirteen years ago.
And it was at the Labour Party conference. I am sure he watched
it on television. Not the same as seeing it live, of course, but
we can't all be lucky, can we?

Anyway, there I was, balcony seat, left-hand side, Blackpool

Winter Gardens, when Tony Blair made one of the most significant political speeches of the postwar era. The one in which he announced that he intended to rewrite Clause Four of the Labour constitution.

And sitting next to me was George Osborne, a young researcher sent by Tory HQ to monitor proceedings. When the speech was over, we went to lunch. We agreed that politics had been altered fundamentally. If Mr Blair succeeded in turning Labour into a centrist party, the Tory party would have to change, moving towards the centre itself, or lose. And keep losing. A few years later, on bike rides to the House of Commons, Mr Osborne set about persuading his close friend David Cameron that this analysis was inescapable.

But the depressing thing is that so many people on the right still appear to think that they can escape it. Never mind having their own Tory Clause Four moment, they haven't yet come to terms with Labour's Clause Four moment. I watched the grammar school row unfold with my mouth wide open. How can they not get it? What's wrong with these people?

Listen. Before the 1997 election I was having a discussion with a Conservative friend (David Willetts as it happens) about how bad the result would be. As bad as in the Labour landslide of 1945? Or worse, as bad as when the Liberals swept to power in 1906. We were both wrong, it was a catastrophe for the Tories unequalled since 1832. It was just as bad in 2001. And pretty much the same in 2005.

So you don't have to have a PhD in political strategy to realise that the Conservative Party now has to change. It has to compromise many of its long-held opinions in order to get some new people, people who are uncomfortable with existing Tory policy, to join in and give it support. It has to broaden its coalition. A lot. It simply can't win, or even come close to winning, if Labour is fighting on the centre ground and the Tory party isn't. Margaret Thatcher beat Michael Foot and Neil Kinnock not Blair or Brown. Labour has changed and the Conservatives have to respond. Simple, yes? But so many Tories still don't seem to understand.

Amazingly, hilariously, petulantly, tragically, doltishly, persistently, bizarrely, infuriatingly, arrogantly, obtusely, fantastically, so many Conservatives appear to believe that no compromise, or at least very little, is needed. Yes, in theory, they accept the need for change. It's just that in practice they oppose every compromise with reality and the voters that anyone suggests. This is, as Mr Cameron put it, delusional.

One of the great ironies of the Tory debate is that the people who accuse Mr Cameron of being all style and no substance also believe that the Tories can win by changing style and refusing to change on substance.

But of course, they can't. My old friend Norman Blackwell, with whom I worked closely and happily when he was head of John Major's policy unit, has spoken up in defence of the Tory 1997 policy of having a grammar school in every town. He thinks that policy is a good one. Of course he does. If he didn't, he wouldn't have put it in the manifesto, now would he? But I am sure that he noticed that the campaign in which this policy had a starring role did not have a happy ending.

So what policies in the 1997 manifesto does Norman, or any other of the grammar school critics, think should be changed? None is not a tenable answer.

This weekend Michael Portillo described Graham Brady, the frontbench spokesman who resigned over grammar schools, as a plodder. He then suggested Mr Brady had won the argument. I think both these judgments are wrong. I wasn't persuaded by what Mr Brady had to say but I have always held him in high regard. He is no plodder, but he has been hugely self-indulgent.

Yesterday morning a *Times* Populus poll showed that 36 per cent of people supported Mr Brady's grammar school policy while 60 per cent backed that outlined by David Willetts. Even if Mr Brady was right, how often does he think the Tory party should go to the country advancing big-ticket manifesto items that the vast majority of voters do not like?

Grammar schools isn't Clause Four. It's only one issue among many where the Tories will have to change. But what does Mr Brady think – that in an election, schools policy won't come up?

He has been praised by many for a principled resignation. I just think he wants the Conservative Party to be the best-dressed corpse in the morgue.

Moving towards the centre is painful for Tories. It starts with accepting something they are very reluctant to accept – that Tony Blair was a substantial figure who has changed the basis of political debate. And it continues with something even more painful – giving ground on policy, accepting that some arguments are lost and others will have to be returned to on another day.

Some may think that there is a brilliant, attractive, right-wing synthesis, a magical narrative that obviates the need for any concessions to the centre. Well, if there is, please don't keep the secret to yourself. Share it with the rest of us.

Tories have a choice. They can be a tight, right little party or they can win. They can't do both. Make up your mind. Which is it going to be?

Tying the knot? For you, we promise £5,000

The right way to deliver the Tory marriage policy

18 July 2007

Have you ever attended Weight Watchers or Slimming World? Or bet on a horse? I'm sorry. I don't mean to be personal. It's just that if you have, I have good news. Even if you put all that weight back on when you stopped going, or lost all your money when Dobbin refused at the first fence, your experience can still be put to use. It can help you to understand how the Tories can solve their dilemma over marriage.

Let me set the dilemma out. There is strong evidence that living in a house with a stable family and two parents is good for children – it makes them more likely to do well at school, less likely to commit crime and so on. There is also good reason to believe that marriage helps to produce longer, more stable relationships than cohabitation does.

Naturally, therefore, Conservatives want to encourage marriage. David Cameron promised to recognise marriage in the tax and benefit system and it is commonly thought that his policy will be some sort of tax allowance paid only to married people. Retreating from this promise wouldn't just make Mr Cameron look a fool – it would also be a blow to marriage itself. It would signal that marriage as a norm is no longer politically defensible.

But sticking with the promise brings no end of problems. There is, for instance, a technical difficulty – many of the people the Tories wish to influence don't earn enough to pay tax. That, however, is just the start. The policy discriminates against single parents, divorced people and widows. The Tories can't get round this – discrimination is how the thing works.

It also appears to judge the relationships of non-married parents and denigrate their ability to care for their children, angering millions of potential Tory voters. And much of this anger will be justified. Marriage may be better for children, but only on average and once all other social factors have been adjusted for. There are, therefore, no end of examples of non-married parents raising their children in a far superior way to married contemporaries. Britney Spears was married when she took to driving with her son on her lap.

For a party trying to persuade people that it is modern and 'for all', it's a bit of a nightmare. David Cameron was happy to drop grammar schools because he had decided supporting selection was the wrong policy. This is different – he thinks recognising marriage is right, it is central to his idea of healing a broken society and, anyway, he's stuck with his words. But that doesn't make the politics any better. So what should he do?

Begin by thinking how a policy to encourage long and stable relationships might actually work. This is where betting on horses and attending slimming clubs come in.

Numerous social experiments show that making public commitments has a very strong effect on those signing up to them. And you can see the application of this research all around you.

Organisations seeking compliance from their staff often get them to set out their goals for the coming year in writing. When you enter a competition on the back of a cereal pack, you usually have to send in a postcard, answering a tie-breaker question, 'I like this cereal because . . .' The purpose is not to break ties, but simply to get consumers to write down that they like the product. Slimming clubs use the power of commitment to get you to move towards a publicly announced target weight.

One of the most interesting features of the academic work on commitment is this – once you have made a choice, you instantly become more confident, more convinced that it was the right decision, than you were before you made it.

This is called post-decision dissonance, since you ask. A study of gamblers, for instance, showed that immediately after placing a bet they became far more confident that their horse would win. Marriage works in exactly this way. The public commitment is a powerful force that keeps the couple together. And the feeling that so many people have immediately after their wedding? The feeling that things are different? Why, that's post-decision dissonance.

So a sensible public policy would do two things to encourage stable relationships. The first is to provide just enough of an incentive to tip cohabiting couples willing to consider marriage into actually getting married. The second is to make marriage a social norm, showing confidence and respect in the institution so that those having children feel that people like them generally marry. Once the couple is married, social psychology – the power of commitment – takes the strain.

How would you do this? Well, paying money makes sense. It might provide that incentive, that little extra push, at the margin and help to establish the norm. But once the money has done the trick, once the couple has got married, why would you keep paying them?

There is no evidence, or theory, that suggests that paying people continual instalments of small sums of money (or taking it off the tax bills of those who pay tax) would increase the longevity of their relationship. In fact, I am surprised so many pro-marriage advocates believe in it. After all, if simply paying people worked to extend relationships, you wouldn't need to bother with marriage at all. You could just pay couples to stay together.

So the right policy is to pay people one lump sum – a dowry – when they get married. A dowry of, say, £5,000 would be a real incentive to formalise a relationship and a public political statement of faith in the institution of marriage.

There are, of course, technical details to be worked out – timing of the payment, the eligibility of divorcees and so forth. But the Government might be able to pay out even more: the money only gets paid to newlyweds (and civil partnerships), so you can afford an amount big enough to make a difference. And it reaches those who don't pay tax, too.

Just as attractive are the political advantages. The one-off dowry doesn't discriminate against anybody who is already a single parent, say, or widowed. It doesn't judge their relationships or even appear to do so. It keeps Mr Cameron's promise, encouraging people to get married, but doesn't divide society into taxpayers who conform and those who don't. It's liberal and Conservative at the same time.

The dowry. Dilemma solved.

Our high inheritance taxes must go, pass it on

Why it's right to keep it in the family

At the October 2007 party conference, George Osborne announced that, if made chancellor, he would cut inheritance tax. The announcement was wildly (and to some, unaware of the polling, surprisingly) popular. In the weeks before the speech there was quite an argument among Tory modernisers about the rights and wrongs of it. So at the end of August I weighed in with this.

22 August 2007

I've been wondering when I should start worrying about inheritance tax. I could wait until after I am dead, I suppose, when the bill arrives. Or I could start now. After a bit of thought, I've picked now. When you are alive it's easier to express yourself clearly, I find.

My choice may seem a no-brainer to you, but it will have taken the Government by surprise. Ministers expect me to die first and worry later. That is the only explanation I can think of for their constant repetition of their favourite inheritance tax statistic. What are you getting so worked up about they ask.

Only 6 per cent of all estates will have to pay inheritance tax. You're off the hook.

And, of course, they are quite right. Last year inheritance tax was, indeed, paid on only 6 per cent of estates. The Government keeps increasing the threshold (the amount below which you don't have to pay), and says that it intends to carry on doing so. It says it will do this rapidly enough, as fast as house price inflation, so that in years to come inheritance tax will still fall on only this small proportion of estates. You see. What's the problem?

I'll tell you what the problem is. The problem is that I don't know when I am going to die.

Yes, it is possible that by the time I die the tax threshold may be so high that my estate is no longer eligible. But it's also possible that I could die tomorrow, and if I did my estate would have to pay tax at existing rates and the existing threshold.

This explains the discrepancy between the small number of estates paying the tax and the potency of the issue. According to research by Scottish Widows, 37 per cent of households now have an estate with a value above the threshold. Every one of these people feels themselves an inheritance taxpayer even if only a few of their estates will ever pay. The Government expects people to shrug off the tax because years later they will discover, upon dying, that everything was fine, after all.

So the tax on inheritance raises a relatively small amount of money (£3.6 billion) from a relatively small number of people while making a big impact on the behaviour, plans and fears of a very large number of people. Not an ideal combination.

Now I know the response to this. It is that the people who own estates aren't really the taxpayers at all. The burden falls on those who inherit. I can spend all I like of my own money and I won't have to cough up a penny. Sure, if there's anything left, my children will have to pay. But why shouldn't they? They've done nothing to deserve the cash. They're lucky to get anything.

This argument seems so obvious and strong that those who deploy it are, I think, baffled that everyone doesn't simply agree. The case for inheritance tax isn't simply left wing – it redistributes wealth – but also right wing – it taxes dumb luck rather than meritorious effort, and doesn't really distort the economy because those who earn the money don't pay the tax.

Which is pretty powerful, except that it ignores human nature.

Most parents do not think of their children as just another set of economic actors. They look at them as an extension of themselves. They don't think just of their own interests but how it will affect their family and future generations. And a good thing too. The purpose of public policy should be to encourage this spirit, rather than to undermine it.

The idea that when you tax the passage of wealth from one generation to the next you are not taxing useful economic activity is simply wrong.

In a brilliant speech entitled 'The Clash of Generations', delivered a couple of years back, the Tory MP and thinker David Willetts argued that, while all our debates on fairness concern social class, the big issue of the future is equity between generations.

Our welfare system rests on the willingness of one generation to support the other at different stages in the life cycle. The pensions of today's pensioners are paid for by young earners, and this burden will increase with demographic change. Yet this willingness could be undermined by a perception that the young are getting a raw deal. As the baby-boomers reach old age they will do so having benefited hugely from the house price boom, while their children struggle to get on to the housing ladder and achieve a similar standard of living to the one they grew up with.

The transfer of assets from one generation to the next is one of the ways that the delicate social pact between generations will be maintained. It may not be a redistribution from rich to poor, but that's not the only kind of redistribution that matters. Inheritance is a redistribution from old to young. And beyond that, the idea that the family's wealth stays in the family is one way that we signal the obligation that the past has to the present and the present has to the future.

Perhaps you don't think such signals matter? Well, in the debate on the environment we are constantly being encouraged to think of those who will inherit the Earth. What sort of planet, we are asked, will our children, our grandchildren, live on?

What if I were to reply that it didn't matter? That I'll be dead by then and the state of the Earth my children inherit is just dumb luck? What if I were to reply that the economically rational thing to do is to refuse to pay out to prevent climate change because an entirely different set of people, my children not me, will suffer from any consequences?

It's easy from this to see that in the long run we're not all dead. We live on in future generations. And if I am expected to think this way in respect of the environment, then I should be allowed to think this way in respect of my estate.

And when you think about it like this, what could be more natural than to abolish inheritance tax and raise the money instead from the myriad ways that we pollute the Earth?

Israel acts because the world won't defend it

The scenes from Gaza are heartbreaking. But the whole conflict could be avoided if the Palestinians said one small thing

At the end of 2008 hostilities between Israel and Hamas resumed after a lull and Israel sent soldiers into Gaza to eliminate the threat from rockets and tunnels.

7 January 2009

It was strictly forbidden to have a notebook in Belsen, but my Aunt Ruth had one anyway. Just a little pocket diary – an appointment book with one of those tiny pencils. And in it, in the autumn of 1944, she noted that Anne Frank and Anne's sister, Ruth's schoolfriend Margot, had arrived in the concentration camp.

My mother and my aunt had been watching through the camp wire when the Franks arrived. Mum remembers it well, because they had been excited to spot girls they knew from the old days in Amsterdam. They had played in the same streets, been to the same schools and Ruth and Margot attended Hebrew classes together. The pair had once been pressed into service to act as bridesmaids when a secretive Jewish wedding had taken place at the synagogue during their lesson time.

But Ruth and Margot did not grow up together. Because while Ruth and my mother lived, Margot and Anne never left Belsen. They died of typhus.

I am telling you this story because I want you to understand Israel. Not to agree with all it does, not to keep quiet when you want to protest against its actions, not to side with it always, merely to understand Israel.

There are two things about the tale that help to provide insight. The first is that all these things, the gas chambers, the concentration camps, the attempt to wipe Jews from the face of the Earth, they aren't ancient history, and they aren't fable. They happened to real people and they happened in our lifetime. Anne and Margot Frank were just children to my aunt and my mother; they weren't icons, or symbols of anything.

The second is that world opinion weeps now for Anne Frank. But world opinion did not save her.

The origin of the state of Israel is not religion or nationalism, it is the experience of oppression and murder, the fear of total annihilation and the bitter conclusion that world opinion could not be relied upon to protect the Jews.

Israel was the idea of a journalist. Theodor Herzl was the Paris correspondent of the *Neue Freie Presse* when he witnessed anti-Semitic rioting against the Jewish army captain Alfred Dreyfus who had been falsely accused of espionage. Herzl was then among the small corps of journalists who in 1895 witnessed the famous ceremony of disgrace in which Dreyfus was stripped of his epaulettes.

The experience was one of the things that led Herzl to abandon his belief in assimilation. He became convinced that Jews would only be safe if they had their own national home. Herzl became the first leader of modern Zionism. For many years many Jews resisted Herzl's conclusion. My grandfather was among them. But the experience of Jews all over the world in the first half of the twentieth century – not just in Europe but in the Middle East too – rather bore out Herzl.

So when Israel is urged to respect world opinion and put its faith in the international community the point is rather being missed. The very idea of Israel is a rejection of this option. Israel only exists because Jews do not feel safe as the wards of world opinion. Zionism, that word that is so abused, so reviled, is founded on a determination that, at the end of the day, somehow the Jews will defend themselves and their fellow Jews from destruction. If world opinion was enough, there would be no Israel.

The poverty and the death and the despair among the Palestinians in Gaza moves me to tears. How can it not? Who can see pictures of children in a war zone or a slum street and not be angry and bewildered and driven to protest? And what is so appalling is that it is so unnecessary. For there can be peace and prosperity at the smallest of prices. The Palestinians need only say that they will allow Israel to exist in peace. They need only say this tiny thing, and mean it, and there is pretty much nothing they cannot have.

Yet they will not say it. And they will not mean it. For they do not want the Jews. Again and again – again and again – the Palestinians have been offered a nation state in a divided Palestine. And again and again they have turned the offer down, for it has always been more important to drive out the Jews than to have a Palestinian state.

It is difficult sometimes to avoid the feeling that Hamas and Hezbollah don't want to kill Jews because they hate Israel. They hate Israel because they want to kill Jews.

There cannot be peace until this changes. For Israel will not rely on airy guarantees and international gestures to defend it. At its very core, it will not. It will lay down its arms when the Jews are safe, but it will not do it until they are.

And if you reflect on it, doesn't recent experience bear this out? Just as Herzl was borne out? A year or so back I met a teacher while I was on holiday and fell to talking with him about Israel. He was a nice man and all he wanted was for fighting to stop and to end the suffering of children. And he had a question for me.

Why, he asked, doesn't Israel offer to give back the West Bank and Gaza? Why doesn't it just let the Palestinians have a state there? If the Palestinians turned it down, he said, then at least liberal opinion would be on Israel's side and would rally to its assistance.

So I patiently explained to this kind, good man that Israel had, at Camp David in 2000, made precisely this offer and that it had been rejected out of hand by Yasser Arafat, not even used as the basis for negotiation. I told him that Israel was no longer in Gaza, having withdrawn unilaterally and taken the settlers with it. The Palestinians had greeted this movement with suicide bombs and rockets. Yet the teacher, with all his compassion, wasn't even aware of all this. And liberal opinion? Sad to relate, my new friend's faith in it was misplaced. It has turned strongly against Israel.

Israel has made many mistakes. It has acted too aggressively on some occasions, has been too defensive on others. The country hasn't always respected the human rights of its enemies as it should have done. What nation under such a threat would have avoided all errors?

But you know what? As Iran gets a nuclear weapon and so the potential for another Holocaust against the Jews and world opinion does nothing, I am not so sure that the errors of world opinion are so much to be preferred to the errors of Israel.

If you don't like the voters, they won't like you

Ed Miliband needs to win back the centre
ground, but he won't succeed unless he knows
what makes it tick

In May 2010 the coalition was formed and David Cameron
became prime minister. On 25 September Labour elected
Ed Miliband as party leader. Three days later, during the
Labour conference and on the day of his leader's speech,
I wrote this, which appeared the following day.

29 September 2010

I think that it is high time Ed Miliband visited an American
airport. He can wait until this conference thingy is over – Hilary
Benn is speaking on sustainable communities on Thursday, and
he won't want to miss that – but the moment that the chair
starts thanking the police and the staff and so forth, Ed should
high-tail it.

American airports are a magnet for cult groups. And in their
hands they carry small bunches of flowers. As travellers pass,
group members attempt to give them flowers. They are really
persistent, refusing to take no for an answer. And then, when

they have successfully handed over their 'gift', they ask for a donation. Now you would think that having suffered the irritation of having to accept unwanted flowers, the last thing that the victim would want to do is make a donation. Wrong. It turns out that travellers who finally take a bunch are more likely to give money. They are. There have been studies.

Watch and learn, Ed. People reciprocate favours. Any kind of favours, even ones they didn't really want in the first place. In his classic book *Influence*, Robert Cialdini explains how people will reciprocate the receipt of a cheap pen included in a letter seeking a charitable donation, they will reciprocate the concession of a point in an argument, and they will reciprocate liking.

In other words, people are more likely to have affection for you if you show affection for them. Successful car salesmen sometimes exploit this in the crassest way possible, sending birthday cards with the message 'I like you' written inside. Or they might do it subtly, by suggesting that they are similar to you. Spotting your golf-club tie, they talk of golf; spotting your son's football kit, they reveal that they support the same team.

Looking back, I think that one of the crucial political steps from William Hague's leadership of the Conservative Party to David Cameron's came with an understanding that liking is reciprocal. Swing voters wouldn't like the Tories until the Tories liked swing voters. Mr Hague's Conservatives didn't look like swing voters, didn't talk like swing voters and couldn't understand swing voters. The reaction of swing voters to this was predictable.

Tony Blair writes in his memoirs of his bewilderment that the Tories used to attack him for enjoying both fish and chips and linguini with sun-dried tomatoes. He points out that millions of other people enjoy both these dishes.

Mr Blair, of course, 'got' the Tories. His father had been a minor Conservative politician. A friend relates that the moment when he bonded with the former Prime Minister was when he told Mr Blair that his parents always voted Conservative.

And then came Mr Cameron. He understands people who voted for Mr Blair. He rather likes Mr Blair himself. He likes swing voters and they like him back. Funny that. That liking suffused everything he did. It was more important than policy change in helping the Tories to reconnect.

Anyway, I think the reciprocity of liking might turn out to be Ed Miliband's big problem. Ed, like his brother, is an intelligent, rather nice man. He's a little serious sometimes, perhaps, but maybe that is just because he cares a lot about the politics of belonging and it weighs him down or something. I don't, however, think he much likes or understands people who voted for David Cameron.

He regards supporting the Conservatives as a very odd thing to do. He gives you – and I am not the only person to experience this – a sort of compassionate but rather irritated look, as if you are a bit dim, perhaps, and certainly a great disappointment to him.

I suspect that this incomprehension will be reciprocated. And it will prove a big problem for him, one that he will struggle to overcome. Because voters are very sensitive. They can detect immediately what a politician thinks of them.

Oh, and there's two more things. The first is this – a politician can't fake it. You can't pretend to like someone or claim to 'get it' if you actually don't. Authenticity is essential.

After 1997 Conservative politicians knew what they were supposed to say, the boxes they needed to tick. And they said it, they ticked the boxes. But this didn't mean they really understood, or quite believed, what they were saying. They would use phrases such as 'I know we seemed out of touch', rather than 'I agree we were out of touch'. Many of the words Mr Cameron later used about changing the party were being spoken from the moment of the 1997 defeat, but the sentiment wasn't the same at all.

The Labour leader's speech yesterday reminded me very much of those early Tory speeches. The more this week that Mr Miliband has said that he gets it, the less I have believed that he does. The more he said he 'understood' voter concerns (rather than shared them) the more I wondered whether he really does. I think it was a speech where his instincts were telling him one thing while his script said something else. And this uncertainty transmitted itself to the audience.

So you can't fake it. And there's a second discipline – you can't change voters. In the words of Billy Joel, you have to like them just the way they are. At the heart of Mr Miliband's speech, and of his political strategy, is the idea that you can move the centre ground, pick it up and put it down a little to the left. The starting point of the two successful modern attempts at party reform – Tony Blair and David Cameron's starting point – was that you cannot shift the centre ground.

Events might, but you can't. You have to accept where the centre ground is, and live with that discipline.

Early in his speech Mr Miliband asserted: 'The most important lesson of New Labour is this: every time we made progress we did it by challenging the conventional wisdom.' The truth was the exact opposite.

New Labour made progress by, at long last, after many years of defiance, accepting the conventional wisdom.

Yesterday's speech veered erratically between conviction and calculation and back again. I think Ed Miliband is going to find it hard to avoid his leadership doing the same.

Gay marriage – such a conservative idea

Party support for this proposal would not just atone for past failings. It would chime with core Tory values

This article appeared at an early stage of the gay-marriage debate and before the Conservatives had committed themselves. It was part of my effort to persuade them to support the idea.

16 February 2011

I want to start with a little history. I think it is necessary.

It was a cold Saturday morning in 1954 and Peter Wildeblood stood in the dock at Lymington Magistrates' Court charged with 'conspiracy to incite certain male persons to commit serious offences with male persons'. In short order, the diplomatic correspondent of the *Daily Mail* was convicted and sentenced to eighteen months in jail. Thus did that great newspaper play an important role in the legalisation of homosexuality.

For the jailing of the *Mail*'s man, and his friends Lord Montagu and Michael Pitt-Rivers, produced an outcry. As occasionally happens in politics, this prosecution suddenly revealed a great injustice that had been there all the time, unnoticed. And the Home Secretary responded to the fuss by setting up a commission under Lord Wolfenden that, when it finally reported in 1957, recommended that homosexual acts should no longer be illegal.

Yet it took a further ten years before this happened. It needed a Labour government, great ingenuity by its Home Secretary, Roy Jenkins, in the mid-1960s and huge rows in the Cabinet before government time was found for the Commons to debate and agree the legalisation of homosexuality.

I start with history for three reasons. The first is that while some argue that gay rights has been an onrushing tide, brooking little opposition, insisting that 'we' bow to political correctness dictated by 'them', the truth is that progress has been very slow; that decades have passed between the recognition of injustice and its correction.

The second is that the history of the suffering of gay people – of jailing, of police intimidation, of discrimination, of street violence against them – and the story of the long and difficult struggle for gay rights illustrates that this is for us in this country the great civil rights cause of our lifetime.

And finally, I start with history because I fear that it shows that the role of Conservatives in advancing this civil rights cause has not been glorious. Tories ended slavery, championed the Factory Acts, broadened the franchise and brought equal votes for women. But in 1967 almost all Tories either voted against legalisation or stayed away. (Although, fascinatingly, of the very few Tories who voted for the Bill, one of them was Margaret Thatcher.)

Now, in office, Conservatives have an opportunity to make their own contribution to a cause they so long spurned. The Liberal Democrats are advancing the idea that gay couples should be allowed to marry in religious establishments. Conservatives in the Government should champion this proposal and not merely tolerate it, for it is a profoundly conservative idea that gays should marry.

What, after all, is conservatism? It is an attempt to distinguish between on the one hand social customs and fashions that can change, and on the other the fundamental ideas and institutions that define a community and therefore must be preserved.

Conservatives get stuck when they muddle up the two, when they, for instance, begin to regard a particular form of dress (a tie, a dinner jacket) as a point of principle. The best Conservatives are those who see the distinction most clearly and who, like Benjamin Disraeli, are able to make great leaps of imagination, broadening the franchise to a new middle class to preserve a stable nation of property holders. Being able to tell the difference between changing social customs and fundamental institutions requires Conservatives to be acutely aware of how society is evolving, always sensitive to the latest developments and trends. Fogeyism is bad conservatism. It misses the point.

Conservatives will often be late to champion reform, as they cautiously weigh up whether changing something might undermine fundamental liberties or the character of the nation. Yet once they have made up their mind they should move boldly and firmly.

When civil partnerships were first suggested the idea was advanced that providing a legal status for gay couples might undermine heterosexual marriage. The means by which this would happen were obscure. I think the idea was that it would hold marriage up to ridicule, or something. But whether or not this was ever a sensible argument, it is apparent that the fear is groundless.

The opposite point should recommend itself to Tories. Marriage strengthens commitment between couples and therefore brings stability into the lives of those who enter into it. The advantage of extending that to gay people is obvious.

Nevertheless, there is an objection that the difference between marriage and gay civil partnership needs to be maintained, because marriage is intended for procreation. Another odd argument. Lots of people marry when they don't intend to have children, cannot have children or are too old to have children. Should all these people be forced to have civil partnerships?

Against this is the important fact – not an irrelevant or small thing this, by any means – that to deny gay people the right to be married in the full sense is to deny people the dignity and respect they deserve. And who better than a Conservative can understand the desire of an individual for dignity, respect and social status? This is a Tory aspiration at its core.

What, finally, of the religious objection? I am not very good at praying. My wife complains that I fidget in synagogue. The children complain that I fidget. But for all my failings in the devotion department, I do have one conviction about prayer of which I feel confident. It would be very disappointing for the Jews to have prayed for thousands of years and learnt nothing. Sometimes you have to sit there for hours. Surely some thoughts must have struck us in all that time.

For me, at least, that thought is a steady, strong belief in the fundamental equality before the law and under God of my fellow humans and a determination to love what is different about them as well as the things that I share. I do not expect, or demand, that all others share it, but I am as sure as I can be that this belongs in my religion. I would want Conservatives to champion my free expression of this religious belief.

Soon it will be mainstream to say 'leave the EU'

Greece has made stark the choices facing Europe
– and now questioning the whole project is not a
fringe position

At the end of 2011 Britain's membership of the EU still seemed secure. It wasn't opposed by any mainstream politician and the Conservative Party still leaned against an in/out referendum. But the Greek financial crisis made me think this would soon change. Written just after the Greek government had promised a public vote on an EU financial package, I predicted that the momentum of the single currency would soon force the UK to seek to negotiate new EU rules, that there would be mainstream politicians supporting leaving and that we would have a referendum on it.

2 November 2011

Sweat dripping from his nose, his collar soaking wet, Hugh Gaitskell finally sat down after speaking for 105 minutes. The Brighton ice-rink erupted. The Labour leader's rejection of entry into the Common Market on the terms proposed by the Government in 1962 received an extraordinary ovation.

But there was something odd about the scene. For Gaitskell's friends on the centre right of the party were dismayed. Some stayed silently in their seats. Others rose (to acknowledge the man) while keeping their arms folded (to signal disapproval of his words). Meanwhile, his party enemies exulted. Gaitskell's rival, Harold Wilson, called for the speech to be printed, and the left-wing union leader Frank Cousins said that the transport workers would pay for it.

Surveying the scene as her husband acknowledged the applause, Dora Gaitskell turned to a friend and commented: 'But Charlie, the wrong people are clapping.'

The wrong people are clapping. Almost from the moment that Harold Macmillan first proposed entry into the Common Market it has enjoyed the support of the broad mainstream of British politicians. Some (Harold Wilson, Jim Callaghan, Rab Butler) were less enthusiastic than others (Roy Jenkins, Jo Grimond, Geoffrey Howe) but in practice and in power they have backed membership. Opponents have been on the extremes, been the 'wrong people'.

Perhaps if Gaitskell had lived, it might have been different. But by the end of January 1963, just three months after his Brighton speech, he was dead. No comparable figures at the height of their power – and this includes Margaret Thatcher – have reached the same conclusion.

The alliance that has supported membership proved vital in 1975, when the question of continuing in the Common Market was the subject of a referendum. Six months before polling day those who wanted to leave had the support of 41 per cent of voters, those who wanted to stay 33 per cent, uncannily similar to polls this weekend on the same question. But the campaign pitched both ends (Enoch Powell, Tony Benn and Michael Foot) against the middle and the middle won, convincingly.

Now, after months of crisis in the euro and after the news from Greece about its referendum, one has to ask: for how long will this alliance hold? For how long will it remain the case that questioning Britain's membership of the EU will be something that cannot be done by a mainstream political figure?

The creation of the eurozone and the troubles that have engulfed it have changed the EU for ever. There can be no going back to the status quo. The EU that survives the great disruption will be a very different body. And our relationship with it will be very different.

Gaitskell warned of the danger that entry into the Common Market could mean the 'end of Britain as an independent European state. I make no apology for repeating it. It means the end of a thousand years of history.' But he acknowledged that this would be the result only if those who wanted a federal Europe had their way. He accepted that, while there were some who had that objective, attaining it was a long way off. His warning about a thousand years of history was, therefore, his most effective piece of rhetoric but always seemed rather an abstract point.

It doesn't now. Now the point is very real. Now it stares us in the face.

During the eurozone crisis, a euphemism has been used repeatedly. The euphemism is that the future success of the euro requires 'a greater degree of fiscal union'.

What this actually means is that Europe will have to have sufficient common resources to deal with a future crisis. And this in turn means that it will have to have a wide range of common tax and spending policies so that the fund does not end up as a transfer from responsible countries to irresponsible ones. How long will Germans agree to pay for Greek public sector workers to have, say, better pension terms than they do?

Greece has revealed the consequence of this. You cannot proceed to common policies without popular consent. But it is madness to allow one country that democratic right unilaterally, saying yes or no in a referendum to a deal that someone else is paying for. Fiscal union requires shared democratic control. To make a single currency work you have to have a state.

If the eurozone countries proceed in an orderly fashion to attempt to create a state, it would change the dynamic of the single market and the functioning of the political institutions of the European Union. Britain would stay outside to protect its thousand years of history, but it would still feel the impact. For a European state would require a fundamental renegotiation of the relationship between those in the eurozone and those outside.

Much more likely is that the process would not be so orderly. As has happened in the past, the aim of creating a state would be disguised, in order to reduce the prospect of popular resistance. Instead, the eurozone would attempt to solve its problems by using the institutions of the EU and existing treaty powers, a stealthy power grab. This, too, would alter our relationship sufficiently as to call it into question.

And then there is a third option. The eurozone might not find a way to deal with its problems, either directly or by stealth. It might find that asking German taxpayers to pay everyone else's debts, and everyone else to agree German policies, just won't work. Ever. Collapse of the euro would be calamitous, and the consequences for the EU hard to predict, but that doesn't make it impossible.

So what is about to happen – whether orderly, disorderly or catastrophic – will change the terms of our membership and is likely to break the alliance that has always supported it. There will – probably – remain strong arguments for being in the EU and much to be lost by leaving. But the politics will have changed; it will no longer be a fringe position to question membership.

I was hugely amused at the brilliantly short speech of the MP Charles Walker last week, calling for a referendum: 'If not now, when?' He had managed to find in four short words and a comma almost the only question on Europe that actually has a clear answer.

'Not now' is the answer. Not now because we don't know what sort of Europe we would be voting for or against. Not now, but it's coming.

If we don't cut the deficit now, when will we?

Politics is about seizing the moment. If the
Government abandons its fiscal policy it will
never resume it again

By the end of 2012 the Government's policy of so-called
austerity was under great political pressure. I argued that
while now may not have been the time for a European
referendum, it was the time to keep going with spending
control.

19 September 2012

About a year before his death Martin Luther King delivered a
lecture on the 'fierce urgency of now'. His subject on that
occasion was the Vietnam War, but the need to act, rather than
delay, was one of the great themes of his short, heroic life.

King had been swept into the civil rights movement almost
by accident and realised the role that contingency played in
politics. The Montgomery bus boycott began his campaign
and once it had started, it had started. There was no going
back. To stop, to pause, would be to lose. Many, indeed most,
of King's lectures and speeches are replies to those telling

African Americans to wait, to be patient, to seek a better moment.

He answers with talk of the fierce urgency of now. 'The tide in the affairs of men does not remain at the flood,' he said, 'it ebbs. We may cry out desperately for time to pause in her passage, but time is deaf to every plea and rushes on.' We cannot miss the moment, we cannot wait – that was his message.

What he was identifying, this great man at this extraordinary time, was a rule of politics that is true for much more prosaic people in even quite banal circumstances. In politics, 'is this the right moment?' is frequently asked and almost as frequently it is the wrong question. Because whether it is the right moment often doesn't matter. It's just the moment and that's all there is to it.

Let me give an example. Ed Miliband is frequently criticised for having run against his brother for the Labour leadership. I don't agree. Obviously it would have been easier for David and Ed to run one after the other. But that was never going to happen; the chance wouldn't come again. When the leadership vacancy arose that was Ed's moment. It wasn't the right moment, just the moment.

And that's where we are on cutting public spending and trying to end the structural deficit. It's the moment.

Last week, the prince of American political investigative reporting, Bob Woodward, published his latest book. *The Price of Politics* takes the reader inside the rooms inhabited by America's leading politicians as they worked to agree a budget deal.

A little over twelve months ago, the US faced a serious crisis. The legal limit on its national debt would be breached in a few days. If Congress did not agree to lift the debt ceiling, the country would start to default on its borrowing. But agreement proved almost impossible.

The meetings, recorded in painstaking detail by Woodward,

dragged on and on. The Republicans wouldn't agree to raise taxes; the Democrats said that in that case they wouldn't agree to reform benefits. There were moments of hope and then they disappeared.

And the crisis still isn't solved. Unable to agree a deal, the politicians lifted the debt ceiling anyway, setting up a so-called super-committee to identify cuts. This committee failed too. America faces a further round of fraught negotiation at the end of this year.

In interviews promoting his book, the normally neutral Woodward has been surprisingly critical of Barack Obama. He says there have been 'gaps' in his leadership. He claims that where Presidents Reagan and Clinton 'worked their will', this President did not. He tells numerous stories of Mr Obama's poor handling of Congress, at one point relating that congressional Democrats pressed the mute button on their phones, allowing Mr Obama to give a lengthy pep talk while they ignored him and carried on with their meeting.

I am not sure that this is entirely fair. It's hard to be very impressed by the picture of the President that Woodward draws, but to compare his performance with that of Clinton and Reagan is to compare him with executives acting in much easier circumstances to achieve much simpler goals.

The main message of *The Price of Politics* is not the incompleteness of Mr Obama. It is that cutting spending and long-term government borrowing are almost impossibly hard. Even in America where there is strong political pressure to restrict the size of the State.

Lending money to the governments of prosperous countries such as the United States is considered to be risk-free because governments have unlimited power to raise revenue. What the American debt crisis showed is that this power is in fact only theoretically unlimited. In practice, politics intervenes. Governments require consent to cut spending and increase taxes and that may not be forthcoming.

Governments cannot go on borrowing larger and larger amounts because at some point – and it is hard to be certain in advance when it will be – those doing the lending will conclude that the country, even if it has the wherewithal, does not have the political will to control its spending and tax.

And this is why I am so resistant to those who argue that Britain should loosen its fiscal policy in response to its low rate of economic growth.

We cannot keep on adding to the borrowing indefinitely. And yet to stop doing so is politically very hard. Summoning up the will and retaining the minimum of political support is incredibly difficult. And fragile.

There are all sorts of arguments for a pause in the fiscal assault. Because corporate tax receipts are so low, the overall deficit is actually growing even though the underlying structural deficit is being cut. Shouldn't we ease up a little? But by how much? £10 billion a year? £50 billion? More? How much would be enough to make an appreciable difference to growth?

And once we stop, once we return to a policy of borrow and spend, how will we ever summon up the will to stop again? The ability to assemble a coalition (with a small c) ready to accept public spending restraint is something that has eluded almost every other Western government except ours.

It is easy for an economist to argue for delay, perhaps a change in timing, but as with a lot of economic thinking, this ignores the politics. It assumes that when later the 'right moment' arrives the coalition will still be there, and the political will with it.

And that assumption is complacent. Whether or not you think now is the right moment, it's the moment.

If Scots file for divorce, we'll need a good lawyer

Cameron and Miliband would find it hard to hammer out a deal with Salmond

This article appeared the day before the referendum on Scottish independence. Much of it could as easily have been written about Brexit.

17 September 2014

'Of course, once you calm down, if you ever calm down, the real torture begins: dividing the assets, selling the house, pleading your case to some overworked thirty-year-old guardian ad litem who decides who gets your kids and on what terms, fighting over the pets (no joke: a custody fight over a Great Dane named Rajah lasted months), negotiating child support payments, making alimony payments, dragging yourself to a therapist and your kids to child psychiatrists, and allowing some black-robed judge to have the last word on your future. I always make sure that I have a Kleenex box handy in my office.'

Divorce, as the celebrated lawyer Gerald Nissenbaum makes clear in his memoirs, is hell. And that's the reason I think that if Scotland votes 'yes', it may not be the last referendum we have on the topic. If you can spare me a moment, I will take you through the logic.

If Scotland files for divorce, the rest of us are going to need a lawyer. The whole thing will be very messy indeed. And they will hire Alex Salmond, who, you have to grant, is likely to be very good. Who will we get? Issues that we have hardly discussed will suddenly become central political questions, and highly controversial. Let me give you a few examples.

What do we do about all the government offices we have based in Scotland? Not just the staff, and their employment rights and the continuity of public services, but the physical assets? What about the armed forces based there and their equipment?

What, of course, about the North Sea oil revenues and maritime rights? What about the BBC? What about galleries and museums? Where will the borders go and who will be allowed across them? What will the immigration rules be? What attitude will the rest of the UK take to a Scottish application to the EU? There are also the tricky questions about British defences, particularly the siting of Trident.

Then there are pension rights accrued in the public sector and the payment of state pensions. And there will be any number of complications about tax revenues and who they belong to.

And this is all before you get to the big-ticket items. What portion of our national debt, and the interest payments on it, belongs to Scotland? And what happens about the currency and Scottish financial institutions?

All of this and more will become instantly a major part of the coming election campaign. A 'yes' vote will not change the date of the general election but it will change the question. We will be hiring someone to handle the negotiations. Which will leave both of the main party leaders with serious problems to resolve.

While the best advice of divorce lawyers might be to take a deep breath and try to construct a settlement that is fair to all, their clients often find this advice hard to follow. And certainly in the early days after Scotland chooses independence, political opinion in England, particularly, is likely to favour a pretty robust approach to what is 'ours' and what is 'theirs'.

Where does this leave David Cameron? If Scotland votes to end the Union, the Prime Minister will face serious calls to resign. The Union would be gone after hundreds of years and on his watch.

His response, doubtless, will be to argue that this is not a time for useless gestures. A prime minister has work to do, and he needs to get on. He will immediately start explaining the negotiations that need to take place. And will immediately run into the argument that will be made against him all the way to election day.

It is this: why trust David Cameron to negotiate with Alex Salmond when the last time he did so, it did not go well? Mr Salmond got, broadly, the timing he wanted, the referendum phrasing he wanted, the electorate he wanted and, above all, the answer he wanted. It is not necessary to accept these criticisms yourself (I don't) in order to appreciate that they constitute an argument that will have political force.

Then there is Ed Miliband. He would not wish to fight any election in which his perceived leadership qualities became a central issue, since these qualities do not poll well. Yet this is a secondary problem when put alongside the agonising dilemma that he will have about his Scottish MPs.

If Mr Miliband promises not to govern in 2015 using his Scottish MPs – in other words only to govern if he can do so with just English and Welsh members – he is quite possibly sacrificing the chance to govern at all. Yet if he does not make this promise, he would be telling English voters that he intends to negotiate with Scotland using Scottish MPs as the casting vote over the deal he strikes. I believe that this offer would be impossible to sell.

So Mr Cameron has a terrible problem, and Mr Miliband one at least as bad, possibly worse. I think both of them might plump for a similar solution. They might offer English, Welsh and Northern Irish voters a referendum on the outcome of the negotiations.

Nobody could, or should, deny Scotland the constitutional status it votes for on Thursday. That would be unthinkable. The rest of the UK will not stop the Scots divorcing us if that is what they want to do. Yet a vote on the terms would seem reasonable. And would solve big political problems for both party leaders.

Mr Cameron would be able to say that whatever doubts might be had about the deal he would do, the people would have the final say. He wouldn't, for instance, agree to a currency union with Scotland without a vote any more than he would agree to a currency union with France without one. Made swiftly, a referendum promise might repel the calls for resignation and outflank UKIP, both of which will be immediate problems.

For Mr Miliband, it might be possible to offset his little Scottish MPs difficulty. He could argue that these MPs, far from being a problem, would be useful because they understand Scotland. They know where the co-respondent to the proceedings has hidden the assets. Yet they wouldn't have the power to approve the deal; that would lie with the people of the rest of the United Kingdom.

Just a thought. In case.

Labour's hypocrisy has brought us to this crisis

The balance of power in Britain may be seized by a party that wants to break it up. That's not something we can ignore

This article appeared as the 2015 election campaign reached its conclusion. The Tories had been accused of endangering the Union by pointing out that Ed Miliband might have to govern in alliance with the SNP. A series of very effective Tory adverts suggested that Mr Miliband would be under the control of Alex Salmond and other nationalists. As it became clear that the SNP might win dozens of Labour seats, some Labour politicians began to blame this possibility on the Tory campaign. They said it was the Tories, by warning of nationalist power, who were driving a wedge between England and Scotland. I was having none of it.

29 April 2015

So this – if I have understood it correctly, and I think I have – is the argument.

In a little over a week, Britain may elect a government entirely dependent for survival on a left-wing separatist group that thinks

Michael Foot would have been a good prime minister. The balance of power will then be held by a party that wants to break up the country. And laws in big areas – schools for instance – will only be passed with the permission of MPs whose own constituents will not be affected by them.

All this may be about to happen but I shouldn't bring it up. Because if I do so, it might undermine the Union.

That, as I say, is the argument. Well, I'm sorry, but no.

Before we get going I just want to point out that I am a Tory living in Pinner. If Labour's Douglas Alexander [the shadow foreign secretary] with his 17,000 majority is going to lose his seat to some twenty-year-old nationalist sitting her finals [Mhairi Black], it's not my fault. The idea that this catastrophe is happening because the Tories and David Cameron are talking about it – and they should therefore stop doing so – is patently absurd. This gets things precisely the wrong way round. Mr Cameron is talking about it because it is happening.

It is Labour that is losing these seats. Labour that dominated Scottish politics for a generation. Labour that crafted the institutions on which the SNP has built its power. Labour that ran the Better Together campaign. And if Labour collapses in Scotland, it is Labour's fault.

I have previously stayed relatively quiet because I felt embarrassed to offer my opinion when there were all these Scottish experts about, explaining to me that things were different and I didn't understand, and I should be ever so careful because, you know, none of us want to weaken the Union.

Well, fine experts they turned out to be. They have stumbled from disaster to calamity, taking in the view of fiasco and debacle along the way. And a few days from them visiting the consequences of this dismal failure upon me and my family I think it is time to say something. Weaken the Union? I couldn't do a better job of weakening the Union than all of them, that's for sure.

On 30 March 1989, the first meeting of the Scottish Constitutional Convention met on the Mound in Edinburgh. With the Scottish Labour Party by far the most significant political actor, the convention members signed the Claim of Right. 'We, gathered as the Scottish Constitutional Convention, do hereby acknowledge the sovereign right of the Scottish people to determine the form of government best suited to their needs.' The sovereign right.

In their book *The Strange Death of Labour Scotland*, Gerry Hassan and Eric Shaw explain how this historic moment came about. They trace the collapse of the main pillars of Labour's Scottish domination – council housing, trade union power, local government hegemony and the strength of the Catholic Church – and show how, as these crumbled, Labour felt the need to become more self-consciously Scottish as a way of maintaining relevance.

The centrepiece of this Scottish strategy was to begin to argue that the Conservative government had no mandate in Scotland. When this argument was first made it was a fringe one and highly controversial.

In a 1983 memorandum that became famous in Scottish left circles, the pugnacious Labour MP George Foulkes argued that Labour must be bold and 'go beyond more vigorous resistance to new legislation on Scottish affairs . . . challenging the legitimacy of administrative directives and circulars which the majority of Scottish MPs have not endorsed'. His conclusion was resisted by the leadership.

Yet over the next five years, this controversial claim – that laws made in London were not really politically legitimate, and Scotland had a sovereign right to govern itself – became a mainstream doctrine. In the panic that followed the loss of the Glasgow Govan by-election to the SNP in 1988, the Labour Party moved to make the Claim of Right.

And its language became more intemperate and extreme.

Robin Cook, one of the party's leaders, said that 'to all intents and purposes Scotland is an occupied country in which the ruling power depends for its support on a powerbase which is outside the country'.

It was precisely the claim that the Conservative government lacked legitimacy – that very word – that Labour used to drive the Tories out of its Scottish seats. And now that they are being clubbed to death by the SNP with the weapon that they crafted, they contrive to complain that it is all the fault of the Tories. Do me a lemon.

The latest bit of nonsense is the idea that Scots have turned from Labour to the SNP because David Cameron talked of English votes the morning after the referendum. Doesn't this conveniently forget that the SNP won a majority in Scotland in the 2011 Scottish Parliament election, winning more than 45 per cent of the vote? Isn't that why we had the referendum in the first place?

No. This wipeout of Scottish Labour is one thing they don't get to blame on the Tories.

You simply cannot spend a quarter of a century arguing that Scotland has a claim of right to determine its own affairs, questioning the legitimacy of a majority that originates in England, crafting institutions to accompany this rhetoric, and then say that the very same arguments are unreasonable when someone gently asks questions about English laws.

The SNP changes the nature of the problem of English laws. While Labour dominated Scotland, it is true that its Scottish MPs might have created laws in England that didn't apply in Scotland, didn't apply in their own constituency. And this would have been a matter of concern.

Yet at least these Labour MPs were unionists who cared about England as part of their country. The position with the SNP would be entirely different. They would be relied upon to sustain and support policies in a country they don't want to be attached to, and in whose outcomes they have no interest. English education law is foreign policy to the SNP.

It will exercise this power in the service of a leftist ideology that England has often rejected and doubtless will reject again.

Is it really wrong to raise this? To point out that we could be days away from it? To ask people to think what it would be like, and to try and avoid it? I can't think that it is.

Is it a scare story? Well, it certainly sounds pretty scary to me.

Shy Tories are not really shy . . . or Tory

Cameron won because he persuaded the sensible,
silent majority (who don't give a fig for politics)
that he's on their side

On 7 May 2015 there was a general election with the polls
showing the parties neck and neck, heading to another
hung parliament. Instead David Cameron's Conservatives
won a majority.

13 May 2015

Back in the days when I earned a living advising William Hague,
I rang up a friend to boast about the success of that afternoon's
Prime Minister's Questions. The joke we'd crafted had worked
brilliantly. The question had put Tony Blair on the back foot.
It had all gone so well.

'Did you hear it, Michael?' I asked. 'Of course I didn't hear
it, I've got a job,' he replied. 'I'm in the office. I am working.'
He had a job. He was working.

I'd like to discuss this question of shy Tories. I don't want to
examine why the pollsters got it wrong. We don't yet know the
answer. It is shy Tories themselves I am interested in. They
played a very big part in this election.

In fact, I think that shy Tories elected David Cameron and that he is their prime minister. And he and his party will remain theirs as long as they realise two things about them. First, that they aren't really shy. Second, that they aren't really Tories.

Most people in this country – and particularly those willing to vote for a centre-right prime minister – aren't that bothered about politics. They are at the office. They have a job.

These people know what they think but they don't particularly want to advertise it. It's not really anyone else's business. They'd like people to share their views but they aren't going to spend a lot of time persuading others. These aren't shy people. They are sociable, successful, frank. They might be the life and soul of a social occasion. But they don't have much time for people who sound off. They make the world a better place for themselves, for their families, for their communities and they expect that from others. They admire – quietly – those who make something of themselves. They despair – quietly – of those who expect to take without contributing.

They don't think that talking loudly about equality is the same as being kind. Caring for the vulnerable is a practical not a theoretical issue. They are in touch with the modern world but don't feel they need to wear a badge saying so. They listen carefully to business leaders without thinking them saints or geniuses.

They don't want to paint their opinion on the side of a war memorial, or even post it on Twitter. They don't want to make a big issue about it with friends and professional colleagues. They wouldn't sign up to give their opinions on the internet (who on earth would want to do that?). They politely turn away a phone canvasser.

And on 7 May they went out, quietly voted for David Cameron and his Conservative Party, went home and watched television.

Yet it is wrong to think of them as Tories. These are people who just want a moderate, competent government which keeps the economy on track. One which ensures that there are decent public services that don't cost the earth.

They don't want to remake mankind, or indulge some student idea about predistribution. They haven't the slightest interest in moving between the different varieties of capitalism, whatever the hell that involves, or improving the politics of belonging. Nor are they fanatical about Europe, ready for jihad on the BBC or interested in abstract questions about the optimal size of the state.

These people are David Cameron's majority and will be as long as he doesn't forget it. After the 2001 general election result – a second heavy defeat – a small group of Conservatives, about five or six of us, would meet from time to time over a pizza to discuss what could be done. I was one of the group, along with David Cameron, George Osborne, Michael Gove and Nick Boles.

The answers seemed to us obvious. The party couldn't win an election until it appealed once again to the moderate, practical people of the country. People who had no interest in political obsessions and ideological positions. They wanted a party comfortable with the modern world, and living in it. One that guaranteed a stable and successful market economy but could be trusted with the NHS and schools.

Conservatives had to be able to win the support of Liberal Democrats and people attracted by Tony Blair.

It was as the spokesman of this idea that David Cameron ran for the leadership and won it. And it was as the spokesman of this idea that he became the shy Tories' prime minister in 2010. In doing so, he produced a remarkable result, winning a huge number of new seats on a massive swing. He then capped off this achievement with a bold move to create a coalition, which produced a stable and reasonably popular government that lasted a full term.

Yet, despite this, both Cameron and his idea have been heavily criticised on the right. He hadn't won a majority even against Gordon Brown, he wasn't going to win even against Ed Miliband. If only he had been more robust he would be doing so much better. Cameron's biggest mistake was this, Cameron's biggest mistake was that, Cameron's biggest mistake was the other.

Wrong, all of this. All wrong. Cameron's modernising conservatism has won a famous victory and he is a famous victor. And that's the end of it. The argument for shifting the party has been triumphantly vindicated, full stop. I've read one or two people suggesting he only won because in the last few months he finally decided to be a conservative. These very same people were arguing only a few weeks earlier that he wasn't conservative enough.

He won because moderate people felt they could trust him when they feared Ed Miliband. Even though some votes were lost to UKIP, even more were won from Lib Dems.

This argument has to be made because of the future, not the past. The people who make up David Cameron's majority are as distinctive as those people who made up Clement Attlee's or Margaret Thatcher's.

They want a moderate, mainstream government that puts the economy right. They want to deal with the deficit in a manner not only timely but pragmatic. They want the northern powerhouse and more school reform. They want apprenticeships, tax cuts and growth. They want the NHS to be protected but also sustainable. They want an EU referendum but don't want to feel the Government is consumed by it.

The Prime Minister should just get on with the job. Quietly. Competently.

Intelligently. Moderately. And his voters will go to the office and get to work. He's got a job to do and so have they.

As Greece shows, threats will get you nowhere

In his EU negotiations the Prime Minister is more likely to win concessions by trustworthy and generous behaviour

Upon re-election David Cameron set out to renegotiate the terms of British membership of the European Union, which he then proposed to put to the British people in a referendum. He was being urged to threaten the EU that he would advocate leaving if it failed to make sufficient concessions. I drew lessons from the failed period in office in Greece of the game theorist Yanis Varoufakis who resigned as finance minister in July 2015.

15 July 2015

The moment I learnt that Greece had appointed an expert in game theory as its finance minister, I knew it meant trouble. Yet I also thought perhaps we would learn a lesson or two that might help Britain's own negotiations. And so it has proven.

It has always amused me that John Von Neumann, the man who in 1928 originally developed game theory as a formalised method of playing poker, was not, in practice, all that good at cards.

Yet while amusing, it is not entirely surprising. Game theory – the development of optimal strategies to act in situations where others are also creating strategies and may have different objectives to you – is immensely complicated in theory and even more complicated when you try to apply it.

It is only ever possible to find a clean, confident solution to a game-theory problem when you simplify it a great deal for academic use. And even then the optimal solution often involves everybody going to jail or killing each other. In game theory, a satisfying end to the game, providing it with a stable equilibrium, can come when everyone playing it is dead.

Von Neumann became one of the leading proponents (the logician and mathematician Bertrand Russell was another) of a preventive war against the Soviet Union. He argued that the United States should drop a nuclear bomb on the Soviets before the Soviets developed their own bomb. He could, he said, show mathematically that this was a sound idea. 'If you say why not bomb them tomorrow, I say why not today? If you say today at five o'clock, I say why not one o'clock?'

So the fact that Yanis Varoufakis is the author of a classic game-theory textbook always seemed to me to promise that tears would flow.

Varoufakis believed that if his negotiating partners – the Germans, the IMF, the Commission – concluded he was a bit bonkers, a bit reckless, they would appreciate that he might crash the Greek economy and bring down the whole edifice of the euro on top of him. Persuading your adversary that you are mad is a classic game-theory gambit. Richard Nixon tried using it in Vietnam.

Instead – predictably – what actually happened is that the Germans, the IMF and the Commission decided that if Varoufakis was bonkers and reckless maybe, erm, they shouldn't lend the bonkers guy any money. He might be bonkers enough not to pay it back.

Appointing as finance minister the professor of double-bluffing in the university's department of bankruptcy studies turned out to be a disaster for Greece, securing a far worse deal than would have been available at the outset of discussions.

What does this mean for Britain? It means that something that is often asserted as common sense turns out to be quite the opposite of that.

It is often suggested that David Cameron ought to tell European leaders that if he cannot secure a good deal for Britain, he would lead his country out of the EU. If he doesn't threaten that, goes the argument, how can he expect to make progress? They have to know that he is serious. Surely this is obvious.

Greece's experience shows the flaw in this apparently simple reasoning.

When game theorists model single encounters between individuals with differing interests, the outcome is commonly that for both sides it is rational to cheat the other.

Yet when the game is repeated, this is no longer the case. In repeated games, the best strategy often turns out to be generosity and reciprocation. Trust plays the critical role. People reward trustworthy and generous behaviour by themselves acting in a trustworthy and generous way.

In his recent book *Give and Take*, the psychologist Adam Grant notes that being a 'giver' rather than a 'taker' can be surprisingly effective. Seeking advice from the person you are dealing with, using tentative rather than assertive ways of speaking, seeing things from the other person's point of view, all work to secure better sales, bigger promotions and higher salaries.

Grant is not advocating being a doormat. He acknowledges that 'givers' will often try to walk all over 'takers'. But he does argue that people tend to reciprocate concessions and that trust is powerful.

By refusing to threaten to leave the European Union, David

Cameron is sacrificing relatively little in the negotiations. After all, other nations are aware that Mr Cameron may lose a referendum if the deal isn't right. So the threat is there without him making it explicitly.

And there is much to gain by not making it explicitly. The Greek crisis has demonstrated that the EU is incredibly anxious to remain together and it will do much to make that happen. It has also demonstrated that, in the end, there are limits to that instinct and you can reach those limits pretty quickly when trust breaks down.

By maintaining a sense of trust and community, David Cameron can achieve a much better deal than by an ultimatum. This doesn't mean that the deal he gets will necessarily be acceptable to him or to the British people. It doesn't – in the end – take away completely his right to say no to it or take away at all the country's right to do that. It does mean that while negotiations proceed it is better they do so in an atmosphere of cooperation rather than in an atmosphere of crisis and last-chance saloons.

There is an eccentric proposal with which Boris Johnson's name has been associated, that Britain should seek two referendums, turning down a first deal and then, after coming back for more, voting through an amended treaty.

Yet the others in the negotiations are only human. They have egos and pride. They have voters to satisfy. They have their own national interests. They have their own newspapers to give quotes to and editorial writers to convince. Understanding that – looking at how they feel about the negotiations – is vital to getting a good deal.

How would they feel about us coming back for more? When trust is exhausted and they begin to feel that much is being asked without much being given, the risk of a two-referendum approach is huge.

For those who couldn't care about Cameron's talks, and don't think they will yield much anyway, none of this matters, of course. And most of the people urging him to threaten withdrawal fall into this category. They actually want failure.

Yet those who want the negotiations to succeed should not be urging David Cameron to play one of Varoufakis's games.

Let's face it, the EU rescued us from failure

Would Britain risk joining if it wasn't a member?
No chance. That doesn't change the fact we've
had a 40-year success story

This article appeared towards the end of the EU referendum campaign. I had told readers earlier in the campaign that I supported remaining and had written about how my family history – and the premium I placed on peace in Europe – had influenced my decision.

14 June 2016

'Europe was to be our deus ex machina; it was to create a political argument with insular socialism; dish the Liberals by stealing their clothes; give us something new after 12–13 years; act as a catalyst of modernisation; give us a new place in the international sun. It was Macmillan's ace, and de Gaulle trumped it.'

This is how Michael Fraser, one of Supermac's advisers, described the moment when General Charles de Gaulle doomed Harold Macmillan. On 14 January 1963, the French president said '*Non*' to Britain's application to join the European Economic

416

Community. The Prime Minister resigned later that year and it was another decade before we were allowed in.

That critical moment in our relationship with Europe sheds light on the critical decision we face next week. It helps answer the question: if we were not already in the European Union, would we choose to join it?

Daniel Hannan, the Conservative MEP, posed this question the other day, and it's a powerful way of making the argument for voting Leave. It deserves a careful reply from those of us who wish to remain. And in any case, it's always best to tackle an opposing argument at its strongest point.

I had better begin with an act of surrender before attempting to advance. All other things being equal, if the British people were now being asked to join for the first time I don't believe they would. An understandable desire not to take unnecessary risks provides a large part of the support for remaining in the EU, and even that support is under great pressure. Without it, Daniel Hannan is unquestionably correct in assuming his side would win.

Yet those words 'all other things being equal' are being made to do a lot of work. They stand for an assumption that if we had not joined the community, things would be much the same as they are today. And that is an audacious assumption.

Let's go back to Macmillan. Days after becoming prime minister in 1957, he sent Michael Fraser a note. It read: 'I'm always hearing about the middle class. What is it they really want? Can you put it down on a sheet of notepaper, and then I will see whether we can give it to them.'

This apparently flippant request expressed Macmillan's entirely serious understanding that the country he had inherited was changing – socially, economically and in its position in the world – and that the governing class didn't know how to adapt. If he was going to succeed he would need to respond.

Britain was, not to put too fine a point on it, failing. It was being overtaken economically by Germany and overpowered by France. The end of Empire was coming and the Commonwealth seemed unlikely to provide a secure source of either economic or diplomatic power. The Americans, crucial to our defence and international clout, were clear that their primary interest in any kind of special relationship was our ability to act as a bridge with other European countries.

It seemed obvious to Macmillan, and indeed the bulk of the Conservative Party, that outside the European Community Britain faced economic and diplomatic eclipse. He recognised that joining would involve some sacrifice of control and independence. He knew, too, that other members wanted a more politically integrated Europe than Britain did, but he thought the gains outweighed the risk.

So what happened when, after ten years of attempts, we finally joined? Since 1973 we have grown faster than Germany, France, Italy and even the US. And in the single market era we have grown by 62 per cent while Germany has grown by 35 per cent. And Switzerland, which is outside the EU but a member of the European Free Trade Area? 48 per cent.

It is easy to respond by suggesting that this growth has occurred despite the EU rather than because of it. We have done well entirely because we have adopted a different economic model to our partners. Yet consider the admission that this response involves. It admits that the EU does not dictate our laws and economic model. We have been able to diverge, rather than converge, with our neighbours.

We have also managed to maintain a strong relationship with the US on exactly the basis that Macmillan posited. We act as a bridge to Europe and are valued for that reason.

There is another point worth adding. It is not just us who would be different if we hadn't joined the community. The EU would be different too. We were critical to the creation of the single market and to enlargement.

So a big part of my answer to the question, 'If we were not already a member of the European Union, would we choose to join it?' is that when we were not a member we did choose to join it. We thought it would help correct weaknesses that we saw no other way to correct. And it did help tackle those weaknesses.

This country is tangibly more prosperous, more powerful, more tolerant, more welcoming, more democratic, more hopeful; simply a better place to be than it was in 1973. And despite sharing power with other EU member states, we are still distinctively British and different politically, economically and socially from our neighbours.

However, this is not enough by itself. Although Macmillan anticipated that we would be in tension with other members who would want to integrate more than we did, this has since become reality. Joining now involves much more serious power sharing than it would have done in 1963.

The best response to this is that virtually every democratic European country eligible to join has wanted to do so as soon as possible. They have, each one of them, perceived the trade-off as worthwhile. They believe it makes them richer and stronger.

The argument that we are different, that they had to join because they are weak and we wouldn't have to because we are strong, makes, once again, that big assumption. It assumes that if we hadn't joined the EU we would be as strong as we are now economically and diplomatically.

But Macmillan didn't think we would be and neither has a single serving prime minister since.

Killer flaw at the heart of the Brexit campaign

The voters that Leave needs to deliver victory in
tomorrow's referendum would be the ones hit
hardest if we left the EU

22 June 2016

You gotta dance with the one that brung ya. Ronald Reagan's
aphorism, taken from a 1920s country song, expresses a general
truth about politics. On the way to victory you acquire allies and
incur obligations, and when you get there, you cannot ignore them.

Politicians, like the heroine of Erica Jong's *Fear of Flying*,
might dream of consummation without commitment. Like her,
they may see it as 'the purest thing there is'. But like her, they're
doomed to discover that such a relationship 'is rarer than the
unicorn. And I have never had one.'

It's because you gotta dance with the one that brung ya that
we are having this referendum in the first place. David Cameron
was not free to ignore the demands of his political base. And
it is because you gotta dance with the one that brung ya that
I believe that leaving the EU promises only failure.

There is a tension between the politics and economics of
Leave that would prove fatal were they to win.

During this referendum two nations have emerged out of one: Remainia and Leavia. The inhabitants of Remainia benefit from globalisation, have university degrees, live in cosmopolitan cities and do not fear international political and economic engagement because they are the ones doing the engaging. They are more willing to embrace change but are often complacent about its costs.

The inhabitants of Leavia feel intensely every pound earned or withdrawn, have less formal education, are more wary about international forces and more distant from power, live in settled communities and are more resistant to change.

In the most recent YouGov poll, voters in the highest social class ABC1 split 53 to 38 per cent for Remain, while those in the lower C2D2 class split 52 to 29 per cent for Leave.

Naturally not every Remain or Leave voter is typical. To say that having a degree is correlated with wanting to remain in the EU is far from suggesting that only non-graduates want to leave the EU. And it certainly doesn't mean that being in favour of Remain is necessarily a sign of greater intelligence.

Whatever the personal background or inclination of those running the Leave campaign, their pitch has been solidly aimed at the inhabitants of Leavia. They are counting on them to deliver victory tomorrow.

The expectation of these voters, certainly their hope, is that leaving the EU can restore to this country control over its own destiny. They are hoping for greater protection from the social and economic change brought by globalisation. They seek more work, better-funded public services, less power to corporations and the elite and, above all, less of the immigration that they believe puts pressure on their wages and communities.

This is the politics of Leave. What about its economics?

While there is a dispute over its scale, most Leave supporters accept that if we go there will be instability and, therefore, a cost in the short term. They proclaim themselves willing to pay it. And that's fair enough, if more than a touch insouciant. While the cost may be considerable, and more keenly felt by inhabitants of Leavia than Remainia, it's entirely reasonable to argue that it would be justified by the long-term benefits the Leave campaign believes would occur. After all, we shouldn't make a decision that will have an effect lasting many decades purely on the basis of its impact over the next two years.

Consider, however, how these long-term benefits might be obtained and you begin to see the problem.

By leaving the European single market, Britain makes itself a less attractive place for big businesses to invest. This is hard to dispute, and in any case they are overwhelmingly telling us themselves. It will also make it harder for us to trade. So unless we act, we will be poorer. The Leave economic argument is that by freeing ourselves from the EU we will be able to act. The Remainiacs aren't getting this, they argue. We won't just be sitting here, suffering. We will be taking back control.

Now think what this might mean in practice. To be a success outside the single market, to be attractive to businesses and to investment, we would need to be a European offshore low-cost competitive Mecca for companies. We would have to offset the increased cost of doing business here that leaving brings (in the form of barriers, both tariff and non-tariff, to European trade) by cutting our own costs even more sharply.

We would need to have lower taxes on foreign rich people than the Continent, pay lower wages to unskilled people than elsewhere in Europe and cut public spending further to keep taxes down. We would need to make old people work longer. Oh, and we would need a huge influx of immigrants, both skilled and unskilled, to ensure that we had a very competitive workforce.

We would also need new trade deals to replace the ones we had abandoned. In Europe, for all its faults, corporate interests are balanced by those of workers but in any other trade deal we would need to overlook these. Our regulation would have to be more attractive to corporate elites, not less. It would be vital that corporate lobbying was even more successful than it has been in the past.

I have always been respectful of those who say they wish to escape the EU to turn to the world, as long as we are clear what it means. It seems to me monumentally unlikely that we would be able to implement such a programme in the event of voting to leave the EU. Politically it would be hard to advance at any time. After a victory won with the votes of Leavia it would be impossible.

I'd go further. It would be something of a betrayal of the legitimate expectations of the people voting for the Leave option. They would have a right to expect that if they win they are winning for more social protection for themselves and their families, for less corporate power, for more democracy and fewer immigrants.

Yet if Britain were to go down such a path, the strongest Leave supporter would surely acknowledge that Brexit would be an economic disaster.

The politics of leaving go one way, and its economics go the other.

If Labour split, what sort of new party would be formed?

The failure of the SDP shows how hard it is to create a centre-left party with the right identity to appeal to voters

In the summer of 2016, with Jeremy Corbyn's leadership highly unpopular with Labour MPs but nevertheless secure, there was much talk of a new centre party to be formed before the next election. I thought history shed some light on the prospects of such a split.

16 August 2016

On my first day in my first job I had to ask my new boss if it would be all right if I left early. I explained that I was on the national executive of the Social Democratic Party, and that I held what was effectively the casting vote in a major political row.

This excruciating conversation might have been made mildly easier if the 'major political row' had been comprehensible to any outsider. Instead it concerned some procedural rules governing a ballot on whether the SDP should merge with the Liberal Party.

Yet almost thirty years later it occurs to me that what we were rowing about is once again relevant. Not the details, of course, but the broad question of party splits and the relationship between liberals and social democrats.

Most of the coverage about the Labour Party's dire position concerns whether the 'moderates' will or should split from the 'Corbynistas' if Corbyn retains the leadership. My own experience suggests it is all a bit more complicated than that.

When some years ago David Owen, one of the SDP's founders, sent me an early draft of his memoirs, I understood for the first time that he had seen the SDP as essentially doomed – certainly in deep trouble – before I even joined it at the beginning of 1982. What had doomed it, in his view, was the decision to form a tight alliance with the Liberal Party.

Owen's conception of the SDP, which was formed in 1981, is that it would be a tough-minded, hawkish party of the left. It would appeal to an aspirational working class, particularly in the north, who had tired of bureaucratic socialism and saw the point of Margaret Thatcher, but were not Tories.

When the future Labour Foreign Secretary was a student working on a building site he had been struck by the reaction of his fellow workers to the Suez Crisis. It had been instinctively nationalist, uninterested in political protocol, and robust. It was these people he wanted the SDP to appeal to.

Roy Jenkins, former Labour chancellor but also biographer of the Liberal prime minister H. H. Asquith, wanted a centre party that reflected his own liberal instinct. This would be a southern party of the middle class, disdainful of Thatcher, fastidious rather than bulldog-like on international issues, avowedly centrist.

Everything about this Jenkins view – the electoral relationship with the Liberals in particular, but also the claret-drinking image – drove Owen crazy. But for all that he later did to shape the party, Owen was right that by 1982 Jenkins had won the battle.

The SDP would be a liberal party. It lost almost all its northern and working-class seats, was not able to compete in the south because the Liberal Party took all the best constituencies, and ended up being swallowed up by its partner.

Owen and Jenkins were rowing over whether liberalism and being a Labour moderate or even a centrist were the same thing. Jenkins felt that practically and philosophically they were. Owen felt that practically and philosophically they were not.

In his history of the Labour Party, *Speak for Britain!*, Martin Pugh argues convincingly that liberalism has always been only one strand of Labour, and not its most important one. From its earliest days a very large part of the party has been conservative on constitutional questions, culturally sentimental and nostalgic, cautious on issues of individual freedom, opposed to mass immigration, monarchist, nationalist, patriotic and militaristic.

When Jenkins, as home secretary, moved in a liberal direction, many older Labour MPs worried this would alienate their working-class support, particularly among Catholics. Others thought it merely irrelevant. James Callaghan responded to the legalisation of homosexuality with bewilderment. He admitted that he hardly knew what homosexuality was and said he hadn't come across it.

In 1976 when Harold Wilson retired, it was Callaghan – Eurosceptic and immigration sceptic – who won the leadership, beating Jenkins handily. When supporters of the latter canvassed fellow MPs in the tea room one of those MPs responded: 'Nah, we are all Labour here.'

All of this is more than history. The Owen critique of the Jenkins position remains a sharp one and directly relevant to Labour moderates. If they decided they could no longer stick Corbyn, what sort of party would they create?

What is the electoral base of a straightforwardly liberal party? Labour voters least likely to be impressed by Corbyn are most likely to be hawkish on defence, tough on immigration and sympathetic to Brexit. There will be middle-class dissidents too, but smaller in number because many of those already vote Conservative and are likely to carry on doing so.

In the absence of a large Conservative defection, a liberal Labour Party would struggle. If a liberal party decided, for instance, to be the party against Brexit and for free movement, how would it hold seats in the north, or indeed outside London?

What then of the prospects of a split that created a more traditional Labour Party? Owen's experience shows how hard it would be to make that succeed. It would require a very large proportion of Labour MPs to go with it, and to agree to a populist platform that many of them are nervous about. And even then it might struggle to win northern seats where party tradition is strong. One of the problems with traditionalist voters is that they are, well, traditionalist.

Owen argues that resigning to fight by-elections might have helped the SDP, and he has a point. It is difficult, however, to be optimistic about the prospect for independent Labour.

What all this indicates is that the great trick in politics is not to split. It is to unify. The great achievement of Ramsay MacDonald, Jimmy Thomas and Keir Hardie, of the Fabians and the unions, of the intellectuals and the activists, is that they managed to assemble a diverse coalition and keep it together, even when the odds against doing so were very great.

Neil Sedaka was wrong. Breaking up is not very hard to do. It's easy to disassemble a political alliance. It's putting one together that is challenging.

Splitting from the Labour Party may end up being necessary. I'd certainly argue that it was in 1981. But it would represent failure. It isn't obvious what sort of moderate party would emerge. Chuka Umunna's liberal party? Or John Mann's traditional one? These are very different propositions, and it isn't clear how either would succeed.

We must stand up to the populist blackmail

Veiled threats over judges' Brexit ruling show why
movements that claim to speak for 'the people'
are so dangerous

6 December 2016

No. I try to see the best in everyone and in their arguments.
Sometimes I worry that I do it to a fault, cutting people slack
when they don't deserve it. But there are moments when resistance is the only option. And this is one of them. So, no.
Absolutely not.

The suggestion that the courts must rule in favour of the
Government over Article 50 because to rule otherwise would
stoke resentment among supporters of Brexit is completely
outrageous.

I think actually it is a case study in populism and what is
wrong with it.

It is, to start with, a threat, a lightly veiled piece of blackmail.
The blackmailers are offering acceptance of the ruling of judges
only if they get the result they want. Otherwise we can expect
'anger' and the never quite specified consequences of that anger.
Such blackmail can never be accepted.

It is also a misrepresentation of what courts are for and what they are being asked to rule upon. Courts have to interpret the law, and the point of law the Supreme Court is interpreting is not whether we leave the European Union. It is whether the power of governments to agree treaties extends to their power over Article 50.

The suggestion that we mustn't have due legal process because it might delay Brexit is also childish. Leaving the EU is complicated and has profound consequences and needs to be done properly and legally. It should be done expeditiously, of course, but it is absurd to start complaining that we voted in June and haven't left yet.

However, none of this begins to explain how dangerous the attack on the court judgment really is.

Parliament must accept and respect the result of the referendum and we must leave the EU. I also hope that the Government wins its court case. I think the prerogative power to agree treaties is important and I fear the consequences of its dilution. In particular, as a free trader I worry about the power to agree trade deals.

To hope for such a result, or to argue that this would be the correct outcome legally, is, however, entirely different from suggesting that the result of the referendum sweeps all before it and that judges should lay aside their legal opinion in order to avoid the fury of Leave voters.

In a very insightful new book, *What is Populism?*, the Princeton academic Jan-Werner Müller looks at the political ideas that unite such disparate political figures as Donald Trump and Hugo Chávez, Recep Tayyip Erdogan and Geert Wilders, Beppe Grillo's Five Star Movement and Nigel Farage's UKIP.

The professor argues that the central claim each of them makes is that they embody the will of the people. That will is simple, clear and unified and obviously associated with the national interest.

The crucial first populist step is to ensure that 'the people' are limited to those who share the same conception of the country's destiny. Anyone who does not must be considered not a real person. They are a member of 'the elite' or of 'the Establishment', they are liberals or they are metropolitan. These groups don't do 'real' jobs, or have 'real experience'; they conspire against 'real' people. They 'just don't get it'.

Other groups may be excluded: immigrants, say, because they aren't 'real' nationals. The attempt to show that Barack Obama wasn't really born in America was much more than just an effort to deny him the presidency on technical grounds.

Or half the country can be dismissed as 'Remoaners'. Nigel Farage described the Brexit vote as a 'victory for real people'. Quite similar to Trump's extraordinary comment at a rally in May that 'the only important thing is the unification of the people – because the other people don't mean anything'. Through this process of exclusion, the populists produce a homogeneous people with a common interest.

The next stage in advancing populism is to attack anybody who challenges the exclusive right of the populist party to define or interpret the national interest. It is vital, for instance, to attack the mainstream media and use social media to communicate with people directly.

Parliament, of course, allows diverse representation and the clash of interests. Politicians interpret these different interests and attempt to weigh them and compromise between them. This is everything populists despise. A lot of talking and accommodation of different views when the will of 'real' people is perfectly clear.

So it is essential to populism that politicians – 'the Westminster bubble' – be subjected to continuous attack. These people have never done a 'real' day's work in their lives. What do they know? And anyway, why should Parliament debate anything when we already know what people think?

The populist Hungarian party Jobbik always couples 'politician crime' with 'gypsy crime'. The UKIP donor Arron Banks flits from attacking 'so-called intellectuals' and the 'metro elite' to suggesting that the Austrians didn't get it right in their presidential election, rejecting the anti-immigrant far-right candidate because 'they haven't suffered enough rape and murder yet'.

The attack on the courts is therefore just one part of a bigger argument. Judges proceed by precedent and rules and make judgments that balance the rights of individuals against the decision of the majority. Yet this assumes that balance is required. Haven't 'real' people made themselves perfectly clear? If judges can't see that, it is because they aren't proper people themselves. They are the Establishment, the elite, the metropolitans.

Müller's analysis explains also why so many populist political positions are simple and pure. It's just 'common sense'. 'People', you see, are tired of political correctness. If the people are cohesive and share a common interest it is not hard to serve that interest. Politics is only difficult if the values and interests of different constituencies clash with each other.

But here is the point, the crucial, unavoidable point. The populist claim is wrong. Wrong and dangerous. All of us are 'real' people living 'real' lives. We all have interests and views and they clash. We must argue and compromise and no one has the 'actual person' trump card.

Our institutions – Parliament, government, the courts – must serve a plural society, they must balance interests and protect rights. We have decided to leave the EU. We must leave the EU. We will leave the EU. But if you think that in the process we are going to allow anyone to undermine a liberal, pluralist, political democracy based on the rule of law you've got another thing coming. No.

This election will sweep away the old politics

In a major realignment, the Tories are targeting the white working classes as Labour woos well-educated metropolitans

My record in the 2017 election was relatively poor. Thrown by the sparkling local election results, the polls and a strong consensus among political commentators, I initially shared the view that Mrs May would win a big victory. I should have been able, given my view that most politics is about big economic and demographic forces, to do better. And as polling day came closer, I did indeed begin to appreciate that something more significant was going on.

In my final column before the election I asked readers to imagine what might happen if Mr Corbyn were to win: 'Sure, conventional wisdom is that they won't win. But conventional wisdom said they wouldn't come close. Conventional wisdom can be wrong. This is not a drill.' But the most interesting column I wrote during the campaign is this one.

30 May 2017

'One should never bribe till a quarter to four.' The Marquess of Salisbury had never liked electoral reform. He agreed with critics who thought that expanding the franchise would turn elections into 'sordid auctions'. But, as his biographer Andrew Roberts puts it: 'Once it had passed, Salisbury saw little point in being too fastidious to take part.'

So just before the election of 1892, in the days when the close of polls was at 4 p.m., he agreed to introduce free elementary education. It was a concession to the Liberal Unionist Joseph Chamberlain, who had become the spokesman for the new voters. Together Chamberlain and Salisbury created the Conservative and Unionist Party.

Salisbury had risen as the most unbending of conservatives. Yet his 'villa Toryism' was a programme of domestic reform designed to appeal to the new ring of suburban seats.

Salisbury was doing something that Peel and Disraeli had done before him and Baldwin, Thatcher and Cameron did after him. The great strength of the Conservative Party has been its willingness to adapt to the voters, evolving with public opinion.

Such an adjustment is going on now, and it is changing politics.

Far from being a dull election, I think this one may come to be seen as the beginning of a realignment in politics that changes the political map and our concepts of right and left. It is a change that was reflected in the Brexit referendum, and helps to explain Donald Trump's victory.

If you understand this realignment, some of what seems mystifying in the election becomes much easier to comprehend. Understanding helps, also, in making judgments about what the result might be.

In 2015 the Conservative Party won almost every seat where

voters were prosperous and generally white. This yielded a majority, but only a small one. To win a proper working majority it needs to succeed outside this enclave. Seeing Britain becoming more prosperous but also more diverse, David Cameron hoped to add some of these liberal metropolitan voters to the Tory columns.

Since the Brexit referendum, the Tory plan has changed. Labour is now vulnerable in seats where voters are generally white, but not prosperous. Here there are voters who are scep- tical of the Conservatives as the party of the rich, and want the state to help them. But these voters are conservative on immi- gration, Europe and security.

At the same time, Labour is changing too. It wants to add well-educated liberal voters, from diverse communities, often living in cities. In other words the political map is changing. The Tories are pursuing less prosperous, less educated voters and Labour is doing the opposite. Over time (and perhaps over quite a bit of time) the right–left battle may become less the traditional economic one between the well off and less well off, more a cultural battle between urban dwellers, educated people, and everyone else.

This realignment is already well advanced in the US. Over almost four decades Ronald Reagan's coalition has become Trump's very different grouping. The Democrats are now ahead among college-educated voters, while the Republicans lead among those who, at best, graduated from high school.

A new poll for NBC and the *Wall Street Journal* shows that there have been big swings even since 2010, with the Republicans gaining among the rural poor and the Democrats among the urban middle class.

These changes alter where the election is won or lost phys- ically and which sort of voters and places the parties can rely upon. In 2016 Hillary Clinton ended up campaigning in the wrong areas. As a result she won the popular vote but lost the presidency. She was the victim of a realignment that her oppo- nent understood better than she did.

Keep this all in mind as we take a look at manifesto week and the rest of the campaign. Because the parties behaved exactly as this analysis would lead you to expect.

If the Tories are seeking these new, less prosperous voters, in areas where few Tories have succeeded before, what would you expect them to do? Make a sharp move towards a message that Conservatives will use the power of the state to help people. Tick. Emphasise your leader rather than the Tory brand. Tick. Make promises on the living wage and energy prices. Tick. Emphasise Brexit and refuse to retreat on immigration. Tick. Eschew the usual big business letter on the economy. Tick.

And what would you do on social care? Take the money from people who inherit homes rather than from the just about managing. Erm, tick.

Now what would you do if you were Labour? You'd emphasise education, support people with big houses and offer free childcare to working women no matter how rich they are. And you'd make your biggest offer to? University students, of course. The promise (at a quarter to four, as it were) of free tuition fees was at least as important as the social care fiasco in shifting the polls.

Like the existing coalitions of support, these new ones are hard to keep together. The social care proposal took money from current Tory voters to give to potential ones and it only lasted four days. Meanwhile Labour has been struggling over its immigration policy, with its traditional voters thinking one thing and its new liberals thinking something else.

The extent to which the parties succeed in their efforts at realignment will determine the result. While some polls show a Tory landslide, others suggest it is very close. Much of the variation is explained by the estimate made of the turnout among young people. In other words, for Jeremy Corbyn to do well he has to get university students voting in record numbers.

Meanwhile the Tory majority will depend to a large extent

on them winning in constituencies where they have previously been a long way behind. Realignment will mean that the swing to them comes there rather than in the seats they hold. But will it be large enough to clinch victory?

The biggest barrier to them taking these seats are people who say that 'if my dad knew I was thinking of voting Conservative he would roll in his grave'. The focus groups being run for the *Huffington Post* and Edelman throughout the campaign have come across these voters again and again. In the last week the Conservatives will turn back to Brexit and leadership in order to try to get these voters to commit.

The 2017 election will see a step along the path to the realignment of British politics. The only thing remaining to be discovered is how big a step.

True socialism always ends with the Stasi

Leftwingers who boast that they'd never kiss a Tory don't seem to realise the flaw it reveals in their own ideology

In the week before this column appeared, the rising young Labour MP Laura Pidcock announced that she could never be friends with a Conservative, because she saw them as the enemy.

30 August 2017

Laura Pidcock doesn't like me. I don't take it personally because it isn't personal. I've never met her and she's never met me. But I'm a Conservative and she doesn't like Tories.

Fair enough. It's a free country. For the time being. And the new Labour MP for North West Durham is entitled to pick her friends. She's not alone, anyway. Her attitude – that Tories are 'the enemy' and 'I have absolutely no intention of being friends with any of them' – is quite prevalent on the left.

Hatred of Conservatives is common currency on social media, and at Labour conferences you can buy mugs with the words 'Never kissed a Tory' on them. The *Guardian*'s deputy opinion editor, Joseph Harker, complained only that Pidcock didn't go far enough. His aim (tricky for an opinion editor, even of the *Guardian*, one would have thought) was to avoid Blairites and Liberal Democrats too.

Not unreasonably, many Conservatives are quite hurt. It's never nice to be thought evil by someone. And the misunderstanding, that Tories are like Mr Burns out of *The Simpsons*, is quite frustrating. There is also something quite amusing about people who check someone's position on free schools before they kiss them.

Yet my reaction to Ms Pidcock's unfriendly (though, it should be acknowledged, civil) comments, and to abusive criticism on Twitter, is somewhat different. I am relaxed about her social attitudes, I don't agree that they make it hard for her to do her job, and I'm sure (indeed I know) that there are a few Tories with a similarly short-sighted view.

But I think nevertheless that this attitude to Conservatives is of profound importance, and points to a big hole in socialism.

Ever since 1956, when news of Nikita Khrushchev's so-called secret speech began to leak out to the West, socialists have been trying to find an alternative form of socialism. One that works. One that does not lead to the errors of Stalinism that Khrushchev identified at the 20th Congress of the Communist Party of the Soviet Union.

Social democratic parties and new liberals had succeeded in reforming capitalism, with a welfare state and progressive tax systems, but after decades of trying still had no model for replacing it. The only attempts that had been made had produced dictatorship, murder and relative economic failure. A new left, the secret speech indicated, was needed.

For more than sixty years since then, this has been the project of socialist intellectuals and politicians from Ralph Miliband to Tony Benn. The new Left has, with progressives and liberals, been involved in important campaigns to end colonialism, to promote gay rights and women's equality, and to reduce and eventually eliminate racial discrimination. But how successful has it been in identifying and propounding an alternative to capitalism?

Completely unsuccessful. After six decades of thought and political action there remains not a single successful example of a socialist society anywhere in history and anywhere in the world. Most recently they all got very excited about Venezuela. We were told by Jeremy Corbyn that we could honour Hugo Chávez by treating him as an example to us all.

This does not, of course, mean that there haven't been successful centre-left governments or that there are no alternatives to whatever policy the Tory party puts in its manifesto. I am not equating Yvette Cooper with Mao Zedong. I am simply saying that for all the slogans about the evils of capitalism, nobody has come up with a workable, sensible alternative. Not ways of changing it, you understand. An actual alternative.

Remember the kid with all the badges in class who tried to explain to you what socialism was, and you couldn't quite understand how it worked? Well we are still basically there, and the failure in comprehension wasn't yours.

And this is where Laura Pidcock comes into it. Paul Mason, the former BBC journalist and political ally of the Labour leader, recently published a book called *Postcapitalism: A Guide to Our Future*. It attempts bravely to articulate what modern socialism, operating without central state planning, might look like.

I confess I was hanging on for dear life trying to grasp his scheme, but I think I got there in the end. He sees a future, as did the Occupy movement, as did the authors of *New Left Review* and the Bennites, in which market exchange is replaced by friendly, voluntary cooperation and free provision. Wikipedia is his model.

Reading his book on the Tube, I was wondering how he might get someone, for instance, to clean station platforms or do an extra shift without being paid. But socialists do have an answer to this of sorts. Amity.

Without the market competition that makes us ruthless and has us jostling for position, we will all muck in. Someone will notice that there is a need for someone to work in the human resources department of the organisation that produces the ink that is used on Twix wrappers, and they will pop in and do it. For nothing.

I am sorry if this sounds preposterous but it's not my idea, is it? And if I've misunderstood how it all works, then answers on a postcard please. But I think you will see where Pidcock fits in. Socialism depends entirely on love and complete trust in the willingness of every person, after capitalism, to cooperate in a spirit of friendship.

So where are you left if there are whole groups of people with whom friendship is impossible, on account of their view of the world? Counter-revolutionary elements who don't accept their socialist responsibilities. Either these people make socialism impossible, or they have to be eliminated on the grounds of their counter-revolutionary position.

Pidcock would probably laugh at this. She's just saying she doesn't want to chum up with Sajid Javid, and here am I suggesting that she wants to obliterate him. And she's probably right to laugh. But not because socialism wouldn't require such obliteration. It would. It's just that socialism is so vague and incomprehensible she probably won't get anywhere near it.

The other day I was listening to a (really quite shocking) interview that Jeremy Corbyn's adviser Seumas Milne gave to George Galloway. Have a listen on YouTube. It's amazing.

In it, Milne regrets the passing of East Germany, really he does. Then he adds that obviously we wouldn't want the Stasi back. But he misses the point. You can't have East Germany without the Stasi.

Jeremy Corbyn's worldview is made for anti-Semites

Hatred of colonialism, capitalism and Zionism
are so intertwined in left-wing minds that distaste
for Jews comes easily

Rising concern in the Jewish community about left anti-Semitism under Jeremy Corbyn's leadership came to a head in March 2018. Controversy erupted over an anti-Semitic mural – a crude cartoon of Jewish bankers playing monopoly on the backs of suffering workers – to which Mr Corbyn had lent support on Facebook. The main communal Jewish organisations held a protest rally in Parliament Square. A number of Labour MPs attended, and so did I. Luciana Berger was at that point still in the party and trying to pull it round.

27 March 2018

I have only been on two political demonstrations in my life. The first was a rally against apartheid more than thirty years ago when P. W. Botha was in London meeting Margaret Thatcher. I held up a banner and marched just in front of a group from the Socialist Workers Party who were chanting,

'Soweto and Palestine, one struggle, one fight.' The future Labour MP Chris Mullin tried selling me a copy of *Tribune*, of which he was the editor. I'm sure Jeremy Corbyn was there somewhere.

My second demo was on Monday. Neither Chris Mullin nor Jeremy Corbyn was present.

Over this last weekend a controversy broke out about Mr Corbyn's support for an anti-Semitic mural, and something snapped in the Jewish community. Hardly a day seems to go by without an anti-Semitic incident involving members of the Labour Party. Too many of them involved the leader himself. And now this.

So the main communal bodies gathered on Parliament Square before delivering a letter of protest to a meeting of the Parliamentary Labour Party and I showed up to offer support.

The atmosphere was a mild air of surprise commingled with depression. We were standing outside chanting. Had it really come to this? And might it rain? I think I counted as an experienced veteran of demonstrations by comparison with everyone else.

When some people pushed to the front, others at the back started joking: 'They do know there's no food up there?' The mic didn't work properly, leading people to start shouting 'Can you repeat that?' as if attending a supper quiz. The police did not require riot shields.

There was even a small counter-demo because this, after all, was a Jewish event. A Jewish night out involves five people, six cars and seven opinions. Having a little dissent made it feel like the synagogue AGM. In other words it was demo amateur night. Because this wasn't a synthetic political protest organised by rent-a-crowd. It was an authentic display of concern and more than a little desperation, a spontaneous statement of anger and bewilderment by organisations representing the overwhelming majority of Britain's Jews.

442

I think the moment that captured this desperation best was when the brave Labour MP Luciana Berger called on us all to join the Labour Party. There was something tragic about Luciana's request. I could see her point. She needs allies for the fight. But on the other hand, how likely is victory? Jeremy Corbyn is going nowhere. So neither is anti-Semitism.

Let's leave the question of whether Mr Corbyn himself is anti-Semitic. As the Labour MP John Mann correctly put it: 'I don't know.'

It is certainly hard to believe that the Labour leader could have even glanced at that street mural of stereotypical Jews playing Monopoly on the backs of the poor and not appreciated it was anti-Semitic. The columnist Euan McColm brilliantly compared it to seeing the Nazi eagle and swastika and saying 'I only glanced at it and thought it was a parrot carrying an electric fan'.

But OK. Why don't we choose to believe him for a moment or two? Let's concentrate instead on the argument that the mural was making, Jew or no Jew.

Searching for a new direction after Khrushchev's secret speech on the crimes of Stalin in 1956, the Left began to champion insurgent movements and nationalist revolutions in emerging economies. Leaders like Fidel Castro and Ho Chi Minh (and later the Sandinistas and Hugo Chávez) represented an alternative both to Western capitalism and Soviet communism.

The guerrilla fighter became a romantic figure to them, the economics professor in battle fatigues profiled by *New Left Review*, the three-hour speeches of dictators anthologised. And along the way, the Palestinian cause was added.

Malcolm X had a good deal to do with this. On the run from his enemies in the Nation of Islam, the African-American separatist leader escaped to the Middle East, undertaking a pilgrimage which led him towards orthodox Islam. And also towards pan-Africanism, a socialist idea championed in newly independent African countries. It mixed unorthodox socialist economics with the argument that Africans were a single people victimised by colonialism.

Already convinced that Jews were economic exploiters, Malcolm now brought this together with his new doctrine. The 'Zionist dollar' was bankrolling colonial oppression. Returning to the United States he helped spread this politics to those that were inspired by his defiance and demeanour. It has been very influential on the new Left.

Over time, Zionism ceased to refer simply to the creation of Israel and criticism of it ceased to be criticism merely of that state's government. Zionism became the symbol of colonialism: the worst example of it, the greatest sin, with Zionists the greatest sinners.

Zionism became a shorthand for colonial oppression, and anti-Zionism a statement of opposition to Western capitalism and of confidence that there is a workable popular alternative to the free-market economy. Nazism was imperialist so Zionism must be like Nazism, and Hitler and the Jews were collaborators. This was the politics championed by Ken Livingstone, Jeremy Corbyn and John McDonnell as they worked together in the early 1980s, each with their own emphasis. It is all over the articles they produced for *London Labour Briefing* and *Labour Herald*. And it defined the allies that they accumulated.

Believing that there is a global conspiracy of bankers, Zionist colonialists and the freemasons to oppress the workers of the world is a dangerously bonkers idea. And it is also bound to attract and sustain anti-Semites. The man who painted Corbyn's mural is just one example.

Jeremy Corbyn wasn't on those Facebook groups of anti-Semites by accident, nor did the mad conspiracy mural come to his attention by happenstance. He belonged to these groups because he shares their conspiracy-driven way of looking at the world, even if he wouldn't always use the same language.

While the Jewish community gathered in Parliament Square, Mr Corbyn's supporters were busy angrily rejecting the charge against him and Labour. Mr Mullin said the Jews were 'ganging up' on his friend. The suggestion was made that this was a plot to derail Labour's local election campaign. In other words 'We aren't anti-Semites, so why are the Jews plotting against us?'

Yet the truth was much sadder than that. The crowd was full of Labour supporters who feel they cannot now accept Luciana Berger's invitation. And that Mr Corbyn can't do anything about the problem, because he is the problem.

And where does that leave you if you are on the left and a Jew? Or even a friend of the Jews?

Boris Johnson's tax-cut promise is sheer folly

The ex-Foreign Secretary's eye-catching policy
echoes previous doomed Tory pledges that voters
won't fall for any more

After his Cabinet resignation and as he began to build his
case for being leader, Boris Johnson argued in his column
that 'Instead of canvassing tax rises, we should say that
tax henceforward will not go up. That's it. No new taxes
and no increase in rates.'

12 September 2018

Towards the end of 1974, President Ford's deputy chief of staff,
Dick Cheney, went for lunch at the Two Continents restaurant
round the corner from the White House. He was there to meet
conservative economists who had a message for the new president. Among them was Art Laffer with a paper napkin. After
trying a more abstract presentation, Professor Laffer drew a
curve on the serviette.

It was all pretty simple, he told Cheney, starting to draw.
If your tax rate was 0 per cent then the Government would
have no revenue. But it was also true that if your tax rate was

100 per cent, you wouldn't raise any revenue either, because no one would bother to make any taxable income.

Voilà – the Laffer curve. As you raise tax rates, revenue goes up until you hit the peak. After that, higher rates actually reduce revenue.

It was a very enticing napkin. Essentially it suggested that tax cuts could pay for themselves; in fact the more you cut them, the more revenue you collect. There it was, engraved on tissue paper, the founding document of the conservative tax revolution.

And if you are thinking, 'Hang on a minute, it can't be as simple as that,' you are right.

On Monday, Boris Johnson outlined the latest part of his leadership programme. The Conservative Party should commit itself to introducing no new taxes, while cutting the rates of some existing taxes and holding the rest steady. He also proposed raising tax allowances.

While his obvious aim is the Chancellor and his autumn budget, Mr Johnson is advocating a long-term position. 'We should say that taxes henceforward will not go up.' And he cites Laffer in support. There may need to be short-term savings (through Brexit allowing us to change public-procurement rules, apparently) but tax cuts will be soon increasing tax yields, napkin-style.

Mr Johnson is not the first Conservative to promote this idea. The party offered a tax guarantee in the late 1990s before abandoning it. Then, in the 2005 leadership contest, David Davis said that, if elected, he would promise £38 billion of tax cuts by 2014–15. And in 2015 David Cameron guaranteed not to raise income tax, VAT or national insurance for five years.

These promises are foolish. And the more watertight they are (Johnson's much more than Cameron's) the more foolish they are.

Before we get on to Laffer, there are two big problems with sweeping tax guarantees. The first is cyclical, the second structural.

The cyclical problem is that you are trying to set tax rates without knowing whether economic circumstances make them appropriate. Take the Davis plan of 2005. His theory – quite intelligent and plausible – was that people need to know where the Tory party stands. You can't make a tax offer at the last minute. It needs to be part of your brand. This is now probably Mr Johnson's thinking too. The trouble, as I pointed out at the time, is that you can't make budgets in 2005 to cover circumstances in 2015. What, I asked, if there was a crash sometime between these two dates? And a big deficit crisis?

Then there is the structural problem. David Willetts made this argument persuasively in a lecture to the Resolution Foundation think tank earlier this year. The past thirty years have been a demographic 'sweet spot': there have been many working-age contributors and relatively few pensioners and children. This means larger revenues and lower pressures on public spending.

Now, however, we have reached the peak. The boomers are growing older, and the number of future workers is relatively smaller. Today, for every ten working-age adults there are seven young and old people needing their support. By 2030, this figure will be almost nine.

This means that it is going to cost more and more just to maintain the existing welfare promise. By the end of the decade, the cost will rise by £20 billion and by 2040 it will be £60 billion. As Lord Willetts puts it starkly: 'The age of tax cuts is over.'

Which brings us back to Laffer. Because if you can cut tax and raise revenue at the same time, then the Willetts objection disappears.

Unfortunately, the idea that tax cuts pay for themselves is seductive, but false. In fact, the Laffer curve doesn't even guarantee it. It simply states that logically, at a certain rate, it must be counterproductive to raise tax rates further. It doesn't say what that rate might be. It is quite likely to be true only at very high marginal rates. Or on certain limited taxes (it may work on high rates of corporation tax, for instance).

Take the famous 1981 Reagan tax cuts, which were heavily napkin-influenced. Even conservative economists believe that they only recouped a third of the money lost to the Treasury by rate reductions.

So the Conservative Party would be unwise to follow Mr Johnson's advice and return to a sweeping tax promise. But it will be sorely tempted to do so. After all, Tories will fret, if we don't make a promise like that, how will we differ from Jeremy Corbyn?

This isn't even a sensible question. Parties should take political positions they believe are right, and not be rushed into making errors just to avoid looking like their opponents. If you do this, you allow the other side to occupy the most fertile political ground and push you off it.

But even if it were a sensible question, the answer isn't all that hard. Labour under Mr Corbyn will be proposing vast and damaging taxes on business and huge spending programmes which will prove difficult to finance. A moderate, fiscally sensible approach will differentiate itself from Mr Corbyn quite clearly. The Conservatives will still be able to campaign as the lower tax party.

Tax cuts can be popular and they have been. But they can't be all the Conservative Party has to say. Even if that has worked in the past, it won't work in the future.

People want a decent standard of living, of which prudent public finance and low taxes are only a part. They want a robust economy that isn't floated on debt. They want good public services that are properly financed and a welfare state that they can rely on.

And there isn't a magic money tree for tax reductions any more than there is one for public spending.

Corbyn's grand plan is to replace Parliament

Devolving decision-making to the party conference is a key part of the project to restore power to the workers

Before the 2018 Labour conference Jeremy Corbyn promised to be bound by any decision it took on a second European referendum. What did he mean by this?

25 September 2018

'There are some of us, Mr Chairman, who will fight and fight and fight again to save the party we love. We will fight and fight and fight again to bring back sanity and honesty and dignity, so that our party with its great past may retain its glory and its greatness.'

In October 1960 the Labour leader Hugh Gaitskell made one of the most memorable speeches in his party's history. During a tense address to the conference in Scarborough, he pressed on despite being booed and heckled. He pledged himself to carry on fighting the policy of unilateral nuclear disarmament which the party was just about to adopt.

His concluding words have become famous. Less well known is

the argument that immediately preceded them. 'It is not in dispute that the vast majority of Labour members of Parliament are utterly opposed to unilateralism and neutralism. So what do you expect them to do? Change their minds overnight?' What would people think of us, said Gaitskell, if we acted like 'well-behaved sheep'?

Over the weekend Jeremy Corbyn affirmed his adherence to the opposite doctrine: 'What comes out of conference I will adhere to.' This was reported (and fair enough in the circumstances) as a story about a second Brexit referendum. But it was a far wider commitment than that. And it was the most important thing by far that anyone has said here in Liverpool.

Corbyn explained that he 'was elected to empower the members of the party. So if conference makes a decision I will not walk away from it and I will act accordingly.' He said that he was 'bound by the democracy of our party'. Confirming that this position was not limited to Europe, John McDonnell applied the same principle to his position on nuclear weapons. Ironically, given Gaitskell's fight, McDonnell declared himself an opponent of the deterrent who accepted that he had 'lost that debate' at conference. 'So democracy prevails and that [maintaining the deterrent] would be the policy of the Government itself.'

This is an astonishing constitutional doctrine. It declares Labour MPs, including the leadership, to be delegates of the Labour Party and its conference. A majority Labour government, and its prime minister, would be controlled by the party rather than by its own judgment and the judgment of Parliament.

It is tempting to see this as merely a doctrine of convenience. Two years ago Corbyn and his supporters did not control the party conference. Now they clearly do. It's their party. But in Parliament they are still in a minority. So all this party democracy stuff is just a way round a pressing problem?

As I say, a tempting conclusion. But also unfair. The assertion of the sovereignty of the party is a longstanding Corbyn view and at the heart of his socialism.

It is often said, glibly, that the election of Corbyn and McDonnell would be a return to the 1970s. But quite the contrary. The origin of many of the ideas of the two men is their shared view that the 1970s were a disaster. Thatcherism was one response to this fiasco, their socialism is the other.

Led by Tony Benn, the socialists determined that the problem that had upended the 1974 Labour government had been a lack of democracy. True democracy. That is, democracy as expressed by working people controlling their own lives and owning the means of production.

The ruling class had used Parliament in the 1970s to deny the workers this control and to protect ruling-class privileges. They had created corporatism. Big business persuaded the state to protect its interests and the unions were recruited to police the deal and keep the workers in line. That's why things had gone so wrong.

You can't, the socialists concluded, tackle the wealth of the rich if you don't first attack their power. And this remains the Corbyn and McDonnell position.

So their programme has two linked parts. The first is to democratise the economy. Big businesses will, over time, be run by their workers who will have an increasing role on boards. The media will elect editors and be controlled by staff rather than by owners. Utilities will be nationalised and run by local councils and trade-union representatives. Trade-union laws will be repealed and union power restored.

Wages – and this, just to emphasise, is the Shadow Chancellor's actual policy – will be determined collectively and democratically sector by sector. This will not be the incomes policy of the 1970s, because then the unions collaborated with the Government. This time the Government would be truly democratic and wouldn't want to restrain the workers.

Yet all this can't happen unless Parliament agrees. Which means that Parliament has to be made to reflect the views and interests of working people. This is the second part of the programme.

McDonnell has always been frank about his support for extra-parliamentary action if it is required to 'encourage' MPs to make the correct democratic choice. After all, the ruling class has its own tools of extra-parliamentary action such as the IMF, the civil service and the judiciary. Why not the workers?

Tony Benn used to worry about simply abandoning the notion of parliamentary rule altogether. What then could prevent dictatorship? His way of solving the problem was to make parliamentarians accountable to a democratic Labour Party. And this explains Corbyn's weekend comments. It also explains the decision in Liverpool to make it much easier for local party members to deselect their MPs.

The Labour Party must, the socialists argue, be organised so that it is the authentic voice of working people, representing their democratic interests. It will then exercise control of Parliament on behalf of working people. True democracy and parliamentary democracy will be unified.

It is true that this programme means that all political and economic decision-making by the state or private enterprises will either be a Labour Party meeting or be very like one. Hours of compositing in conference arrangements committees lie ahead for all of us. But even this is a feature and not a bug. For who will have the fortitude to participate in such proceedings, save for the most redoubtable champions of the interests of working people?

If some of this reads like satire, it is certainly not intended as such. The man who asks us all to make him prime minister has just announced that if we accede he intends to be the mere instrument of his party conference. The party has added that in a war the deployment of nuclear weapons will be subject to the agreement of the 'wider community', whatever that means.

So I'm not engaged in satire. Satire is redundant.

Acknowledgements

It is impossible to acknowledge everyone who has helped or inspired me to write these columns. But there are a few people I would like to mention.

My colleagues at *The Times* to start off with, beginning with the editors. Sir Peter Stothard who first hired me, then Robert Thomson and James Harding and now John Witherow. They have both encouraged and tolerated me and I'm really grateful.

On the comment desk Anne Spackman, Tim Montgomerie and Mike Smith have been wonderful editors, and my columns have benefited immensely from the work that Robbie Millen, Tim Rice, Paul Dunn, Richard Preston and Cliff Martin have done to improve them. Thanks also to Helen Glancy and Rebecca Callanan. And to Nicola Jeal and the features team for their amazing assignments.

I also learned so much from arguments and debates with David Aaronovitch, Oliver Kamm, Phil Collins, Hugo Rifkind, Mary Ann Sieghart, Giles Whittell, Joe Joseph, Camilla Cavendish, Michael Gove, Raphael Hogarth, Henry Zeffman, Murad Ahmed, Robert Crampton, Matt Chorley, Simon Nixon, Alice Fishburn, Alice Miles, Rachel Sylvester and Alice Thomson. And been guided by Keith Blackmore, Ben Preston, George Brock and Emma Tucker.

Andrew Cooper, George Osborne, Greg Clark, Matthew Gould, Robert Cialdini, Steve Martin, Karren Brady, Stephen

Pollard, Bernard Hughes, Henry Stott, Jonathan Haskel and Robert Shrimsley have been important sources of inspiration.

I often write with an imagined audience in my head. I think how my sister Tamara, her husband Michael Isaacs, my brother Anthony and his wife Judy Fishman might receive a particular idea or line. And I'm lucky to write for *The Times* because I love its readers.

This book wouldn't be here without Craig Tregurtha, my brilliant agent Toby Mundy and its editor Arabella Pike, as well as the William Collins team, Jo Thompson, Katherine Patrick, Katy Archer and Alex Gingell. Thanks also to Sir Michael Parkinson, Laurence Myers and the family of Sir George Martin for permission to quote their emails.

And nothing would be worthwhile at all if it weren't for Sam, Aron and Isaac. And Nicky, who has had to bear the burden of me standing in the kitchen on a Sunday morning every week for fifteen years and saying: 'This week, this week I really don't know what to write.' She tells me it'll come to me. And, on that as on everything, she is always right.

Index